AMERICAN
ANTHROPOLOGY
The Early Years

FRANCIS LA FLESCHE 1857–1932
(See Chapter 6, "The Contributions of
Francis La Flesche.")

AMERICAN ANTHROPOLOGY

The Early Years

1974 Proceedings of
THE AMERICAN ETHNOLOGICAL SOCIETY
Robert F. Spencer, *General Editor*

Edited by
JOHN V. MURRA
Princeton, New Jersey

WEST PUBLISHING CO.
St. Paul • New York • Boston
Los Angeles • San Francisco

Printed in the United States of America

Library of Congress Catalog No.:   76–12975

ISBN 0–8299–0097–7

Foreword

That the history of a discipline is by no means a dry-as-dust pursuit is indicated in the papers which follow. If anthropology today sometimes questions its own aims, this was definitely not the case in its earlier developmental years. The field of anthropology, however, still depends for its disciplinary focus on what has gone before, on the methods of comparison and description developed by its pioneers. It was this awareness which led Professor John V. Murra, as out-going president of the American Ethnological Society, to develop the 1974 symposium on aspects of the earlier phases of American ethnology and anthropology.

The symposium was held between April 26 and 28, 1974, at Clark University, Worcester, Massachusetts, a site in itself significant when it is recalled that Franz Boas was once a member of the Clark faculty. The American Ethnological Society met in conjunction with the Northeastern Anthropological Association and expresses its appreciation to the officers and program chairmen of the latter group.

Robert F. Spencer, Editor, AES

University of Minnesota

*

Contents

vii

AMERICAN
ANTHROPOLOGY
The Early Years

*

INTRODUCTION

*

1

American Anthropology, the Early Years

JOHN V. MURRA

Institute for Advanced Study, Princeton, New Jersey

One of the true privileges the American Ethnological Society
bestows upon its officers is the opportunity to choose the theme of
the spring meeting the year after one has served as president. I did
not hesitate when choosing the early history of the AES and of U.S.
anthropology as the topic for 1974.

I am not a historian of our craft. When I receive my copy of the
History of Anthropology Newsletter, I nod my head in recognition
or amazement. All those kinsmen resurrected, reevaluated, scru-
tinized. Events, influences, skullduggery, interests, and alternative
readings of the evidence are *us* because they are part of our past. I
am glad of the research chronicled in the *Newsletter* because it

reinforces my own attitude toward anthropology; I pretend it is my only ethnic, religious, and ideologic affiliation. This stance may not be a scientific one and may be the reason why I do not conduct research in the history of anthropology. But I am a commited, critical, patriotic consumer of the work of those who do.

In one of the papers that follow, John R. Cole welcomes the challenge of Dell Hymes *Reinventing Anthropology.* Hymes asks, would we do it again, if we had a chance? Like Cole I answer yes, though my reasons are somewhat different.

The most important contribution of earlier U.S. anthropologists was their devotion to recording the achievement of native Americans. I realize that some of their work was done for the purpose of converting them to some European creed; that some of the studies were financed by Congress to facilitate the alienation of lands, rivers, oilfields, and forests; that the U.S. cavalry engaged in genocide while others tolerated ethnocide. But it is also plain that none of this negates, eliminates, or supersedes the achievement, unique in the world, of *The Omaha Tribe* by Fletcher and La Flesche, described in Margot Liberty's paper below; or of the thousands of pages of texts printed in the vernacular; or of Paul Radin's *The Winnebago Tribe.* The presence of the Annual Reports of the Bureau of American Ethnology on the remainder shelves and their low prices startled the war–time refugee Claude Lévi-Strauss (1966:124). Has anyone recently reread A. L. Kroeber's entries in the *Handbook of California Indians?* The wide availability of linguistic, economic, ceremonial, and autobiographical data collected by anthropologists will some day be revealed as a major ingredient in the successful self–rediscovery and revitalization of native American culture.

If we see anthropology primarily as a recovery of such cultural achievement and a defense of such human endurance in the face of homogenizing and destructive forces, the "four-field" definition of our endeavor in the U.S. will be seen as indispensable. Who would imagine a study of Chinese civilization that neglected the written record, ignored linguistic variability, thought it could get along without the excavation of settlements from earlier dynasties, or missed the social organization of contemporary agricultural communes? All four and many more approaches must obviously be coordinated if one is to fathom the achievements of the Chinese. Anthropology argues that the same array of procedures is indispensable to understand the kingdoms of Meso-America, lacustrain East Africa, or the Andes at the time of the European invasion; Hawaii or the highlands of Papua; Europe in the tenth century; or the Navajo and the Lumbee.

If we try to pinpoint when U.S. anthropology became apologetic about its accomplishments, there may be disagreement. I leave it to the historians to chronologize this propensity for guilt. As a foreign, if U.S.-trained, anthropologist, I would argue that contemporary apologetics are closely related to the careless abandonment of our four-field commitment and genuflection before an ahistorical "science of society." At the end of his long, anthropology-filled life, A. L. Kroeber looked back over the road we had come and mused:

> There is some risk that the growing habit of university [administrators] to group us with the social sciences will tend to influence students to believe that anthropology is intrinsically a social science and has always been such, plus only certain odd sidelines and specialties of its own. It therefore seems important for everyone concerned with anthropology to recognize that its specific social science aspect is historically recent — scarcely a generation old. . . . And so far as it has a social science ingredient, it prevalently treats the data of this historically, which the core social sciences do to only a minor degree . . . . [1954:767,764]. It also seems unlikely that the social science ingredient will absorb or displace the older natural science and humanistic components.
>
> If at times some of you, like myself, feel somewhat ill at ease in the house of social science, do not wonder: we are changelings therein, our true paternity lies elsewhere. (1959:404).

Obviously anthropology cannot proceed without also internalizing the methodology of *The Eighteenth Brumaire of Louis Bonaparte, The Elementary Forms of Religious Life, The Interpretation of Dreams, Essai sur le Don,* or *Pre-capitalist Economic Formations.* Still, we have our own tasks, undertaken by no one else.

Human evolution in its inseparably biological and cultural dimensions; the millions of years when we fished, hunted, and gathered; linguistic diversities and uniformities; the emergence of stratification, kings, exploitation, and war; preindustrial urbanization or ideologies; the defense of ethnic diversity, of options in economic and political organization to the point of ethnogenesis—all these are undertaken and studied by no one if not by anthropologists. None of this has to be reinvented; it is our heritage and no one else's.

The following papers are grouped into two parts: the first deals with the early days of the American Ethnological Society and of U.S. anthropology; the second provides some insight into Robert Redfield's work.

Not all of the participants in the first symposium were anthropologists. Two were historians (Robert E. Bieder and Curtis M. Hinsley) and we are grateful for their joining us. In their present sequence the papers oscillate between a period or group to individual pioneers. We begin and end with papers devoted to the Society itself.

The second symposium was planned to deal with the history of a single department. I thought the first twenty years of the one at Yale, organized by Cornelius Osgood, would provide valuable insights into one way of organizing U.S. anthropology. Unfortunately, the moment was premature. When I reported this to the membership meeting in the fall of 1973, Bernice A. Kaplan suggested that we substitute the evaluation of one man's career for the history of the department. She suggested Robert Redfield, and there was support in the audience.

The second part, then, includes the papers read and some of the comments taped at the special session on the last day of the spring meeting. Among those invited who could not take part were Alfonso Villa Rojas, Sol Tax, and Lisa Redfield Peattie. I would like to reproduce the letter from Prof. Villa:

> *Con profunda pena me veo en el caso de comunicarte que no me será posible asistir a las sesiones de la Sociedad - Americana de Etnología, que tendrán lugar en la última semana de este mes, debido a que todavía no estoy del todo bien del ojo que me*

operaron y, por lo tanto, no me han podido poner - el lente de contacto que es indispensable para una buena visión. No tienes idea de lo que lamento haber perdido esta estupenda oportunidad de rendir homenaje al Dr. Redfield, a quien tanto debo; además, me hubiera dado gran gusto charlar con usted y con los demás amigos como Tax, Leslie y otros a los que hace mucho tiempo no veo.

I am distressed to have to let you know that it will not be possible for me to take part in the meetings of the AES, to be held at the end of this month. I am still not fully recovered from the operation on my eye so that they were unable to fit me with the contact lense, indispensable for good vision. You have no idea how much I regret to have lost this opportunity to express my respect for Dr. Redfield to whom I owe so much. . . .

The papers we do offer should be a good beginning for the evaluation of Robert Redfield's work and influence.

The taping and the transcriptions of this final session were made possible through the interest and hard work of June Collins and Charles Frantz.

LITERATURE CITED

Kroeber, Alfred L.
> 1954 The Place of Anthropology in Universities. American Anthropologist 56(5):764-767.
> 1959 The History of the Personality of Anthropology. American Anthropologist 61(3):398-404.

Lévi-Strauss, Claude
> 1966 Anthropology: Its Achievements and Future. Current Anthropology 7(2):124-127.

✻

BACKGROUNDS OF AMERICAN ETHNOLOGY

*

2

From Ethnologists to Anthropologists: A Brief History of the American Ethnological Society

ROBERT E. BIEDER and THOMAS G. TAX
Newberry Library and University of Chicago

On February 15, 1870, E. G. Squier circulated a form letter which stated, "At a meeting of *'The American Ethnological Society'* held in this city in October last, it was agreed to dissolve that society with the view of organizing another, to be called *'The Anthropological Society of New York'* " (Squier Papers, LC 2/15/70).[1] What could have led the members of the American Ethnological Society to reorganize their twenty-eight-year-old institution? To answer this question we will examine the history of the AES and the reasons for its ultimate failure.

Most histories of the American Ethnological Society name Albert Gallatin as its founder (Mitra 1933:65; Adams 1879:645; Hallowell 1960:92; Hale 1850:30). However, John Russell Bartlett's "Autobiography" told a somewhat different story. Bartlett wrote in 1842 that he "suggested to Mr. Gallatin the idea of a new society, the attention of which should be devoted to Geography, Archaeology, Philology and inquiries generally connected with the human race. This would involve subjects which did not come within the scope of the Historical Society, and hence would not in the least interfere with it" (Bartlett n.d.:30). Gallatin and Bartlett, both officers in the New-York Historical Society, were protective of that organization's interests, and saw no conflicts with the goals of the American Antiquarian Society of Worcester, Massachusetts, perhaps the leading ethnological society in the United States at that time. Bartlett pointed out that the Antiquarian Society was largely local in its orientation, whereas the proposed New York organization would be global in focus (Bartlett n.d.:30). Bartlett recorded Gallatin's agreement with the plan and his suggestion that they broach the idea to other gentlemen of similar interests. The resulting organizational meeting was held in Bartlett's house on November 19, 1842. Bartlett reported in his "Autobiography" that those present were Albert Gallatin, John L. Stephens, Frederick Catherwood, Rev. Edward Robinson, Rev. Francis L. Hawks, Charles Welford, Henry R. Schoolcraft, George Folsom, and Alexander I. Cotheal. These men formed the nucleus of the American Ethnological Society and named Gallatin president (Bartlett n.d.:33).

Having no headquarters, the group met in the homes of its members. President Gallatin's increasingly poor health, however, soon led the Society to assemble regularly in his home. These meetings combined social gatherings with learned discussions. The members would congregate about seven o'clock in the evening, dine at Gallatin's table, and then indulge in postprandial ethnological discussions. Records of these meetings are scanty, but an idea of what they were like can be gleaned from Bartlett's "Autobiography," from the correspondence of the members, from the Society's occasional volumes of *Transactions* and *Bulletins* and from the unofficial minutes frequently published in *the Literary World.* Apparently the Society construed the term *ethnology* to include a mixture of geography, philology, history, archaeology, travelogue, and at times, literary criticism. As Bartlett recalled, "Our President always had a great deal to tell us connected with geographical studies, new voyages and travels or reminiscenses of his early life. New books, maps, antiquarian objects, etc., were always laid before the members for discussion. Papers, too, were generally read at these meetings" (Bartlett n.d:34). Recitals of the letters of foreign ethnologists, travelers, and missionaries played an important part in the meetings, and were often substituted for more formal, prepared papers.

Throughout the 1840s, the papers presented most frequently focused on archaeology, philology, and general ethnology. Occasionally members presented ethnological maps and papers devoted to physical anthropology, literature, and Biblical history. The largest category of papers in these years was the archaeology of the Americas, most frequently dealing with the mounds of the southeastern United States. The antiquities of the Middle East were also well represented. Discussions of both American Indian and Middle Eastern languages occurred with nearly equal frequency, and often included attempts at deciphering ancient inscriptions, both genuine and spurious.[2]

After Gallatin's death in 1849, the Society began to falter, but more complex causes led to the rapid deterioration of the organization. The Society's weakened condition is evidenced by the reduction in both the quantity and quality of the papers presented. During the 1850s and 1860s, the Society met infrequently, and its meetings resembled social clubs more than scientific assemblies. Most papers given were mere travelogues with little ethnological content. The members sometimes discussed topics as little related to ethnology as medieval literature. At one meeting in 1851, two works were presented for discussion. One, R. G. Latham's *The Natural History of the Varieties of Man,* received little comment. The other paper, a work on a Norman poet, sparked a lengthy discussion of twelfth–century literature and the general history of European letters *(Literary World* 1851:371–374). Perhaps because several clergymen held influential positions in the American Ethnological Society, religious subjects were frequently discussed after 1850. The Society often engaged missionaries to speak about their experiences in exotic lands. Their interest in the peoples of Africa, Asia, and Oceania tended to give the Society a global perspective, somewhat at the expense of American Indian studies. The publishing program of the Society declined due to lack of money and scarcity of papers of publishable quality.

In large part, the Society's early prominence rested on the solid achievements of its *Transactions*. Two full-sized volumes were issued, the first in 1845 and the second in 1848. The first and only part of a third volume followed in 1853, but a fire destroyed nearly all copies and the volume was not reissued until 1909. The wide distribution of these volumes helped to promote the Society both at home and abroad. Several members acquired international reputations from their articles and initiated correspondence with leading European ethnologists. The weakness of the Society in the 1850s and 1860s was reflected in its underdeveloped publishing program. By the 1860s, the Society was only able to muster enough support to bring out a few brief *Bulletins,* and after that only one known publication appeared, that being in 1869 (Berendt 1869).

While similar societies in other countries were vital and expanding, the AES was moribund and lost much of the prestige it had acquired in the 1840s. In earlier years, the Smithsonian Institution had submitted several important manuscripts to the Society for criticism, most notably two "Smithsonian Contributions to Knowledge" by Squier, one co-authored by E. H. Davis. However, by the 1860s, when Lewis Henry Morgan submitted his *Systems of Consanguinity and Affinity* to the Smithsonian, Secretary Joseph Henry asked the American Oriental Society to review it for possible publication (Henry in Morgan 1871:iii). That the AES, seemingly the obvious choice for the job, was overlooked, is a strong indication of its severe loss of scientific credibility.

On at least one occasion, the Society did attempt to reestablish itself as an important international body. In 1867 it appointed two delegates to the International Congress of Anthropology and Prehistoric Archaeology held in Paris. One delegate, E. G. Squier, served as a vice-president at this meeting while another, John Russell Bartlett, attended as a delegate of both the AES and the American Antiquarian Society (Bartlett n.d.:80). Bartlett, and probably Squier, also attended the International Archaeological Congress held in Antwerp the same summer. Whether Squier and Bartlett knew the French anthropologist Paul Broca before the Paris Congress is not known, but they certainly met him while in France. Squier, at least, was much impressed with the strides Europeans had made in archaeological and philological research. The inactivity of his own American Ethnological Society must have been a source of acute embarassment for him in his dealings with European anthropologists. In any case, upon his return to the United States, Squier attempted to invigorate the AES. By 1869 his evident failure to accomplish much through the traditional structure of the Society led him to suggest drastic alterations. Apparently he thought a reorganization along European lines would be the most fruitful. Broca and his Paris Anthropological Society pointed the way for Squier (Squier 1871:15–17).

Thus, when Squier attempted to make the Society "anthropological" in the late 1860s, he had a clear concept of what he wanted. For him the use of the word *anthropological* emphasized both the new organization's theoretical orientation and its dependency on Europe. Nearly all European societies of that time preferred the term *anthropology* to *ethnology*. Squier adopted Broca's definition in which ethnologists studied man without the benefits of natural history, while anthropologists incorporated craniology, anatomy, geology, and the other natural sciences in their researches (Broca 1871:29–31).[3]

By 1869 Squier's position was significantly strengthened by recent additions to the Society's membership. Most of the members who voted to dissolve the American Ethnological Society had belonged for less than a decade. The committee, chaired by Squier and formed to prepare a constitution and program for a new society, was composed mostly of Squier's allies. Some of the older members probably disassociated themselves from the new Anthropological Institute of New-York, for several prominent names were missing from the membership list of that organization. The Institute met occasionally during 1870 and 1871, but seems to have disappeared by 1872. It published only one issue of its *Journal*, filled with articles by Broca, Squier, and a few others. (Fletcher 1882:120). Most of the articles were ethnological, however, showing how little the "anthropological" science really influenced the membership.

The shortcomings of New York ethnology can be blamed to some degree on the nature of the memberships of both societies. At no time were there more than forty-five resident members of either organization and generally the number actively involved was fewer than twenty. The active members tended to be gentlemen of some social standing in the New York community who knew each other well, and while they all had some intellectual pretensions, they were not "ethnological experts." Nearly all were professional men engaged in a variety of occupations. Of the sixty New York members active from 1842 to 1870, thirteen were educators or librarians, eleven were journalists and travel writers, and ten others were physicians. In addition, seven were lawyers, five entered politics, and five were clergymen. Of course their primary occupations did not prevent them from actively pursuing their ethnological interests, but in most cases they actually contributed little to anthropology. Many of the active members also participated in other learned societies, dividing their time and loyalties. Of the sixty members, twenty-four belonged to the New-York Historical Society and twenty-four were listed on the rolls of the American Geographical and Statistical Society of New York, established in 1859. In addition, fifteen were members of the American Oriental Society of New Haven. Some of them held important offices in these organizations.

Very few of the members, even in the early and most fruitful years of the AES, had any ethnological field experience. While a few members like Paul DuChaillu, Stephens, Catherwood, Schoolcraft, Squier, Davis, and to a lesser extent, Bartlett and Robinson, had done important research in ethnology, by far the majority were simply travelers or armchair ethnologists. Even among those with experience, ideological differences of opinion concerning the nature and purpose of ethnology undermined their productivity, at least so far as the Society was concerned. The basic problem was that the clergy believed that ethnology was important for missionary work in exotic lands; others saw ethnology as an end in itself, and still others used it to bolster favorite racial theories.

Philosophical disagreements had an adverse effect on the Society's fortunes. Many members quarreled about what was pertinent and legitimate for discussion. The crux of the matter lay in the fundamental division between the atheistic polygenists, like Squier, and the clerics, typified by Rev. Francis Hawks. When ethnology included only philology, archaeology, and ethnography, the clergy seemed to have been pleased with the AES. However, as physical anthropology became a topic of common discussion in the Society, discord erupted. The polygenist approach to physical anthropology disturbed both the clergy and other monogenistic members, many of whom were mainly interested in Near Eastern antiquities and insisted on a literal interpretation of the Bible. However, European discoveries of prehistoric man in the late 1850s and 1860s lent support both to antiscriptural archaeology and to Squier's intellectual position that no truth seeker can bring to the study of mankind "the element of faith, or adhesion to dogmas or creeds of any kind whatever" (Squier 1871:16). The racial issue had led George Gliddon to refuse a corresponding membership in the mid–1840s, evidently on the grounds that he found the religious faction unbearable (Bartlett Papers, Gliddon to Bartlett June 16, 1845). The controversy became more acute during the 1850s, and, as Squier later recalled, "the question of human unity could not be discussed without offense to some of the members and its casual introduction was made a ground of impassioned protest" (Squier 1871:16–17). According to Squier, this situation forced the AES to limit itself to innocuous discussion. A pronounced schism never developed, but the differences remained irreconcilable. The evidence suggests that Rev. Hawks and probably some of the other ministers quit the Society in the late 1850s over this issue.[4]

Disputes between members were not, however, limited to differing scientific or ethnological theories. Personality conflicts led to some serious altercations which disrupted the smooth functioning of the Society. Albert Gallatin was once angered at the removal of some personal friends from the membership list in the first volume of *Transactions,* and even had the pages reprinted to reinstate the missing names (Turner to Bartlett, Bartlett Papers 11/5/1849). More seriously, a lengthy feud broke out between Squier and his coauthor, Dr. Davis, over the credit for their *Ancient Monuments of the Mississippi Valley.* Throughout the 1850s, Squier and Schoolcraft were continually at odds. Their clash was motivated less by differences of opinion than over which of them was the dean of American ethnology. Such personal quarrels, usually confined to correspondence, occasionally resulted in venomous printed attacks on published research.

The meager economic resources of the AES also proved detrimental to its scientific activities. Although Gallatin paid much of the cost of the first two volumes of *Transactions,* this support ended with his death in 1849, and it must have given members the unfortunate impression that funds could come from sources other than their own pocketbooks.

It was unfortunate, too, for the American Ethnological Society that it had to compete against the larger and better financed New-York Historical Society. Something akin to sibling rivalry existed between the two groups, with the older Historical Society clearly the dominant New York institution, often receiving gifts from wealthy New Yorkers who neglected the AES. Although the memberships of the two societies overlapped, there was still competition for members, financial support, papers, and recognition. Interestingly, papers given before the Historical Society became increasingly more ethnological in their concerns, while those given to the AES became less so. For example Schoolcraft, Morgan, and Squier all read papers on Indians and ethnology, and Bartlett originally gave his "Progress of Ethnology" before the New-York Historical Society (Collection of NYHS 1842–48).

While the Historical Society had an imposing building at its disposal, the Ethnological Society lacked even a rented room to house its library and collections and to hold meetings. Over the years, the Society tried unsuccessfully to obtain funds from wealthy New Yorkers to build or buy a hall. After thirty years of shifting from house to house, the Society's library and museum was hopelessly scattered and had all but disappeared (Squier 1871:71).

If the Society had financial problems, so too did some of its members. Many of the older members possessed moderate fortunes, but aside from Gallatin, they were generally the least productive as ethnologists. Some of the younger and most active members eventually found themselves forced by financial exigencies to seek employment outside New York City. For about a decade, Bartlett and Charles Welford shared a New York bookstore. When the business could no longer support two growing families, Bartlett sought greener pastures. He first headed the U.S.—Mexican Boundary Commission, which entailed a sojourn to the Southwest, and later entered Rhode Island politics. Squier received an appointment as Chargé d'Affaires to Central America and thereafter was deeply involved with several business ventures. Professor William W. Turner, a philologist by inclination, found a post at the Patent Office in Washington, D.C. Schoolcraft, formerly the Superintendent of Indian Affairs in Michigan, after nine lean years in New York City finally got a commission from the state of New York to conduct a census of Indians. This eventually led to a federal appointment to prepare a statistical history of the Indians of the United States, which necessitated his removal to Washington, D.C. The exodus of these men, four of its most productive members, dealt the Society a crippling blow. Ironically, in most of these cases recommendations by influential Society members led to the governmental appointments.

All of these causes—financial difficulties, feuds, loss of key members through relocation and, of course, death and factionalism—led to the decline of the American Ethnological Society. Its offspring, the Anthropological Institute, fared no better. The failure of the latter organization probably stemmed from New York's inability to support so limited and doctrinaire a body. Clearly, many New York ethnologists had less of an "anthropological" outlook than had Squier. According to Franz Boas, many preferred to associate with the American Museum of Natural History, founded in 1868 (Boas 1943:8). It is possible that even during the short life of the Anthropological Institute, dissident members continued the AES. We know that after the institute's demise, the American Ethnological Society continued to meet irregularly throughout the nineteenth century. Proud of their distinguished past, members of the Society retained their old name, but not until the twentieth century did the American Ethnological Society regain the prominence it had experienced in the 1840s (Bartlett Papers, J. C. Brown Library, Drowne to Bartlett 3/3/71; 4/19/73).

NOTES

[1]Squier's committee wanted to rename the AES the American Anthropological Society, but that name had reportedly been adopted by a Boston and another New York group (Squier 1871:19).

[2]Gallatin's work on the languages of the Americas claimed the greatest amount of space in the Society's *Transactions*. Gallatin's fame and the fact that he underwrote the costs of publishing much of the volume doubtless justified the length of his contribution.

[3]Squier was quite open about the Institute's debt to Europe and Broca. He wrote that "by the consolidation of the Ethnological Society of London with the Anthropological Society of the same capital, the designation 'Ethnological' had ceased to apply to any society of importance in Europe, and the term 'Anthropological' had been accepted instead, for the reasons well explained by Dr. Broca, one of which is, that the new name is more appropriate and comprehensive; and another, that the study of man requires the cooperation of naturalists as well as archaeologists, anatomists as well as antiquaries" (Squier 1871:20).

[4]Hawks became a founder and the first president of the American Geographical and Statistical Society, a body which included ethnology among its interests.

LITERATURE CITED

Adams, Henry
 1879 The Life of Albert Gallatin. Philadelphia: J. B. Lippincott & Co.

American Ethnological Society
 1860-61 Bulletin of the American Ethnological Society.
 1845-53 Transactions of the American Ethnological Society.

Anthropological Institute of New-York
 1870-72 Journal of the Anthropological Institute of New-York.

Bartlett, John Russell
 Papers. John Carter Brown Library, Brown University, Providence, R.I.
 n.d. Autobiography. John Carter Brown Library, Brown University, Providence, R.I. MS.

Berendt, Carl Hermann
 1869 Analytical Alphabet for the Mexican and Central American Languages. New York: American Ethnological Society.

Boas, Franz
 1943 The American Ethnological Society. Science 97:7–8.

Broca, Paul
 1871-72 The Progress of Anthropology in Europe and America. Journal of the Anthropological Institute of New-York 1:22–42.

Fletcher, Dr. Robert
 1882 Paul Broca and the French School of Anthropology. *In* The Saturday Lectures, pp. 113–142. Boston: D. Lothrop & Co.

(Hale, E. E.)
 1849 Memoir of Albert Gallatin. Proceedings of the American Antiquarian Society. October 23, 1849:16–32.

Hallowell, A. Irving
 1960 The Beginnings of Anthropology in America. *In* Selected Papers from the American Anthropologist, Frederica De-Laguna, ed. pp. 1–90. Evanston, Ill.: Row, Peterson and Company.

Literary World
 1847-53

Mitra, Panchanan
 1933 A History of American Anthropology. Calcutta: University of
  Calcutta.

Morgan, Lewis Henry
 1871 Systems of Consanguinity and Affinity. Smithsonian Contributions to Knowledge, no. 17. Washington, D.C.

New-York Historical Society
 1843-49 Proceedings of the New-York Historical Society.

Squier, E. G.
  Papers. Library of Congress; Washington, D.C.
 1871-72 Proceedings Preliminary to the Organization of the Anthropological Institute of New-York. Journal of the Anthropological Institute of New-York 1:14–20.

3

Franklin B. Hough: An Incipient Anthropologist of the Early Nineteenth Century*

ARTHUR EINHORN

Lewis County Historian, Lowville, New York

The late nineteenth and early twentieth centuries saw numerous personalities emerge from totally unrelated disciplines and interests into qualified scholars of anthropology. Their influence and theories

*Mr. Einhorn also chairs the Social Science Department at Lowville Academy and is Associate Professor of Anthropology at Jefferson Community College. Watertown, New York.

have become part of the profession's intellectual bag and baggage, as well as subjects of the discipline's folklore. Several years ago Claude Lévi-Strauss (1969:61–63) published a convincing case for ranking Rousseau as a "father" of anthropology. Those who argue against the anthropological legitimacy of some historical personalities might be applying criteria to the past that only recently became viable professional taxonomy.

As it functions today, anthropology could only have grown out of the work of interested nonprofessionals who engaged in anthropological behavior and whose "marginal" work reinforced the contributions and eventual emergence of major personalties. Early anthropology was not a discipline, nor would it have developed into one had it not been for the men on the sidelines, some long forgotten. Their significance is revealed when we examine it in the light of anthropology's roots in the natural sciences and museums (Fenton 1968:4–5). Western man may have been dealt with in the context of history but preliterate societies were lumped with botany; primitive technology and folklore were collected as most biological and geological specimens.

In the early nineteenth century there were few specialists in the slowly emerging study of anthropology; a real need existed for the generalist, the dilettante, whose mind was stimulated by a wide range of topics and whose awareness responded to the relationships between widely separated artifacts and man.

This paper addresses itself to the life and works of one of those marginal men of early anthropology, although he was better known as a historian, forester, conservationist, and medical doctor. His anthropological contributions seem minor admidst the other work he produced, yet a lack of quantity cannot alter that they were written with quality when anthropology was still ill defined and such anthropological behavior was the exception rather than the rule. The subject was a contemporary of Lewis Henry Morgan and graduated from Union College within a few years of him. Their paths probably crossed many times in Albany at the New York State Legislature, as well as at the Albany Institute and the Smithsonian Institution in Washington, D.C. He was familiar with Morgan's work on the Iroquois, as is shown by the many footnotes and references to Morgan in his publications. This, however, is only a superficial claim to a link with the anthropology of Morgan's time, and before presenting the evidence, it will be necessary to outline briefly some highlights of the man's extremely active career.

FRANKLIN HOUGH'S LIFE

Franklin B. Hough was born in Martinsburg, Lewis County, New York in 1822, the son of Dr. Horatio Gates Hough. Horatio Hough was the first physician in Lewis County and a man whose accomplishments included a short published tract entitled *Diving, or An Attempt to Describe Upon Hydraulic and Hydrostatic Principles a Method of Supplying the Diver with Air Under Water,* (Hartford, Conn., 1813). With Franklin growing up in the household of such a father, he developed many intellectual interests, despite the fact that he resided in a remote and sparsely settled region of New York far from intellectual centers or academia. Lewis Henry Morgan's life was similar in many respects, before and after his college training.

Hough received his primary education at Lowville Academy (located in Lowville, Lewis County) and later attended Union College (Schenectady) where he acquired his A.B. degree in 1843 and his A.M. several years later. For a short while he taught school in Champion, New York, then decided upon medicine as a career. In 1848, Cleveland Medical College (now Case Western Reserve) awarded him the M.D. and many decades later his accomplishments caused the Regents of the State of New York to confer on him the Ph.D. Between his graduation from Union College in 1843 and his death in 1885, Hough wrote, edited, and published over eighty books, pamphlets, and articles on subjects ranging from colonial and American history through physical science, linguistics, archaeology, American Indians, botany, forestry, constitutional law, statistics, biography, genealogy, and miscellaneous other topics. Such prolific eclecticism, ranging all over the academic landscape, suggests the general lack of others specializing in those areas; a characteristic typical of Franz Boas even years later.

When the professional associations most scholars affiliate with today are matched against Hough's activities, he appears almost gargantuan. He belonged to thirty-six professional and nonprofessional organizations in many states of the United States, as well as Canada and Europe. These included a wide range of interests covering forestry, medicine, genealogy, anthropology, and biology. He was also a fellow of the American Association for the Advancement of Science and active in the American Philosophical Society, the Academy of Natural Sciences, the Anthropological Society of Washington, and the New York Forestry Association (this last named orginization being closely tied to his role as the intellectual progenitor of the New York State Conservation Department). Hough also had close ties with the Smithsonian Institution and was several times engaged by congressional commissions and state governments to conduct various studies in population census, medical and vital statistics, and botany.

During the Civil War he had served as a regimental surgeon with the New York Volunteers, and as a result of this experience translated Lucien Bandens's *Guerre de Crimée* under the title *On Military and Camp Hospitals* in 1862 (Graves 1932:250–252).

Over the middle decades of Hough's life he recognized the growing problem of forest resource depletion. In 1873 he presented a paper to the American Association for the Advancement of Science entitled "On the Duty of Governments in the Preservation of Forests" (Graves 1932:251). This paper resulted in a memorial to Congress recommending enactment of conservation laws. President Grant subsequently endorsed the recommendations to Congress, and in 1876 Hough was appointed by Grant as the first federal forestry agent in the Department of Agriculture. Hough's familiarity with forestry had an early foundation, seen in his publication *A Catalogue of Indigenous, Naturalized and Filicoid Plants of Lewis County, New York* (1846). Hough was also interested in geology and is reputed to have discovered the mineral "houghite" (Graves 1932:251). He also donated many geological specimens to the natural history cabinet in the state capitol in Albany.[1]

HOUGH'S WORK AND PUBLICATIONS

Hough's writing career began while practicing medicine in rural St. Lawrence and Jefferson counties in upstate New York. During this time he took up a serious interest in the local history of the region and began researching it. His published county histories are quite long and generally begin with voluminous material focused on the aboriginal and colonial occupation. For this he drew from previously published colonial documents, the works of his contemporaries (e.g. O'Callaghan, Clark, Morgan, and Squier), and his own observations and fieldwork (principally among the Mohawks of the St. Regis reservation in New York and the Caugnawaga reservation near Montreal). Much of the material is broken down into systematic categories and reads well as a regional synthesis representing the state of the art for the mid–nineteenth century.

ARCHAEOLOGY

One of Hough's archaeological county histories (1853) quotes liberally from Squier's (1849) previous work describing earthworks and mounds. But Hough then goes on to enumerate outstanding sites and their locations, adding new sites and interpretations not covered by Squier. He further describes petroglyphs and their locations in the above publication as well as in another county history (1854). There are no clear-cut indications that Hough ever excavated a site, but he certainly conducted a survey of sites and roamed the countryside with open eyes, as is evident when he states, "Nothing is more common than to find along the lands that skirt the fertile meadow bottoms . . . the broken remains of crude pottery . . ." (Hough 1854:18).

Very little of Hough's records of archaeological remains lacks some reasonable inference and interpretation. In referring to several sites with high earthern works, Hough noted, "It may be well to remark, that the observation made by DeWitt Clinton, that none of these remains occur below the level of the lake ridges, fails to be sustained in the instances which occur in St. Lawrence and several which occur in Jefferson counties" (Hough 1853:15), and for astute observation, Franklin Hough must take honors as one of the first to publish a description of post molds left by ancient stockades: "In a few of the trench enclosures of Western New York, the evidences of this (stockades) are not wanting, for the holes which were left by the decaying of the pickets may still be traced" (Hough 1853:19).

It is fortunate that articulate observers like Hough and Squier recorded what they did, for as Hough observed on one site, "Every trace of the work has been long since erased by cultivation . . . [and] . . . great numbers of these [artifacts] . . . have been picked up and carried off by the curious . . . . " (Hough 1853:19). Quite appropriately Hough's archaeological references have been a useful resource for mid-twentieth-century archaeologists,[2] particularly at the University of Buffalo, where a special archaeological project has been under way for several years writing the prehistory of Jefferson County. As one Ph.D. candidate noted, "Hough's site location references are usually more accurate than Squier's."[3]

ETHNOGRAPHY AND ETHNOHISTORY

Hough found much in the French and English colonial literature whereby some Native American history might be reconstructed. In 1866 he translated and republished the original 1787 French edition of *Captain Pouchot's Memoirs of the War of 1755-60*. In this account of one man's view of the French and Indian War, there are several examples of Iroquois oral tradition which Pouchot had written down. In subsequent publications, Hough quoted this material when discussing native tradition; as he also used the works of LaHontan, DelaPotherie, Colden, and Charlevoix.

By 1880, when Hough published *The Thousand Islands of the St. Lawrence,* he was in a position to sort out the confusion of who first set down the "Legend of Hiawatha"—Clark, Schoolcraft, or Longfellow—and concluded it was Clark who had first recorded it from two Onondaga chiefs. Schoolcraft later published it without acknowledging Clark's *Notes on the Iroquois;* Longfellow acknowledged Schoolcraft in what Hough kindly described as a "highly imaginative versification" (Hough 1880:13-14) of the tradition. Hough points out that Longfellow changed the locale of the tradition as well as the essence of it, and finally gives Clark much credit for having recorded it in the first place.[4]

In his earlier *History of St. Lawrence and Franklin Counties,* Hough put together, from many published and unpublished sources and his own investigations, a fairly concise picture of the history of the St. Regis and Caugnawaga Mohawks. He apparently interviewed many Mohawk residents of both reserves, pieced together life histories, and effectively described the lifestyle, pastimes, government, numbers, and condition of those people for the early and middle decades of the nineteenth century, a boon to any student of acculturation and ethnohistory. This material is widely scattered throughout the book, but it is a virtual gold mine of data for the ethnohistorian today.[5]

Among other Hough publications relating to ethnohistory are the following: *Pemaquid in Its Relations to Our Colonial History* (1874), *Easton's Phillip's Indian War* (from original MS with Hough notes and analysis—1858), and numerous other items such as the *Journal of Major Robert Rogers* (1883), *Capt. Leonard Bleeker's Order book* (1865) from the Sullivan Campaign against the Iroquois, and *Sir John Johnson's Invasion of the Schoharie and Mohawk Valley* (1861) from the unpublished originals.

In 1970 a doctoral dissertation was written which relied as much on Hough as on any other source, particularly on the ethnographic material on the St. Regis Mohawks (Frisch 1970). Because of the 1911 fire in the State Capitol in Albany, Hough's material is the only extant data available on the subject for certain periods.[6]

LIFE HISTORIES AND BIOGRAPHIES

Apart from five biographies of white Americans which Hough wrote and published, he fell heir to and edited a life history manuscript sent to him by one of his informants at the St. Regis Reservation. This was published under the title, *Life of Te-Ho-Ra-Gwa-Ne-Gen, Alias Thomas Williams, A Chief of the Caughnawaga Tribe of Indians in Canada*, by the Rev. Eleazer Williams (Albany: J. Munsell, 1859). It is a good document of the colonial period and the French and Indian War. While imparting the highlights of Thomas Williams's life (the descendent of a white captive from New England), the narrative gives many insights into Mohawk and Abenaki culture during the late eighteenth and early nineteenth centuries. Unfortunately, only 200 copies of this work were printed. Eleazer Williams was the object of much controversy when Hough knew him (over his claim to being the Lost Dauphin), and in the introduction Hough Describes Eleazer and the controversy in terms which could only be defined as objectively fair.

Scattered throughout the St. Lawrence County History, noted earlier, are pages on the life of At-I-Aton-Ha-Ron-Kwen, or Col. Louis Cook. One section of sixteen pages is a solid biography of Cook, which, as Hough states, "we have derived from his daughter, Mary Ka-Wen-Ni-Ta-Ke, at St. Regis, through the kindness of the Rev. F. Marcoux, as interpreter, and from a biographical notice written by Eleazer. . . ." "The author has also availed himself of whatever else came his way, among the public archives in Albany."

In Hough's charming book *American Biographical Notes* (1875), he lists not only white U.S. citizens, but also both famous and obscure native Americans, American blacks, visiting Japanese students, Latin American Presidents and prime ministers, native Hawaiians, Hungarians, and Dutchmen in Surinam among others. His coverage, hardly Anglophile, was surely Pan-American in scope, and implies a definite recognition of the family of man. Most of the personalities included in Hough's work were *not* included in other biographical dictionaries of the day, such as Drake's or Allen's.

LINGUISTICS

Although Hough was not conversant in Mohawk, he knew simple greetings and utilized several qualified bilingual informants who worked closely with him in producing a sizable list of Iroquois (Mohawk) place names for a three-county area in northern New York and adjacent Canada. These Mohawk names are accompanied by English translations, as well as common names. In several instances he notes Morgan's and Squier's terms for the same locations in a comparison between Seneca and Mohawk. It is interesting that he coded each of the native terms and translations to indicate which informant provided the information (Hough 1853:178–181). Such meticulous care for data quality was rare in that era.

Entirely in keeping with Hough's humanism, apparent throughout his writings, he believed Indian place names were beautiful both in sound and meaning, and advocated using them instead of the recently superimposed Anglo-Saxon names.

MINORITY ADVOCATE

Not uncharacteristic for the period and region, Hough was an abolitionist in the pre–Civil War era, although his role in the movement is an obscure story. His older brother, Horatio Hough, was a conductor in the Underground Railroad.

In Franklin Hough's edited edition of the *Proceedings of the Commissioners of Indian Affairs for Extinguishment of Indian Title in New York State* (1861) he expresses his empathy and remorse, rather than the usually cold and implicit rightness presumed by many others of the period in the national pastime of manifest destiny. Hough further emphasized his position on dubious land titles by twice noting that the Oneidas were forced into ceding their salmon fisheries in 1802, due to clumsy and indifferent procedures by the state (Hough 1860:21, 23; 1854:38–42). Had Hough been alive in that period he may well have championed the Oneida cause as Morgan so ably served the Tonawanda Seneca.

PHYSICAL ANTHROPOLOGY

As a medical doctor Hough was conversant in osteological terminology. Occasionally when describing Indian burial sites or ossuaries he used technical terms for parts and conditions of skeletal remains. In other instances, as when interviewing informants at St. Regis, he noted human variation in facial traits and hair type. These aspects, though not forming a significant feature of his writings, indicate he was familiar with and aware of them.

CONCLUSIONS

Franklin Hough's interests and writings are really not so unusual when it is considered that in his day the percentage of highly educated individuals in America was relatively small. Men like Hough and Morgan returned to their rural hamlets with college degrees in hand barely forty years after the frontier had moved westward. Amidst the majority of their fellow citizens they were educationally unique and probably intellectually frustrated. Such professional men naturally turned to intellectual endeavors and interests which filled their leisure time and in some instances became contributors to literature, history, or some branch of science.

It is apparent that Hough touched in varying degrees on many aspects of what we today define as anthropology. With his historical orientation he ably used library archives, did fieldwork, asked the right questions, gathered data, and presented a diachronic picture of a region. While he exhibited incipient anthropological behavior, his general interests were too varied for him to concentrate in one area. One wonders what he might have progressed into had he lived closer to Morgan in western New York, or if the Mohawks at St. Regis had been traditional Indians rather than Catholic converts. Would he have delved deeper and further than he did, given the opportunity? Indications suggest that he probably would have. In one passage he stated that he often collected material because it might be useful to others, apart from his own research target. Hough never expounded any theories, although he occasionally attempted light interpretations, a trait Boas would have admired in him.

A special case need not be made for Hough any more than for the many others whose contributions were minor, but perhaps significant to someone in the future. Franklin Hough is not a difficult man to assess in the broad picture of nineteenth-century intellectual activity. He and others like him filled a need by functioning in various social, governmental, and academic vacuums. As science and academia grew, these men grew with the trend and reinforced it with their contributions; in some cases perhaps they even created trends. The intellectual climate of America in the period was certainly a curious and searching enthusiasm, a creative influence on many educated men.

Not to recognize the importance of such individuals to the emergence of specific disciplines, including anthropology, is to ignore the intellectual milieu and process of peer interaction for a given period of history. In a day when only a few professions could claim a specific training harness within academia, there were many unharnessed in the race to understand man and record his past. That only a few would finish the race with a broad recognition of accomplishment is typical statistical prediction. Yet the "also-ran" group should not be forgotten; to them is owed the validity, if not the intensity of the race.

NOTES

[1]Charles Gillette, senior curator, New York State Museum (personal communication).

[2]Marian E. White, "Current Work on Iroquois Archaeology in Northern New York State," paper read at the 1969 meeting of New York State Archaeological Association.

[3]Earl Sidler (personal communication).

[4]Subsequently collected versions of the Hiawatha epic would prove to be superior to the Clark version, but it is important to know who recorded the one he did.

[5]The citations are too numerous to quote here; the original index to the *History of St. Lawrence and Franklin Counties* is inadequate. See new comprehensive index compiled by the St. Lawrence County Historical Association, Canton, N.Y., 1971.

[6]Jack A. Frisch (personal communication).

LITERATURE CITED

Fenton, William N.
    1968 Anthropology and the University. Inaugural lecture at the State University of New York at Albany, May 8, printed program text.

Frisch, Jack A.
    1970 Revitalization, Nativism and Tribalism Among the St. Regis Mohawks. Ph.D. dissertation, Indiana University. Ann Arbor, Mich.: University Microfilms.

Graves, Henry S.
    1932 Franklin B. Hough. *In* Dictionary of American Biography. Dumas Malone, ed. New York: Charles Scribners Sons.

Hough, Franklin B.
    1853 History of St. Lawrence and Franklin Counties. Albany, N.Y.: Little and Co.
    1854 History of Jefferson County. Albany, N.Y.: Joel Munsell.
    1860 History of Lewis County. Albany, N.Y.: Munsell and Rowland.
    1875 American Biographical Notes. Albany, N.Y.: Joel Munsell.
    1880 Thousand Islands of the St. Lawrence. Syracuse, N.Y.: Dains, Bardeen and Co.

Hough, Franklin B., ed.
    1859 Life of Thomas Williams. Albany, N.Y.: Joel Munsell.

1861 Proceedings of the Commissioners of Indian Affairs for Extinguishment of Indian Title in New York State. Albany, N.Y.: Joel Munsell.

Lévi-Strauss, Claude
1969 Rosseau, Father of Anthropology. *In* The Unesco Courier. New York.

St. Lawrence County Historical Society
1971 Index to Hough's History of St. Lawrence and Franklin Counties. Canton, N.Y.

Squier, E. George
1849 Aboriginal Monuments of New York. Smithsonian Contributions to Knowledge. Washington, D.C.

White, Marian E.
1969 Current Work on Iroquois Archaeology in Northern New York. Draft of paper presented at the 1969 annual New York State Archaeological Association meeting.

4

Amateurs and Professionals In Washington Anthropology, 1879 to 1903

CURTIS M. HINSLEY, JR.
Colgate University

In recent years professionalization has become a popular topic among historians and other scholars interested in the histories of their disciplines. Much of the renewed interest, especially among historians of science, resulted from Thomas Kuhn's controversial book, *The Structure of Scientific Revolutions*, which presented a useful model for evaluating professional change within scientific communities. Predictably, subsequent studies have been of uneven quality, ranging from helpful discussions of concepts such as *professional* and *scientist* in differing historical contexts, to confusing works in which the process of professionalization takes on a certain inevitability and an impersonal, suprahistorical quality.[1]

Several years ago George Stocking set forth some guidelines for historians of the behavioral sciences. Pointing out the dangers as well as the utility of presentist assumptions and motivations in such investigations, he advised that we must attempt to understand the past for the sake of the past; the science of any historical period, he reminded, must be understood in its own terms.[2] This is a challenging task. Understanding the emergence of American anthropology as an academic discipline requires that it be approached simultaneously in terms of debate over substantive data and theory, institutional patterns and alternatives, the careers of individuals, and the interaction of these factors.[3] Rather than an impersonal or inevitable process, the movement toward self–consciousness and self–definition among persons involved in anthropological studies in the late nineteenth century was a halting, complex, and highly personal historical phenomenon. In order to comprehend what it meant to be an anthropologist in America in 1880 or 1890 we must seriously consider the works and careers of individuals who, in terms of ultimate disciplinary and theoretical developments, were left behind. Why were they superseded? What happened to them? Why did their concept of anthropology fail to take root and flourish? What explanation adequately accounts for their fate?

Anthropologists studying the history of their discipline have understandably given most attention to tracing theoretical developments. Recently institutional studies have increased, perhaps because they offer concrete signs of professional change. In particular, the establishment of university departments around the turn of the century has been viewed as a critical professional breakthrough.[4] But historical change consists of avenues not taken as well as those chosen. It is important to examine both. The development of university anthropology was a gradual process, not nearly as certain at the time as in retrospect.[5] Two other models—museum anthropology and the Bureau of American Ethnology—presented possible alternatives. The Bureau embodied a concept of scientific anthropology that became a historical reject, a road not taken in the professional development of American anthropology. While it continued to contribute to anthropology (until abolished in 1965), the professional assumptions that dominated the Bureau during its early years diminished with the death of John Wesley Powell in 1902. This paper examines the professional standards and ideas about scientific inquiry that dominated Washington science under Powell, and attempts to account for the fate of the Bureau in terms of those ideas.

Anthropology in Washington during the last decades of the nineteenth century was inseparable from the personality and opinions of Major Powell. The Bureau in particular was largely the personal creation of this man. Powell owed much, it is true, to his predecessors, especially to ethnologist and linguist George Gibbs IV. The corpus of 670 manuscripts that formed the data base for the Bureau's efforts at linguistic classification had been gathered over several decades prior to the founding of the Bureau, particularly during the 1860s and 1870s in response to Gibbs' circulars disseminated by the Smithsonian Institution. Powell also inherited directly from Gibbs the idea of a comprehensive linguistic mapping of America.[6] But whatever his theoretical and material debts, the Bureau bore the stamp of Powell. He was solely responsible for its legal existence.[7] In his twenty years as director he doubled the linguistic inventory; by his death these irreplaceable manuscripts were clearly recognized as the priceless possessions of the Bureau.[8] And while Gibbs only dreamed of a linguistic map, Powell made the map and the classification the outstanding achievement of the Bureau's first decade.

Powell envisioned anthropology as the grand science of man, which he divided into numerous subsciences or lines of inquiry. These divisions, institutionalized in the structures of the Bureau and the Anthropological Society of Washington, reflected the growth and composite nature of nineteenth-century anthropology. According to Powell's broad definition, the science embraced everything relating to man: physical nature, relations to environment, material products, social arrangements, psychology, religions, and so on. The Major's basic classification established four or five categories, which he repeatedly rearranged and subdivided. The

Anthropological Society of Washington, like the Bureau of Ethnology founded in 1879 and dominated by Powell until his death, originally had four sections, each headed by a vice-president: Somatology, Philology, Ethnology, and Archaeology. These were subsequently expanded to five, and later again increased to seven sections.[9] In theory each vice-president of the Society was expected to give an annual report of progress in his section and to insure that his branch received adequate representation in the proceedings of the Society. In practice, however, some sections—notably physical anthropology—were slighted, reflecting Powell's own biases.[10]

The concept of anthropology as a grand, overarching science embracing many diverse but somehow interrelated lines of inquiry encouraged the interest, support, and participation of a broad range of men and women. Most of these individuals pursued vocations only tenuously, if at all, related to any present definition of the discipline. But in the last years of the nineteenth century, anthropology in America was still very much as Joseph Henry, first secretary of the Smithsonian, had described it decades before: a "common ground" of interest and concern to cultivators of the physical sciences, natural sciences, archeology, language, history, and literature alike. The uniqueness of anthropology lay in broad inclusiveness, not in exclusive specialization.[11] By joining the Anthropological Society, an individual gained for himself and for his special line of work a new significance and perspective, a sense of participating in a larger, perhaps universal quest for "the secrets of man's origin, progress and destiny."[12] As the lectures and discussions of the Society indicate, anthropology in Washington in these years was oriented to the present and future as much as to the past—it was here, after all, that Lester Frank Ward first read drafts of his *Dynamic Sociology*. The prestige and sense of involvement in vital affairs that became attached to the title *anthropologist* toward the end of the century in the nation's capital is difficult to recapture, but Otis T. Mason caught it when he quoted a Patent Office employee, who, on hearing of the anthropological relevance of his work, supposedly exclaimed: "I an anthropologist! I thought I was only an examiner. I am going to write a paper on anthropology."[13]

Between 1880 and 1900 the Anthropological Society's membership and proceedings embodied this tradition and approach. The
Society enjoyed a large and diverse membership. It drew heavily, of
course, on the various government bureaus: besides the Smithsonian personnel (including the Bureau and the National Museum),
the Patent Office, Army, Navy, Geological Survey, Pension Office,
and Department of Agriculture were well represented. In addition,
physicians consistently made up for more than fifteen percent of the
membership. Although the leadership of the Society remained in the
close control of Powell and a relatively small group of associates,
the members as a whole participated actively in the lectures and discussions at the biweekly meetings from November through May.[14]
The Society's programs, published first in its *Transactions* and
later in the *American Anthropologist,* reflected the diverse special
interests of the members, ranging from discussion of Henry
George's *Progress and Poverty* and the theory of rent, to debate
over Malthusian doctrine, feudalism in Japan, and medical
mythology in Ireland.[15]

Over at the Bureau offices on F Street the original staff, hand
picked by Powell and to a large extent carried over from the geological surveys of the 1870s, exhibited a similar range of background
and interest.[16] While the Anthropological Society reflected the openness and inclusive nature of Washington anthropology in a social
context, the Bureau embodied Powell's concept of scientific activity
in a functioning organ of government. Like Joseph Henry, his
mentor in Washington, Powell believed that there were many roles
and useful functions in a young science such as geology or
anthropology that was still gathering its basic materials from remote and unpopulated regions of a vast continent. In Powell's
opinion, few individuals were capable of becoming first-rate
scientists; only the best scientific minds might perform the ultimate, highest tasks of synthesis, deduction, and generalization.
But many could participate in the exciting fact-gathering operations. Thus while he excluded very few from a role in scientific enterprise, he discriminated between those who contributed to the inductive data gathering and those who derived generalizations and laws
from the accumulated materials.

This vision of a two-tiered scientific establishment is essential to understanding the early history of the Bureau and of anthropology in Washington generally, because it determined the structure and mode of operations of Powell's organizations. A product of the peculiar needs and exigencies of mid-nineteenth century scientific explorations of the American continent, this view of distinct functions was both democratic in inviting wide participation, and elitist in reserving certain functions to a few individuals. In 1882 Otis Mason—a self-trained anthropologist himself—delivered a public lecture at the Smithsonian that was intended to "bring about a better understanding between scientific specialists and intelligent thinkers." "Who may be an anthropologist?" Mason asked rhetorically, and then answered: "Every man, woman, and child that has sense and patience to observe, and that can honestly record the thing observed." Anthropology, he stressed, was "A science in which there is no priesthood and no laity, no sacred language; but one in which you are all both the investigator and the investigated. . . ."[17]

It is worth noting that Mason's requirements for participation in anthropology were sense, patience, and honesty. Even in the late nineteenth century being a scientist in America was still as much a matter of character and integrity as one of specific academic or laboratory training—especially in a field like anthropology. After all, a man or woman could be taught to use the latest scientific equipment, but dedication to the pursuit of truth and willingness to forego the popular acclaim of the fraud were qualities that transcended the expertise of separate branches of scientific inquiry. In 1880 Powell, like Henry before him, still sought above all trustworthy and honest observers whose reports would form the factual foundation of scientific anthropology.

This vision of scientific enterprise helps to explain two distinctive features of early Bureau anthropology: the presumptuous ease with which Powell's workers moved in and out between anthropology and other fields—usually natural sciences such as geology, zoology, botany, and so on; and the lack of any attempt to undertake systematic training of anthropologists. It is true that academic programs in anthropology did not exist in America in 1880, and so the original Bureau staff necessarily came from other (if any) scientific backgrounds. But this fact obscures more than it explains, because Powell placed far more value on his estimate of character and methods of thought than on academic training.

Perhaps the democratic nature of government science under Powell, which at times approached an antiacademic and antieastern bias, is attributable to his midwestern background.[18] It is remarkable that so many of his colleagues had similar roots. In any case Powell, as he had done on his geological surveys, surrounded himself in the Bureau with men that he knew and trusted: James C. Pilling, his bibliographer and personal friend; Dr. Harry C. Yarrow, whose specialty was mortuary practices; Albert S. Gatschet, trained in classical philology; Garrick Mallery, who specialized in sign language and pictographs; and Otis Mason, who began the synonymy which later, after several metamorphoses, became the Bureau's *Handbook of American Indians North of Mexico.*[19] On his explorations down the Colorado River in the early 1870s, the major had permitted the members of his parties wide latitude in pursuing their own observations, reserving to himself the function and responsibility of drawing together the scientific conclusions of the expeditions.[20] Similarly, in the Bureau Powell assigned problems to the members of his scientific corps, who carried them out largely on their own and without close surveillance by the director.

Powell used their results, as one of his biographers has noted, "like building blocks in his synthetic history of mankind."[21] These results were printed in monograph form as appendices to the annual reports of the Bureau; but the larger theoretical generalizations derived from them appeared in Powell's statements in the main bodies of the reports. For example, in the 1881 report, Powell, commenting on William Henry Holmes' article "Art in Shell of the Ancient Americans," praised Holmes' caution and modesty in offering no theories. The Major then went on to conclude from Holmes' work that "the artistic methods of the Mounds Builders are traceable among the historic tribes of North America . . . ." Two years later Holmes contributed three more significant studies to the report. From these Powell gained a new appreciation of the importance of custom and tradition in the development of art. Holmes had shown, Powell wrote, that aesthetic judgments were not innate principles, but functions of habit and custom. "Objects are not made because they are essentially pleasing," the director concluded, "but are pleasing because they have been customarily made."[22] Such commentaries on the work of his staff provide a valuable means of tracing Powell's anthropological growth. While he rarely cited others in his own publications, in the process of synthesizing the accumulating data of the Bureau, Powell did learn from the labors of his colleagues.

The career of one of Powell's closest associates illustrates the dominant assumptions and characteristics of government science under Powell. William John ("WJ") McGee came to Washington in the early 1880s from the farmlands of Iowa with a background that included less than eight years of formal schooling and brief experiments in farming, blacksmithing, inventing, and finally surveying. His topographical and geological survey of part of northeastern Iowa in the late 1870s brought McGee to Powell's attention. Joining the United States Geological Survey in 1883, he soon took charge of its work on Atlantic coastal plain geology. When Powell resigned from the Survey and retired to the Bureau of Ethnology in 1893, McGee accompanied him, assuming the title Ethnologist in Charge and becoming the ailing Major's confidant, protegé, and heir apparent. As McGee and others later testified, during Powell's final years McGee supervised the daily operations of the Bureau and wrote almost everything that left the Bureau over Powell's signature.[23] On Powell's death, however, Smithsonian secretary Samuel P. Langley passed over McGee, choosing William Henry Holmes instead to head the Bureau. McGee resigned less than a year later, moving to St. Louis to take charge of the anthropology department at the Louisiana Purchase Exposition. He stayed on at the St. Louis Public Museum until 1907, when he returned to Washington to start a third and final career in hydrology, irrigation, and conservation. Until his death in 1912 McGee held a position as expert in the Bureau of Soils of the Department of Agriculture; with Gifford Pinchot he played an important—and largely unrecognized—role in the conservation movement of the Roosevelt and Taft administrations.[24]

McGee was the Horatio Alger figure of the Washington scientific community. As one biographer succinctly noted, he "attained a very notable measure of success with the minimum of formal educational training."[25] McGee's rapid and smooth rise to positions of prominence and responsibility, first in geology and later in anthropology, did not result from his original scientific contributions, which were minimal. As a contemporary observed, not unkindly, McGee's great strength was "the skillful use of the results of others."[26] John R. Swanton, one of the first of a new university-trained generation of anthropologists, was less charitable, recalling that McGee "did not impress me as a profound thinker but as intensely desirous to win scientific consideration, and while aping originality—rather by means of unusual verbiage than new ideas—desperately feared to depart from the 'party line' of his day...."[27]

Criticism of McGee's originality really misses the broader significance of his career. In part his successes in both geology and anthropology reflected the relative openness of these fields in the 1890s, more so in anthropology than geology. As a geological colleague enviously reminded McGee in 1899, he faced fewer rivals in ethnology than in geology.[28] But the explanation for McGee's stature in 1900 as one of the foremost anthropologists in the country lies in his role as an untiring promoter of science in general. McGee belonged to the last generation of a dying breed of scientist, a type, one colleague lamented in 1916, "whom there seems to be a tendency to crowd out now."[29] These men served a concept of science rather than a specific scientific discipline, and they valued generalization based on breadth of experience in several fields more than specialization. McGee summarized this position in 1898: "Worthy has been the work of specialists in the extension of knowledge, during the past half-century; but nobler still have been the tasks of the fewer searchers who have been able to span two or more specialties, and to simplify knowledge by coordination."[30]

Science was first and fundamentally a way of thinking, of assimilating experience. "Consciously organized knowledge," McGee called it, the most recent and highest evolutionary form of human thinking, at once including, superseding, and reducing to "simpler order" all lower forms of responding to and understanding the cosmos, such as animal instinct, human intuition, common sense, even wisdom.[31] Because science as a way of ordering experience was, like the size of the human brain, fundamentally a product of evolution, the limits to an individual's scientific utility and insights were set more by innate moral and intellectual factors than by training. On the lower levels of scientific activity, such as gathering and classifying objects and determining relationships within limited fields, basic honesty and intelligence sufficed. But in the almost ethereal realms where McGee and Powell "coordinated" laws and generalizations from every field of science, a higher order of thinking was required.

This scientific framework, while paying lip service to the "personal equation" of the astronomers, made little allowance for subjectivity in human perception. If two accounts of the same phenomenon disagreed, either there had been purposeful distortion for sensational effect or there had been two phenomena. Human perception, once cleansed of primitive notions and base motives, was unquestionably clear and certain.[32] Once attained, the methods of accurate scientific observation and generalization, crystallized and systematized in the New Geology and New Ethnology of Powell and McGee, yielded absolute or "determinate" knowledge that was unlikely to be overturned. Furthermore, the methods were applicable to any field of science; indeed, on the higher levels breadth of experience and vision were necessary to produce the broadest, most useful generalizations.

Utility was the ultimate goal. To McGee there was no such thing as "pure" science divorced from application to human needs; utility was integral to his concept of scientific activity. As Gifford Pinchot recalled, "[McGee's] vast mental activity was tempered and guided by the informing conviction that what he knew was valuable only as he could make it serve the human race."[33] Science, in McGee's broad sense of certain knowledge applied to human need, was chiefly responsible for the unity and exalted state of American civilization; and it would determine the future social and moral progress of the nation:

America [McGee wrote] has become a nation of science. There is
no industry . . . that is not shaped by research and its results . . . there is no law in our statutes, no motive in our
conduct, that has not been made juster by the straight-forward
and unselfish habit of thought fostered by scientific
methods . . . but greatest of all in present potency and future
promise is the elevation of moral character attained by that
sense of right thinking which flows only from consciously
assimilated experience, — and this is the essence of science now
diffused among our people.[34]

The fate of the world, it seemed at times, rested in the hands of the
scientist—particularly the government scientist, who ideally embodied the virtues of certain knowledge and the highest altruistic
motives on behalf of his fellow citizens.[35]

To this grand cause the Iowa farm boy devoted his life and subordinated his various careers in public service. During the two
decades in Washington McGee gathered to himself all the outward
trappings of scientific attainment, including marriage to Anita
Newcomb, daughter of America's foremost astronomer, Simon
Newcomb; continuous membership in every significant intellectual
society in Washington; and incessant activity in the American Association for the Advancement of Science, the Geological Society of
America, the National Geographic Society, the American Anthropological Association; and numerous other organizations.
Through this web of interrelated activities McGee hoped to secure a
respectable scientific place not only for himself but for the Bureau
and anthropology in general. During his years in the Bureau McGee
devoted much of his and his stenographer's time to these outside
activities. When he came under severe criticism for this practice
McGee defended his actions. It was essential, he believed, that
every collaborator of the Bureau "become connected with general
scientific progress" by participating in the voluntary scientific societies, which he felt were largely responsible for America's
scientific preeminence. The reputation of the Bureau depended upon
the scientific standing of its workers, which in turn resulted from
the number and quality of their official publications and their
voluntary activities. "The fact that salaries are paid out of appro-

priations made by the government," he concluded, ". . . is largely an incident in connection with the scientific development of the individuals who constitute the scientific element in this country . . ." McGee may have worked in the Bureau of American Ethnology, but he served the scientific development of America.[36]

McGee's vision for the development of America's "scientific element" amounted to a process of professionalization, a method of establishing scientific criteria and a community that relied on informal contact, personal encouragement, and advancement. A type of training was involved, but it was largely self-training in the field. In these respects the plan reflected the experiences of self-trained anthropologists like Powell and McGee, and it presented an alternative to the structured university programs of older sciences.

Within the Washington circle, with its recognized hierarchical structure dominated by a small group, this system functioned for a time. But the lack of explicit, nonpersonal criteria for discriminating and defining relative positions led to crises of status, particularly with persons outside Washington. One controversy of the early 1890s focused on the issues of professionalism in a peculiarly personal way and revealed the depth of the dilemma. Although the debate took place primarily within geological circles, one of the substantive issues—the antiquity of man in America—occupied the borderland between geology and anthropology; the major Washington combatants—McGee, Holmes, and Powell— were intimately involved in both fields.[37]

In June, 1892, George Frederick Wright, professor of "Relations of Science and Religion" at Oberlin Theological Seminary, published *Man and the Glacial Period,* a popular summary of an earlier work, *The Ice Age in North America.*[38] Wright had no formal training in geology; he had begun his own local investigations while a minister in New England, first publishing reports in the *Proceedings* of the Boston Society of Natural History. He later undertook investigations of glacial deposits in other states, working briefly with the U.S. Geological Survey and traveling to Alaska in 1886 to examine the Muir glacier.[39]

Wright's books challenged Washington geologists and anthropologists on two points: glacial history and the antiquity of

man in America. The scientists of Powell's Survey contended that
interglacial deposits and other evidence indicated at least two and
possibly more glacial periods in the western hemisphere, separated
by epochs of mild climate. Wright maintained, on the other hand,
that the Survey men had misread the evidence, chiefly because they
were under the influence of European glacial theorists such as
James Croll and James Geikie. He argued instead for a single glacia-
tion marked by temporary retreats, rather than complete departure
of the glacier.[40] Concerning the anthropological question Wright
contended, contrary to Washington orthodoxy, that evidence of
human implements found in the glacial gravels in various sections
of the United States—particularly Ohio and New Jersey—demonstrated conclusively the existence of glacial man.

The Washington corps, led by McGee, Holmes, and geologist
Thomas C. Chamberlin, responded with a vicious attack on Wright
which bore no relation to the intrinsic merits of his book and which
was clearly intended to destroy his credibility with both the
scientific community and the reading public. Wright's de-
fenders—who included Frederick Ward Putnam at Harvard—noted
at the time that the attack was particularly puzzling because the
new book only summarized in a popular form the conclusions that
Wright had drawn in his earlier book. *The Ice Age in North America,* originally published in 1889, had gone through several printings
by 1892, and not a word of criticism had come from Washington.[41]
But when the second book appeared, Chamberlin, in a series
of reviews and comments in *The Dial,* picked apart Wright's glacial
geology, officially disowned him on behalf of the Survey, questioned
the competence of his authorities for the paleolithic finds, and
accused him of misleading the public on a crucial scientific issue.
This last point clearly was Wright's major transgression. "No one,"
Chamberlin lectured him, "is entitled to speak on behalf of science
who does not himself know the way accurately." He reminded the
Oberlin professor that "when an author assumes to teach the people
on behalf of science, he ought to tell them what is science, as distinguished from what rests merely on inexpert testimony." The
responsible scientist did not presume to address a public audience
on scientific issues that were still under debate, since this might

"erect barriers in the way of the reception of the truth when it shall be ascertained. . . ." Publication of a popular book such as *Man and the Glacial Period* "inevitably carries with it the assumption of the fundamental prerequisite of instruction; namely, determinate knowledge." To be sure, the "modern critical geology" of the Survey was gradually reaching conclusions that "will unquestionably stand," but until the final results were in, works like Wright's amounted to a "peculiar blend of plausibility and inaccuracy."[42]

McGee's reviews of Wright's work lowered the level of debate to personal acrimony and name-calling. In brutal language McGee publicly branded Wright a "betinseled charlatan," an "intellectual parasite" and a "commercial swindler," accusing him of "egregious and misleading egotism," "specious misrepresentation," and "sheer mendacity." Privately he informed Chamberlin that "the sooner geologists . . . awaken to the necessity of stamping Wright as a pretender incompetent to observe, read or reason, and devoid of moral sense, the better it will be for the world." He implored his colleague to step on "this interminably buzzing mosquito."[43] As McGee's critics pointed out, his ardor was attributable partly to the fact that he was himself only recently converted from the erroneous views that Wright espoused regarding glacial man. As recently as 1889 McGee had corresponded warmly with Wright, and in an article in *Popular Science Monthly* in 1888 McGee, after reviewing much of the same evidence as Wright, had concluded that the testimony in favor of glacial man was "unimpeachable . . . the proof of the existence of glacial man seems conclusive."[44]

The Washington attack on the Oberlin professor had deeper roots, however, than McGee's need to establish his own geological and anthropological credentials. In the first place, Wright had impugned the reputation of the United States Geological Survey, supposedly the premier example of inductive science in America. Operating free of theoretical assumption, and particularly independent of European theories, the Survey had established the science of geology on a new plane in America—Powell and McGee called it the New Geology. Wright's accusations directly assaulted this vision. On the glacial issue Wright occupied the scientifically more respectable position, appearing as the voice of caution speaking against theoretical commitment. Consequently the Washington scientists found themselves in the unaccustomed position of having to reaffirm their adherence to the "best Baconian inductive process of carefully observed facts, and generalization to inferences."[45] On the antiquity issue, though, the roles were reversed. Here McGee and Holmes appeared as the cautious critics, willing to be convinced but only by overwhelming evidence. Consequently, although the antiquity question was clearly not the main point of Wright's work, they pursued him on this issue, hoping to discredit him at the same time as a critic of Survey geology.[46]

The vehemence of the response to Wright indicated that it was more than simply an attack on theory without facts.[47] Wright's publication of independent investigations and conclusions had violated the concept of scientific enterprise established in Washington. In the first place, *Man and the Glacial Period* was an explicit appeal to a popular audience. Chamberlin had warned the professor that this was a dangerous and unacceptable precedent. Forty years before, Joseph Henry had similarly advised Ephraim Squier against appealing to the public "for that commendation which it is the privilege of only the learned few to grant. . . ."[48] Squier had heeded Henry's advice and published his *Ancient Monuments of the Mississippi Valley* with the Smithsonian, under Henry's careful editorship. But Wright had not listened to Chamberlin; he had published a popular book thereby violating a basic canon of nineteenth-century science. Worse, Wright had presumed to summarize the present state of certain unsettled scientific questions for public consumption. As an observer and contributing participant in science, Wright had been acceptable, but as synthesizer and generalizer he had exceeded his bounds. These functions were reserved for those in certain positions, as Chamberlin readily informed him.[49]

But the difficult questions remained: Who was to determine the fitness and proper function of an independent investigator like Wright? Certainly there was still a place in science for such men, but where was it? Furthermore, who was to judge the expertness of Wright's authorities? Was employment in a government bureau the sole criterion of scientific respectability? After all, George Wright had, like McGee and Holmes, achieved his geological credentials with field experience; in addition, he possessed vastly more formal education than the Survey men. On what grounds, then, were they authorities and he a fraud? These questions the Washington corps attempted to answer by slander and storm because the open yet structured nature of Washington science left no other means of determining status. In the end their science was a moral enterprise in which participants were judged as much by motivation as by accomplishment; they attacked Wright's moral character because that was the ultimate criterion of discrimination.

In the first decade of the Bureau (the apex of Powell's scientific career), his visions were useful in organizing and focusing Bureau work and in framing major anthropological questions. However, from the early 1890s until his death in 1902, Powell receded into his synthesizing role to an extreme degree. The last decade of his life was a long, sad decline and a distortion of the principles of scientific organization that had proved fruitful a few years before. Between 1890 and 1895 many of Powell's oldest and most trusted collaborators departed: Mallery, Pilling, and James Owen Dorsey died, while Henry W. Henshaw moved away. They were replaced by McGee, who cared for and in a sense protected the Major while he prepared to succeed him. But McGee could not restore the invigorating sense of direction of the early years, and by 1900 an air of stagnation had overtaken the Bureau.

While Powell's old guard was gradually passing, no new projects arose to give spirit or focus to the work. The linguistic map and classification appeared in 1891, and although it was conceived as a temporary working model, Powell made few subsequent revisions.[50] The proposed synonymy or dictionary of Indian tribes languished after Henshaw's departure around 1890 and was not revived until Holmes succeeded Powell in 1902. C. C. Royce's "Indian Land Cessions in the United States," which finally appeared in the Annual Report for 1896–1897 (printed in 1899), marked the completion of the third major project of the Bureau's early years. The valuable work that continued to emanate from the Bureau in the 1890s grew either from seeds sown in the early years, such as Matilda Stevenson's continued work in the Southwest; from the efforts of path-breaking and quasi-independent ethnologists like James Mooney; or from influences outside the Bureau, namely Boas's collaborative efforts toward a thorough revision of the Powell linguistic classification on a morphological basis. Indeed, the accomplishments of the nineties sometimes occurred in spite of the Major, whose narrowing interests in psychology, mythology, and philosophy in his last years lay like a heavy hand on investigation in new fields.[51]

Powell died in September, 1902. The following spring, less than eight months after his death, Bureau officials discovered evidence of forgery and embezzlement by a minor employee, Frank M. Barnett. During the summer of 1903 Barnett's misdeeds led to a general inquiry by Smithsonian officials into the operations of the Bureau during Powell's final years.[52] In July the investigating committee took more than a thousand pages of testimony from prominent anthropologists, including William Henry Holmes, WJ McGee, Albert S. Gatschet, Matilda Coxe Stevenson, J. N. B. Hewitt, Jesse Walter Fewkes, Frederick Webb Hodge, James Mooney, and Franz Boas, who in addition to his positions at Columbia and the American Museum of Natural History, had held since 1901 the unsalaried position of honorary philologist in the Bureau. Although the main focus of the inquiry was fiscal matters, the anthropologists discussed freely their scientific interests, their concerns about the methods of inquiry pursued by the Bureau, and their recommendations for the future orientation of government-sponsored anthropology. Their remarks revealed that by Powell's death the Bureau had reached a unique and untenable position in the developing science of anthropology. Political pressures and the dilemmas inherent in government science accounted in part for the decline of the Bureau's anomalous position; but the fundamental reasons for the decline of the Bureau were more professional than political. By 1900 Powell's concept of science and the pattern of inquiry arising from it had served their purposes and were no longer fruitful.

The fundamental question, as chairman Cyrus Adler expressed it, was "whether the work of the members of the scientific staff of the Bureau was being pursued in accordance with some general system, so that it might . . . show definite results in a reasonable time; or whether it was being done upon individual opinion, according to individual tastes . . . ." In other words, was there any scientific planning in the Bureau? Hodge testified that in the early years Powell had set forth three major projects: the history of land cessions, the synonymy, and the linguistic map. But in recent years, Jesse Fewkes admitted, things had just "drifted along." Fewkes contrasted the Bureau work with the "correlated plan of operations" of the Jesup Expedition, which concentrated on the single question of Asian migration routes. At the Bureau, on the other hand, investigations were determined more by personalities than by problems: "If they could get a good man to do work in any field, they got him, and he brought in his results; and they catalogued them under the different sciences." J. N. B. Hewitt testified that there was no close collaboration in the Bureau; "each man had his own work and stuck to it." As a result, Tillie Stevenson concluded, the Bureau had become not "a Mecca for scientific men to come to and to believe in," but "a place at which scientific men all over the country shrug their shoulders."[53]

Boas blamed Powell for the Bureau's loss of direction and contraction rather than expansion in scope. Powell's antipathy to physical anthropology had kept the Bureau from developing into the "Ethnological Survey" of the American population—including blacks, mestizos, and mulattos—that Boas envisioned. In addition to work in physical anthropology, Boas emphasized investigations with "practical bearings" such as the effects of white education and missionary teaching on Indian amalgamation with white society.[54] Similarly, McGee reminded the committee of his own prospectus for an "Applied Ethnology," which he had first outlined in the 1902 Annual Report. McGee, like Boas, proposed a study of minority elements in the American population, including the new overseas possessions, but focusing more on the question of racial mixture and the future fertility of the American population. The extension of Bureau activities into these areas had never occurred, he said, because of the opposition of Powell, who had argued that "We must leave something for McGee, and besides, I am an old man now, and I do not want to do it."[55]

The question of planning arose from the concern of the committee over the tendency of the Bureau to accumulate material and data without publishing it.[56] This practice of hoarding materials—a consequence of Powell's desire to publish only "final" results—had embittered relationships with geologists and anthropologists outside Washington for years. Ten years previously one observer had reminded the Washington corps that the public—not to mention the scientific community—had more interest in the process of scientific inquiry than in the grand generalizations that the arrogant Washingtonians chose to reveal to them. [57] The same proprietary attitude had prevented outside anthropologists such as Daniel Brinton from having access to Bureau materials, and indeed had kept the researches of some of the Bureau's own workers, such as Albert Gatschet, from reaching the public.[58] Boas deplored this practice, which had resulted in large amounts of unfinished and therefore possibly useless materials. While government science should not be limited to publication of mere data without trying to draw "the widest, and consequently most useful inferences," Boas advised, at the same time no scientist in any position had the right to present his conclusions without the facts on which they were based.[59]

Although he spoke more briefly than either Boas or McGee, ethnologist James Mooney, called back from the field for the investigation, addressed and summarized most directly the critical problems of the Bureau. He also gave the committee some lessons in anthropological fieldwork. Unlike some members of the BAE, Mooney had published reports on a regular basis during his eighteen years with the Bureau. Still, he informed the committee, he had large amounts of unworked field notes that would be of little use to another student, since they were "shorthand notes, to be interpreted from my own knowledge and experience. . . ." Using the same terms of salvage ethnography as Schoolcraft, Morgan, and Powell before him, Mooney defended his practice of spending two-thirds of his time in the field at the expense of writing up his notes. The choice between fieldwork and publication was the "constant dilemma" of the ethnographer. If he died his notes would be of limited value, Mooney admitted, but nevertheless "it is better to take the chances of having some of this note material lost, and to spend this present time in investigation." Mooney described from his own experiences the rapidly changing Indian cultural patterns:

> I have been with them [the Kiowas] on this last trip, for a year and a half, and in all that time I have not seen one man in Indian dress in that tribe. When I went to them [twelve years ago] there were not half a dozen families in the tribe living in houses. They were all in tipis and in tipi camps . . . There were not a dozen men who ever wore a hat. They had feathers in their hair, and they painted their faces whenever they went any place. The man with whom I made my home . . . had eight rings in one ear and five in the other. He lived in a tipi and under an arbor in summer, always had his full buckskin on when it was time for buckskin; and he never went to a military post, or to a dance, or to anything else, without spending a couple of hours at least to dress up. Now he is in a house, and has chickens and a cornfield, and stoves and clocks and beds; and he has taken out his rings and cut his hair, and he looks like a dilapidated tramp.

In the face of such rapid change, Mooney added, the ethnologist could not afford to spend time at a desk. "The field work," he concluded, "cannot wait."[60]

Mooney pointed out to the committee the uniqueness of the field experience of the anthropologist. The investigator in the field, he lectured Adler, was not a scientist in the laboratory, because to a great extent the unpredictable data often controlled the nature and immediate direction of the inquiry. "The Indian," Mooney explained to the committee,

> is an uncertain quantity. You get him in one place and in another place. He is not a man whom you can talk with right straight along. You hear little incidental points and they may be all intermixed with another subject, and you may get a point here now, and then two or three months afterwards you may get with another tribe another little point. . . . You are constantly getting little scraps of information all along the line, so that when you come to bring the threads together, it is all through your note-books, and if you have a pretty good memory, you will find that half of it is in your mind. . . .[61]

Mooney's testimony reflected his years in the field, during which he had acquired a patient willingness to let the specific field situation determine the information received. His insight marked a clear advance over the structured vocabulary lists and circulars of inquiry that had guided previous fieldwork. These circulars, arising from a desire to accumulate materials for comparative purposes, drew on interested, devoted, and completely untrained observers for data. Since the purpose of the inquiries was to introduce a system into fact gathering, they carefully channeled inquiry along certain lines, but in the process they discouraged wide-ranging independence and flexibility in field observations. The value of observations recorded through questionnaires from Jefferson to Powell is undeniable; but their very structure narrowed the horizons of inquiry by discouraging integrated, concentrated researches on specific groups. Mooney, with his contemporaries Matilda Stevenson and Frank Hamilton Cushing, broke with this tradition. Rather than depending on a single hasty reconnaissance, Mooney knew from his own work that "a man is not really fit to publish anything until he has made his second or third visit with a people."[62]

Powell had not really advanced in concept over the rationale of the circular. As described earlier, his tendency had been to assign an individual to a "line" of inquiry, and to spread him over diverse ethnographic areas, thereby confirming and accentuating the already strong topical fragmentation. But extended exposure had taught some of Powell's ethnographers that a people's "religion, their sociology, their whole life, is so entangled, so gnarled together that you cannot study one line without the other unless you are familiar with their life."[63] Mooney directly countered Powell's assumptions by suggesting concentration on "life groups" or "types" of Indians, as he called them. The era of the survey and the wide-ranging study of particular subjects was over. Powell's efforts had had great value, for his linguistic map had established general boundaries of most language stocks north of Mexico (except for the Pacific coast). But now with the boundaries established, new methods and questions were needed.

The five hundred or so distinct tribes of North America Mooney divided into fifteen or twenty "well defined tribal groups and types of life." He perceived that "there are certain groups, certain life groups, environment groups, that classify the Indian readily for study and for Museum work. . . ." Anthropologists had built upon and surpassed the broad classification; but at the same time the study of each tribe was neither feasible nor necessary, since the attempt would simply result in "a lot of bad work." Since all the tribes within a single group or type exhibited "pretty similar habits of living and thinking, and similar mythologies and all the rest of it," Mooney suggested that investigators should specialize on "some good typical study tribe for each group," such as he had done with the Kiowa and Cherokee:

> I think a man's best plan [Mooney testified] is first cover a good deal of ground in the way of tribes and territory to familiarize himself with various features of study, and then concentrate on one or two [types]. . . . I do not think that much can be accomplished by skimming around through a dozen tribes. It takes time before you get enough knowledge of the language to check up your interpreter, and to train your Indians to be able to understand what you are trying to get at.[64]

By the summer of 1903 morale at the Bureau of American Ethnology had reached low ebb, as the investigation testimony unanimously affirmed. Swanton found the "atmosphere of suspicion, meanness and political pulling and hauling about the worst for any young man of energy and high scientific ideals."[65] McGee resigned at the end of the hearings, the scapegoat for the shortcomings of the Bureau's last years under Powell. The committee's blistering indictment accused him of unsystematic financial methods; carelessness and perhaps corruption in the purchase of manuscripts; gross negligence in caring for the manuscript collection; and a hostile and disloyal attitude toward secretary Langley.[66] To some extent political exigencies had a hand in the misfortunes of McGee and the Bureau, which depended on annual appropriations from a suspicious Congress. In the two decades since its founding the Bureau had outlived its original purpose—scientific classification as a basis for intelligent control of the remaining American aborigines—and had turned increasingly to work only remotely re-

lated to practical goals. McGee was most closely associated with
the new trend, and the various plans for "applied ethnology" that
he and others offered were attempts to redefine the Bureau in utili-
tarian terms that would appeal to Congressional critics.[67]

But McGee's personal downfall and the political question of
utility masked more fundamental changes. By the beginning of the
new century Powell's concepts of anthropology as a body of knowledge and as a scientific activity had achieved his original goal of
"organizing anthropologic research in America." In providing continuing support for area specialists like Mooney and Stevenson the
Bureau had planted seeds of change from the topical divisions of
Powell to concentration on ethnographic groupings. The result was
a dawning awareness of the complexity of Indian cultural patterns
and of the need for integrated treatment.

Washington Matthews, a former army surgeon and nonbureau
Washington anthropologist, stated the changed situation most
poignantly. In 1903 Matthews prepared to finish his work on the
Navaho and pass his labors on to a young and ardent student, Pliny
Earl Goddard. Recalling his long years in the Southwest with mixed
pleasure and regret, the veteran ethnologist advised his young fol-
lower: "You have advantages in studying them [the Athapascan
languages] which I did not possess. You have youth and are able to
devote your entire time to them. My time was well occupied with
other matters while I was in the Navaho country. I predict great
results from your labor if you do not try to spread yourself over too
wide a surface. The time has come for concentration of effort in
Anthropology."[68]

This reorientation—from a system of gathering data on a topical
basis for ultimate synthesis in Washington, to concentration by the
individual anthropologist on a specific group of people—implied
and accompanied basic changes in the professional structure as
well. Men like Powell and McGee had drawn on the exhilarating
experiences of their own early years of independent discovery in the
unpopulated regions of North America to establish a model of
government science characterized by informal, personal contact and
an accepted hierarchy within the scientific community. McGee's
voluminous correspondence—in the 1880s with prospective geolo-

gists like Robert T. Hill, in the 1890s with young, ardent students of anthropology like Harlan I. Smith—constituted a system of communication and personalized instruction. This method of education has not been fully recognized, but both the instructors in Washington and their students in the field took it very seriously.[69] It was supplemented by active participation in local scientific societies, which played a vital role as the "intermediate link" between scientists and laymen. They were the unique American instrument, McGee thought, for diffusing scientific knowledge among the populace.[70]

Field experience, informal instruction, and voluntary participation in local societies, combined with government-supported research and publication opportunities constituted a matrix of scientific activity, but it was a system of severe professional limitations. As the case of George F. Wright demonstrated, the intrusions of independent investigators from outside Washington, who refused to respect the professional hierarchy and questioned the theoretical orthodoxies of the government workers, presented ultimately insuperable challenges. By the first years of the new century American anthropology was rapidly passing, in both theoretical sophistication and organizational complexity, beyond the horizons of Powell and the nineteenth-century explorers and surveyors.

NOTES

[1]In the first category, see the enlightening examination of early nineteenth-century science in Arthur P. Molella and Nathan Reingold, "Theorists and Ingenious Mechanics: Joseph Henry Defines Science," *Science Studies* 3, no. 4 (October 1973:323–351).

[2]George W. Stocking Jr., "On the Limits of 'Presentism' and 'Historicism' in the Historiography of the Behavioral Sciences," *Journal of the History of the Behavioral Sciences* 1 (1965:211–217); Stocking, *Race, Culture, and Evolution: Essays in the History of Anthropology* (New York: Free Press, 1968), p. 8.

³Regna D. Darnell, "The Development of American Anthropology, 1879–1920: From the Bureau of American Ethnology to Franz Boas," Ph.D. dissertation, Univ. of Pennsylvania, 1969, p. xxxx.

⁴Regna D. Darnell, "The Emergence of Academic Anthropology at the University of Pennsylvania," *Journal of the History of the Behavioral Sciences* 6, no. 1 (January 1970):80–92; John Freeman, "University Anthropology: Early Departments in the United States," *Kroeber Anthropological Society Papers* 32:78–90.

⁵Darnell, "The Development of American Anthropology," p. xxxxiii.

⁶The idea of a linguistic map was not new with Gibbs. See Regna D. Darnell, "The Powell Classification of American Indian Languages," *Papers in Linguistics* (July 1971):73–76; and Mary Haas,"Grammar or Lexicon? The American Indian Side of the Question from Duponceau to Powell," *International Journal of American Linguistics* 35 (1969):239–255. Gibb's contribution has generally been ignored. He outlined his concept of an "ethnological atlas" in letters of November and December 1862 to Joseph Henry, secretary of the Smithsonian Institution, printed in the 1862 Annual Report, pp. 87–93. Responding to Lewis Henry Morgan's "Suggestions Relative to an Ethnological Map of North America," (Smithsonian Institution Annual Report, 1861, pp. 397–398)—a map that was to include not only linguistic families, but also principal archaeological sites, isothermal lines, topographical features, and political divisions—Gibbs proposed two maps, one for topographical features, the other showing linguistic groupings in different colors. In addition to the general linguistic map he envisioned a series of larger-scale collateral "sub-maps" of specific districts like the Northwest coast where language diversity was great. Although he had no organization such as Powell subsequently did, Gibbs had in mind a cooperative effort, organized and supported by the Smithsonian, by a number of independent collaborators already working in various parts of the continent. These included John G. Shea, John R. Bartlett, Buckingham Smith, Ephraim G. Squier, and Gibbs. On Gibb's career see Stephen Dow Beckham, "George Gibbs, 1815–1873: Historian and Ethnologist," Ph.D. dissertation, University of California at Los Angeles, esp. pp. 225–266.

⁷William Culp Darrah, *Powell of the Colorado* (Princeton, N.J.: Princeton University Press 1951), p. 254; Wallace Stegner, *Beyond the Hun-*

dredth Meridian: John Wesley Powell and the Second Opening of the West (Boston: Houghton Mifflin, 1954), p. 240.

[8]In 1903 the value of the manuscripts was estimated variously at $150,000 to $250,000. Report of the Bureau of American Ethnology Investigating Committee, Cyrus Adler to Samuel P. Langley, 9/24/03, Box 3, Barnett Case Records (see note 52).

[9]"Transactions of the Anthropological Society of Washington," vol. 1 (February 10, 1879 to January 17, 1882); *Smithsonian Miscellaneous Collections* 25, no. 501 (1882):6; Daniel S. Lamb, "The Story of the Anthropological Society of Washington," *American Anthropologist*, n.s., 8 (1906):564–579; James K. Flack, "The Formation of the Washington Intellectual Community, 1870–1898," Ph.D. dissertation, Wayne State University 1968; J. Howard Gore, "Anthropology at Washington," *Popular Science Monthly* (1889):786–795.

[10]Powell's antipathy to studies in physical anthropology is well documented. In his annual address for 1881 to the Anthropological Society [*Smithsonian Miscellaneous Collections* 25, no. 502 (1883):113–136] entitled "On Limitations to the Use of Some Anthropologic Data," which also appeared in the Bureau's first Annual Report (1879–80), Powell set forth his reasons for choosing a classification of tribes based on language rather than physical characteristics. He repeated his remarks in succeeding reports. Powell successfully avoided sponsoring somatological work by the Bureau during his lifetime. Within the Society, Dr. Robert Fletcher and Frank Baker repeatedly but unsuccessfully urged on Powell the need for a balanced representation of the various branches of anthropology in the proceedings of the Society. (See, e.g., the minutes of ASW meeting, January 5, 1886, where Fletcher and Powell debated the merits of anthropometry, ASW Papers, National Anthropological Archives, Smithsonian Institution). As Lamb noted (p. 578), in its first twenty-five years physicians constituted about 16 percent of the Society membership; but there was no corresponding emphasis on physical anthropology in the proceedings or publications. Between 1891 and 1895, for instance, less than 4 percent of the articles in the *American Anthropologist*, the organ of the Society, pertained to physical anthropology.

[11]Smithsonian Institution 1860 Annual Report, p. 38. Darnell observes similarly that "the Society drew on general scientific rather than specific

disciplinary interests." ("The Development of American Anthropology" p. 7.)

[12]Otis T. Mason, "What is Anthropology?" Saturday Lecture, March 18, 1882 (Washington, D.C.: 1882), p. 5.

[13]Ibid., p. 13.

[14]Flack (p. 175) observes that "the role of the general membership in operating the Society was clearly a passive one," pointing to the concentration of authority in the unchanging board of managers. He portrays the Society as the result of an uneasy attempt to combine elitist control and popular support. Lamb (p. 579) supports this view, noting that Mason, William Henry Holmes, and Powell read the most papers and that "most members have read only a few papers, or none; they have doubtless been good listeners, however. . . ." Although this view is undoubtedly true in part, and certainly accords with the dominant conception of scientific roles held within the Powell circle, analysis of the authorship of papers presented at the meetings actually reveals wide participation. Between February 1882 and May 1883, for instance, twenty-eight papers were presented by twenty-one individuals; fifteen years later, between 1896 and 1899, similar figures indicate that most papers were single contributions by individuals. In 1899 the Society reached a democratic extreme when thirty-one papers were given by twenty-eight individuals. Papers published in the *American Anthropologist* during these years show comparable diversity.

[15]"Abstract of the Proceedings of the Anthropological Society" (November 3, 1885 to May 15, 1888), *American Anthropologist*, o.s., 1:361–371; Darnell, "The Development of American Anthropology," pp. 5–6.

[16]Ibid., p. 31.

[17]Mason, "What is Anthropology?" pp. 4–5, 20.

[18]On Powell as an example of the "midwestern mind," see Stegner, *Beyond The Hundredth Meridian*, pp. 8–21.

[19]Mason to Frederick Webb Hodge, 1/31/07, Hodge-Cushing Papers, Southwest Museum; Neil Judd, *The Bureau of American Ethnology: A*

Partial History (Norman: 1967); Darnell, "The Development of American Anthropology," pp. 2–4.

[20]Stegner, *Beyond The Hundredth Meridian*, p. 146.

[21]Ibid., p. 269.

[22]BAE 1881 Annual Report, 35; BAE 1882 Annual Report, 63; BAE 1883 Annual Report, 57–63.

[23]Barnett Transcript, pp. 535, 719 (see note 52).

[24]Emma R. McGee, *Life of W J McGee* (Farley, Iowa: privately printed, 1915); F. H. Knowlton, "Memoir of W J McGee," *Bulletin of the Geological Society of America* 24 (1912): 18–29; N. H. Darton, "Memoir of W J McGee," *Annals of the Association of American Geographers* 3: 103–110. On McGee's activities in irrigation and conservation after 1907, particularly in the Inland Waterways Commission, see Whitney R. Cross, "W J McGee and the Idea of Conservation," *Historian* 15 (Spring 1953): 148–162. Evaluations of McGee's anthropological work are: the biographical sketch by Clark Wissler in the *Encyclopedia of the Social Sciences* 5: 652–653; A. L. Kroeber, "The Seri," *Southwest Museum Papers*, no. 6 (1931); and Bernard L. Fontana, "Pioneers in Ideas: Three Early Southwestern Ethnologists," *Journal of the Arizona Academy of Sciences* 2, no. 3 (February 1963): 127–128. See also *The McGee Memorial Meeting of the Washington Academy of Sciences* (Baltimore: 1916); F. W. Hodge, "W J McGee," *American Anthropologist*, n.s., 14, no. 4 (1912): 683–686; and Anita Newcomb McGee to Gifford Pinchot, 6/5/16, Pinchot Papers, Library of Congress, Washington, D.C.

[25]Knowlton, "Memoir," p. 18.

[26]Charles Keyes, "W J McGee, Geologist, Anthropologist, Hydrologist," *Annals of Iowa*, series 3, vol. 2 (1913): 187.

[27]John R. Swanton, "Notes Regarding My Adventures in Anthropology and with Anthropologists," MS.(c. 1944), p. 33–34, National Anthropological Archives.

[28]J. J. Stevenson to McGee, 8/14/99, McGee Papers, Library of Congress, Washington, D.C.

[29]*McGee Memorial Meeting*, p. 90.

[30]W J McGee, "Fifty Years of American Science," *Atlantic Monthly* 82, no. 491 (September 1898):320.

[31]W J McGee, "Cardinal Principles of Science," *Proceedings of the Washington Academy of Sciences* 2 (March 14, 1900):1-2.

[32]Franz Boas began as early as 1888, in his article "On Alternating Sounds," to recognize cultural factors in perception of anthropological phenomena, as discussed by George Stocking in *Race, Culture, and Evolution*, pp. 157-160. Boas's early insights had little noticeable effect in Washington, however.

[33]*McGee Memorial Meeting*, p. 21.

[34]McGee, "Fifty Years," p. 320.

[35]For McGee's emphasis on altruism and public service, see McGee, "The Citizen," *American Anthropologist*, o.s., 7 (October 1894):352-357.

[36]Barnett Transcript, p. 822 (see note 52).

[37]For a brief review of the following events in a larger historical context see R. Alan Mounier, "The Question of Man's Antiquity in the New World: 1840-1927," *Pennsylvania Archaeologist* 42 no. 3 (September 1972):59-69.

[38]George F. Wright, *The Ice Age in North America and Its Bearings Upon the Antiquity of Man* (New York: 1889); Wright, *Man and the Glacial Period* (New York: 1892).

[39]"Sketch of George Frederick Wright, "*Popular Science Monthly* (December 1892):258-262.

[40]Wright, *Man and Glacial Period*, pp. 106-120, 322-326; Wright's main geological conclusions are summarized in the review of his book in *Popular Science Monthly* (December 1892):266-268.

[41]Mounier, "The Question of Man's Antiquity," p. 64; E. W. Claypole, "Prof. G. F. Wright and His Critics," *Popular Science Monthly* 42 (1893):765.

[42]Thomas C. Chamberlin, "Geology and Archaeology Mistaught," *The Dial* (November 16, 1892):303–306; Chamberlin, "Professor Wright and the Geological Survey," *The Dial* (January 1, 1893):7–9. Wright Responded in *The Dial* issues of December 16, 1892 and January 16, 1893.

[43]W J McGee, "Man in the Glacial Period," *American Anthropologist*, o.s., 6 (January 1893):85–95; McGee, "A Geologic Palimpsest," *Literary Northwest* 2 (February 1893):274–276. William Henry Holmes's critical but more restrained review appeared in *Science,* October 28, 1892. McGee to Chamberlin, 11/11/92 and 3/28/93, McGee Papers.

[44]W J McGee, "Paleolithic Man in America: His Antiquity and Environment," *Popular Science Monthly* (November 1888):25. McGee's reversal did not pass unnoticed. Claypole observed (p. 780) that "it is not fair to taunt a man with change of mind. . . . But we do look for a more tolerant spirit from one who has so recently seen fit to change his own faith on an important subject."

[45]McGee to Warren Upham, 3/24/93, McGee Papers.

[46]Holmes believed that his cautious stance on the entire question of ancient man in America—which he stubbornly held until his death in 1933—established his credentials as a scientist. As the same time he felt that in contrast to McGee he had established a reputation for fairness and sobriety. See Holmes, "The End of Paleolithic Man in America, 1889–1894," MS. (1932), in "Minor Anthropological Papers," National Anthropological Archives.

[47]Thomas G. Manning, *Government in Science: The U.S. Geological Survey, 1867–1894* (Lexington, Ky.: University Press of Kentucky, 1967), p. 92.

[48]Henry to Squier, 4/3/47, Squier Papers, Library of Congress, Washington, D.C.

[49]Chamberlin could not veil, however, his own impure desires for fame: "I am compelled [he wrote Wright] to be consistent with my conception of scientific and educational ethics and with the canons of practice which have withheld me from a popular utilization of work whose extent would probably justify me, if anyone, in attempting to secure popular returns." Quoted (by Wright) in *The Dial* (January 16, 1893):380.

[50]Regna D. Darnell, "The Powell Classification of American Indian Languages," *Papers in Linguistics* (July 1971):81–82; Ms. Darnell discusses subsequent changes in "The Revision of the Powell Classification," *Papers in Linguistics* (October 1971):233–257.

[51]Boas later judged that Powell had lost control of the Bureau at an early date because the field of investigation was simply too vast and complex for the series of volumes, or handbooks, that Powell had originally planned. Every worker went his own way; this "chance development" intensified after about 1895. (Boas to Robert S. Woodward, 1/13/05, Boas Papers, American Philosophical Society).

[52]The records of the 1903 BAE investigation (referred to here as the Barnett Case Records or Barnett Transcript) are in the National Anthropological Archives of the Smithsonian Institution. They consist of several drafts of the testimony and a box of accompanying documents concerning various aspects of the hearings, especially the activities of W J McGee.

[53]Barnett Transcript, pp. 838, 288–289, 278–283, 501, 386.

[54]Barnett Transcript, pp. 933–936, 939–940, presents Boas's plan briefly; a fuller exposition is Boas's "Organization of the Bureau of Ethnology," undated (presumably 1903) typescript, Boas Papers.

[55]Barnett Transcript, pp. 253–257. For a full statement of McGee's applied ethnology, see BAE 1902 Annual Report, ix–xiv; and McGee to Boas, 9/18/03, Smithsonian Institution Archives. (Boas presented the plan outlined in this letter to the Smithsonian Board of Regents on behalf of McGee in December, 1903)

[56]Barnett Transcript, p. 940.

[57]Claypole, "Prof. G. F. Wright and His Critics," p. 776. As early as 1891 Mason had described to Samuel Langley the opposition to Powell's Bureau from outside Washington. Mason listed among the opponents F. W. Putnam, Alice Fletcher, and Daniel Brinton. Their reasons for dissatisfaction included "the alleged exclusive spirit of the Bureau in reference to material in its possession and withheld both from publication and from the privilege of investigation." Mason to Langley, 6/23/91, Smithsonian Institution Archives.

[58]Darnell, "The Development of American Anthropology," pp. 81–82.

[59]Barnett Transcript, pp. 927, 942. Boas's comments on Gatschet revealed the great disadvantages of Powell's mode of operations. Gatschet's failure to publish was due to Powell, who kept the linguist moving from one language group to another gathering material for Powell's general linguistic survey. Gatschet consequently never had the opportunity to work up his findings. Powell's worst mistake, Boas remarked, was making Gatschet begin work on Algonquian languages in the mid-1890s, when he was already an old man. This was doubly unfortunate since Gatschet was the foremost philologist in America, "away ahead of us all"; his Klamath grammar was the best of any American language at the time, Boas added.

[60]Barnett Transcript, pp. 973–975.

[61]Ibid., pp. 982–984.

[62]Ibid., p. 969; Don D. Fowler, "Notes on Inquiries and Anthropology—a Bibliographic Essay," Paper presented at 9th International Congress of Anthropological and Ethnological Sciences, Chicago, 1973.

[63]Barnett Transcript, p. 353 (remarks of Matilda Coxe Stevenson).

[64]Barnett Transcript, pp. 966–970. Like Mason, Holmes and McGee, with all of whom he worked closely in setting up Indian "groups" for the National Museum exhibits at the expositions of 1893 and 1904, Mooney placed emphasis on environmental factors in defining the Indian "types." He attributed the social, economic and religious life of his nomadic buffalo group of the plains primarily to two factors: buffalo as the principal game animal and the absence of forested areas.

[65]Swanton to Boas, 8/16/03, Boas Papers.

[66]Report of Investigating Committee (Adler to Langley, 9/24/03), pp. 40–42, in Box 3, Barnett Case Records. The committee placed entire responsibility for the shortcomings of the Bureau on McGee; as Boas pointed out, this was not completely just, since McGee had worked within limits set by Powell (pp. 946–951). Boas concluded that "whatever was good went to the credit of Powell and whatever was bad went to the discredit of McGee" (p. 951). He returned to New York convinced that the

committee was trying to build a case against McGee. Boas to McGee, 8/3/02, and Boas to Charl Schurz, 8/12/03, Boas Papers.

[67]McGee was not unaware of Congressional sentiments. The Bureau, he told Adler's committee, had labored for years in a hostile environment because of the apparently "pure" nature of its science. Barnett Transcript, pp. 253, 821.

[68]Matthews to Goddard, April-May, 1903, Matthews Papers, Museum of Navaho Ceremonial Art, Santa Fe, New Mexico.

[69]Correspondence with Robert T. Hill, Harlan I. Smith and others, McGee Papers. Smith's letters to McGee, Cushing, Holmes and Boas, spread through various collections, are particularly fascinating for their insights into the doubts and fears of a young Michigan man beginning a career in anthropology in the 1890s, e.g.:

> Will this work for which I have given my time and study now for a number of years earn for me from now on a living and at the same time afford a chance for study and improvement? Will the subject of anthropology require so many men as are fitting for it? Will it offer them a living? . . . I often fear that my culture and intellectual capacity will not stand comparison with eastern men that are coming on. (Smith to Frank Hamilton Cushing, 1/28/95, McGee Papers)

Of course the pattern of personalized instruction did not end abruptly with the beginnings of academic anthropology. Boas's strongly paternal attitude toward his students was apparent to the Adler committee in 1903.

[70]McGee to F. P. Venable, 3/25/87, McGee Papers.

5

Daniel Brinton and the Professionalization of American Anthropology

REGNA DARNELL
University of Alberta

There has been considerable concern within anthropology in recent years about the nature of the discipline's "paradigm." The term has attained its greatest popularization through the work of Thomas Kuhn, whose book *The Structure of Scientific Revolutions* has set the tone for the debate by claiming that the social sciences are "pre-paradigmatic," that is, lacking the set of "universally recognized scientific achievements that for a time provide model problems and solutions to a community of practitioners" (Kuhn 1962:x). Kuhn's own training is in the hard sciences, and his primary concern is to demonstrate that the progress of a science is not a simple cumulative process. A paradigm, in his view, provides a uniform theoretical stance for an entire field of study and contains the seeds of its own downfall with the increasing recognition of anomalies not explained by the theory. In spite of the reference to "a community of practitioners," Kuhn's stress is on the intellectual content of successive paradigms in any given discipline.

There are those in anthropology who have argued that the discipline has the intellectual unity of a paradigm in Kuhn's sense, but clearly such a position excludes a great deal of what most of us recognize as anthropology from that paradigm. If anthropology is defined, albeit somewhat tautologically, as what anthropologists do, then it is obvious that the discipline does have models for what Kuhn refers to as "normal science." There is considerably more question, however, whether all of us share the same models. To Kuhn, competing paradigms eliminate normal science. To many practicing anthropologists, the absence of a unified paradigm threatens the scientific validity of the discipline. To others, however, it is a source of pride and professional identity that multiple "paradigms" exist in the present science of anthropology. That is, they perceive the discipline according to a model of "organization of diversity" rather than one of "replication of uniformity" (Wallace 1962). Using the methods of anthropology to study its history, therefore, we are virtually forced to consider paradigms (with the emphasis on the pluralization) and to focus on the social organization and ongoing function of the discipline. It is, then, an empirical question whether the discipline at any given time possesses overall unity in its theory and practice.

Turning to the recent history of anthropology in North America, it is possible to isolate at least four successive paradigms, using the term somewhat loosely: First, there was a period in which information about the aborigines of North America was collected by people who were not primarily anthropologists, such as traders, missionaries, and explorers. Their descriptions were often interpreted by gentlemen and philosophers who themselves had not had contact with native peoples (for example, Thomas Jefferson). This period gave way to one of incipient professionalization in which individuals labeled their work as anthropology and submitted it to evaluation by their peers, but were not themselves trained as anthropologists; the Bureau of American Ethnology dominated this period, although independent scholars such as Horatio Hale, Lewis Henry Morgan, and Daniel Brinton were also important. The third period produced true professionalization, largely through the efforts of Franz Boas and his students. During this period there was considerable intellectual and social unity within the discipline in North America. The fourth period, still in progress, is one in which a variety of theoretical and social organizational perspectives, or paradigms are identifiable.

It should, of course, be obvious that there is an overlap between each of these successive paradigms. Although Kuhn's notion recognizes that this occurs, his emphasis on the intellectual content of paradigms does not encourage examination of overlap, conflict of paradigms, and changing allegiances of individuals, particularly the establishment of a new paradigm utilizing the resources and personnel of the old. For example, Boasian anthropology began very much within the institutional framework of late-nineteenth-century American anthropology which focused around the Bureau of American Ethnology (Darnell 1969). Boas's later activities were, of course, more independent as he developed his own institutional frameworks and personal networks. The relatively unified anthropology which developed around Boas provided a baseline for succeeding diversity within the discipline.

In addition to the changing theories and social organizations of anthropology, which may be visualized as a series of partially overlapping circles, there is a concurrent process, professionalization, which is essentially linear and chronological. That is, professionalization of anthropology and American science in general took place only once. The development of a *profession* rather than merely a *tradition* of anthropology, therefore, continues to influence the structure and organization of the present discipline. This linear development *is* cumulative, although the contents of successive paradigms, as Kuhn stresses, are not. For example, the social organizational transition between the Bureau of American Ethnology and Boasian anthropology was accompanied by an equally important theoretical transition: from cultural evolutionism to historical particularism.

The substance of this paper will examine the career of one important figure in the period of transition to professional anthropology in an effort to clarify the kinds of changes that were taking place toward the end of the nineteenth century. Daniel Garrison Brinton, although he is, for the most part, "a forefather of whom we have no memory" (Hymes 1962), was recognized in his own time as a major anthropologist. Although he himself had no formal affiliation with an anthropological institution and earned his living as a physician and publisher, Brinton had important ties to developments of anthropological activity, for example, the Bureau of American Ethnology in Washington, Boasian anthropology in New York, the founding of the *American Anthropologist* as a journal of national scope, and the establishment of university programs for the training of anthropologists. These are the major trends which produced full professionalization during the decade following Brinton's death in 1899.

During the late nineteenth century, most anthropologists were amateurs with loose affiliations to localized scientific societies in major Eastern cities. The focus of such societies was usually not restricted to a single discipline, and the members were rarely professional scientists. Some important examples were: In Boston—The American Antiquarian Society, The Peabody Museum of Archaeology and Ethnology, The Boston Society of Natural History and the Essex Institute; in New Haven—The American Oriental Society and the Connecticut Historical Society; in New York—the American Ethnological Society, The American Geographial Society, the American Museum of Natural History, and the Lyceum of Natural History; in Philadelphia—the American Philosophical Society, the Academy of Natural Sciences of Philadelphia, the Numismatic and Antiquarian Society, the Museum of Archaeology, and the Oriental Club of Philadelphia; and in Washington—The Anthropological Society of Washington, the Washington Academy of Sciences, and the United States National Museum.

The American Association for the Advancement of Science was the major organization of national scope. The appointment of Frederick Ward Putnam of the Peabody Museum as its permanent secretary in 1873 assured anthropology of an important role in that association. Section H, Anthropology, was established in 1882 as an independent unit. The *American Anthropologist*, formerly an organ of the Anthropological Society of Washington, was established as a national journal in 1898, although the American Anthropological Association was not founded until 1903. During the late nineteenth century, therefore, anthropologically-inclined scholars were virtually forced to affiliate themselves with the local learned societies.

Moreover, at this time there was no way of obtaining training specific to anthropology, because there were no academic programs. Franz Boas was trained as a geographer and physicist. John Wesley Powell, founder of the Bureau of American Ethnology, was a natural scientist turned geologist. Frederick Ward Putnam was a naturalist. Lewis Henry Morgan was a Rochester businessman. Horatio Hale did most of his anthropological research at the beginning and end of a distinguished business career. And Brinton was a Philadelphia physician, whose primary scientific affiliation was the American Philosophical Society.

Brinton was elected to the American Philosophical Society in 1869, at a time when he had done little ethnological work outside local circles to justify his election. Of his more than two hundred publications (see Appendix I and II), forty-eight appeared in the various transactions of the Society between 1869 and 1898, with some clustering between 1885 and 1892. These articles formed a large proportion of the anthropological research of the American Philosophical Society, as well as its being Brinton's most frequent publication outlet. Many of the papers were, of course, originally lectures delivered at meetings of the Society. It is important to compare Brinton's output with that of the American Philosophical Society during the same period. John Freeman has estimated forty-one anthropological papers in the *Proceedings* between 1840 and

1880, twenty-three archaeological, and sixty-five papers between 1880 and 1900, only ten of them archaeological (Freeman 1965). Brinton's contributions, therefore, must be recognized as significant in terms of magnitude alone. Most of his work (Thirty-nine items) falls within Freeman's second period, with its greater emphasis on ethnology. This means that Brinton was himself responsible for well over half the anthropological contributions appearing in the publications of the Society. His role in the American Philosophical Society makes it likely that he was the active agent in the modification of interests toward ethnology, not merely its passive reflector. In addition to his publications and lectures, Brinton served as a curator from 1877 to 1897, as a secretary from 1888 to 1895, and was chairman of the publications committee at the time of his death in 1899.

Brinton's importance in Philadelphia intellectual circles is also indicated by his publications in other Philadelphia-based outlets. Five items appeared in each of the following: the *Proceedings of the Academy of Natural Sciences,* the *Bulletin of the Free Museum of Science and Art,* and the *Proceedings of the Numismatic and Antiquarian Society;* two items appeared in the publications of the Philadelphia Oriental Club. These, plus the American Philosophical Society publications, total sixty-five contributions, encompassing almost one-third of Brinton's total output. Since most of these were originally lectures, the tabulation indicates Brinton's considerable prominence in Philadelphia intellectual life. Brinton's own reputation was, of course, equally dependent on Philadelphia. In the period before full professionalization, there were few outlets for ethnological writings, and most of these were sponsored by local organizations and favored local talent. Brinton may have constituted Philadelphia's claim to ethnological fame, but Philadelphia publications and audiences equally constituted Brinton's medium of communication to establish wider intellectual contacts.

The second most frequent publication outlet for Brinton was *Science,* and the *Proceedings of the American Association for the Advancement of Science.* His column "Current Notes in Anthropology" ran in *Science* from 1892 until his death in 1899. Nineteen independent articles appeared in that journal and nine more in the

Proceedings. Brinton's publications, of course, formed a much smaller percentage of the anthropological interests of this organization due to its national focus. It is interesting to note that Brinton's publications through the American Association for the Advancement of Science began only *after* the formation of Section H in 1882, indicating that his reputation was locally established and expanded late in his lifetime as new institutions developed for anthropological activity.

If a single index of Brinton's national reputation must be sought, it is undoubtedly that he served as president of the American Association for the Advancement of Science. Although not restricted in its focus to anthropology, the association represented the trend in American science toward increasing professionalism. Only three other nineteenth-century anthropologists, Lewis Henry Morgan, John Wesley Powell, and Frederick Ward Putnam, were so honored. In the early twentieth century, only Boas held this position. Brinton's inclusion in this company makes it clear that he stood alongside these men in the view of his contemporaries as a major figure of the period.

Brinton also served a president of the International Congress of Anthropology in Chicago in 1893. He published three papers in its *Memoirs,* their number and topics underscoring his stature at that time. A review of the state of American linguistics indicated that Brinton felt himself able to speak for the field as a whole. A discussion of the independence of the Asian and American races reiterated a personal hobbyhorse which a man of lesser reputation might have had difficulty publishing in 1893. His presidential address dealt with the concept of nation in anthropology and attempted to reach consensus in terminology and theoretical approach within the young discipline; here Brinton made no effort to be original, believing that commonality and acceptability were the issues facing anthroplolgy as a profession.

The major institution for anthropological research in North America during the late nineteenth century was the Bureau of American Ethnology, founded by John Wesley Powell in 1879. Brinton, as the most important of the independent scholars continuing to work until near the end of the century, provides a baseline for assessing the professionalization which the Bureau was attempting to encourage. Brinton's most extensive contact with the Bureau occurred over the classification of North American Indian languages. Powell's 1891 classification, still a conservative baseline for the study of American Indian languages, postulated fifty-eight stocks in North America (later reduced to fifty-five) (Darnell 1971). The classification appeared under Powell's name, but resulted from the labours of the entire Bureau staff to supplement the manuscripts already available at the Smithsonian Institution (Powell inherited 670 of these at the time he began work on the classification). In the same year, 1891, Brinton published a book called *The American Race* in which he proposed an alternative classification consisting of only thirteen units, several of them geographical catchalls. Although the total classification was patently inadequate, partly due to the imitations of a single scholar working alone in his library, Brinton did recognize some stocks that Powell had not, particularly the relationship of the Uto-Aztecan languages. Unlike Powell, Brinton consulted the original reports in German and drew his conclusions from the data directly. Also in contrast to Powell, who considered a grammar a fact of evolutionary level and classified genetic relationship of languages solely on the basis of lexicon, Brinton relied heavily on grammar in his classification. His belief in the basic similarity of all American Indian languages, of course, encouraged him to unite as many stocks as possible. Powell's classification was designed to group closely related tribes for purposes of government administration.

The Brinton classification, in spite of its limitations, is intriguing as in indictor of the developing institutional structure of American anthropology vis-à-vis unaffiliated scholars. Hodge (1931:100) noted that the Powell classification was rushed into print because of competition with Brinton's *The American Race*. Kroeber (1960:4-5) has contrasted the two classifications in some detail:

> There was some conscious competition between Powell's classi-
> fication and D. G. Brinton, whose *American Race* appeared in
> 1891. It was a pubisher's book, and a work of quite a different
> sort from Powell's monograph, although it did group many lan-

guages. . . . He gave only tiny samples of evidence on linguistic relationship, insufficient to be sure; but then Powell wisely published none.

As early as 1885, Brinton had requested the current Bureau classification of tribes, whether "by linguistic stocks or otherwise" (Brinton to Pilling, June 12, 1885:BAE). Pilling's reply made it clear that Brinton did not have access to the tentative results of the Bureau's researches (Pilling to Brinton, June 13, 1885:BAE):

> I regret to have to say that the linguistic classification is still unfinished—indeed in so unsatisfactory a condition that it would scarcely be intelligible to those who are not engaged in its compilation. It is a slow affair, as you may well imagine, and I fear it will be some time yet before it is available for use.

Actually, by 1885, the Bureau classification was substantially complete, although details were added before publication in 1891.

In 1890, just before presenting his own classification (which was written as a series of lectures to the Academy of Natural Sciences of Philadelphia between 1884 and 1890), Brinton wrote a number of letters to Henry Henshaw at the Bureau inquiring about details of linguistic classification. He requested a classification of the Pacific coast stocks, noting that he was preparing a list of linguistic families for use in his lectures (Brinton to Henshaw, August 1, 1890:BAE). Four days later, he wrote again asking about Cherokee and Iroquois, Apache and Navajo, and Kiowa: "These are my inquiries about which my authorities do not quite satisfy me." Ten days later he wanted to know about Beothukan, San Antonio, Coahuiltecan, Caronkaway, United States Shoshonean, and the Texas coast stocks.

In his published classification (Brinton 1891:xii), Henshaw's aid was acknowledged with the Northwest coast classification (reporting on Boas's fieldwork there for the Bureau) and for "various other suggestions." Brinton then stated that he had not used the Bureau's classification, with the implication that he was not permitted to do so. Correspondence in the Bureau archives indicates that this was not entirely accurate. Brinton had written to Henshaw in 1890 indicating his interest (Brinton to Henshaw, November 7, 1890:BAE):

> How is the map of North American Languages getting on? Is the classification of the Bureau yet completed, and could I have a sight of the proofs, or, if not that far along, of the MS copy.

Brinton's next letter indicated that the decision was his (Brinton to Henshaw, November 19, 1890:BAE):

> I am much obliged to you for the courteous offer . . . about the map, etc. At first, I was inclined to come on and look it over; but on second thought, I think I had better not. The information I wish to gain could be made public soon in my lectures, and perhaps in printed reports from them, and this, I can readily see, might not be agreeable to the Bureau. It would, for this reason, be better for me not to see the map; as even if I confined my publication to matters already in my possession, some members of the Bureau might think that I had learned them by the facilities you offer, and I had refrained from giving credit. There are, in fact, only a few points in the ethnology of the United States area about which I am in much doubt.

He then asked about Comecrudo, Choctaw, Eskimo, and Aleut.

The interest of this correspondence lies not so much in establishing classificatory priority as in illustrating Brinton's liabilities as an independent scholar, and his realization that his own work was necessarily formulated competitively with that of the Bureau, to his disadvantage because of their greater institutional resources. Undoubtedly, Brinton's paranoia was rationally based. Of course, the 1885 manuscript classification by James Mooney and A. S. Gatschet gives clear priority to the Bureau classification.

A second important source of professional contacts for Brinton was Franz Boas and the New York anthropology which was beginning to develop at the end of Brinton's lifetime. The two men were on cordial terms personally, although there is no evidence that they were friends. Their correspondence is concerned with institutional matters rather than substantive ones. Brinton was eager for

Boas to remain in the United States and encouraged him in his field-work and employment (mostly in the form of congratulatory letters at various turning points in Boas's career).

Of interest for this symposium is Brinton's letter of congratulation to Boas on the organization of the new American Ethnological Society (November 20, 1887:APS). Brinton asked if the old American Ethnological Society, organized in 1844[2], should not be reincorporated, with the implication that Boas might not know it had existed earlier. The effect is to reinforce Brinton's own status as an elder statesman of American anthropology. Boas replied the next day that he knew about the older organization and had the support of several of its members; although he almost certainly found Brinton's remarks officious, the reply was blandly polite. Boas continued: "Your promise that you will write for our first publication is extremely valuable to me and I am almost sure of success. . . . Your name will be of great help to me." Boas apparently solicited the collaboration of other prominent American anthropologists of the old establishment, but the inclusion of Brinton is nonetheless an interesting indication of Brinton's reputation. From Boas's point of view, full professionalism had to be built on the best of the existing amateur base and could not be brought about by antagonizing scholars like Brinton.

On the occasion of the reorganization of the *American Anthropologist,* (the official journal of the Anthropological Society of Washington) into a publication of national scope, Brinton and Boas were united in their opposition to Bureau control, although for quite different reasons. An abortive plan to establish such a journal in 1896 had conflicted with the interests of the American Association for the Advancement of Science. Brinton had reluctantly endorsed this proposal in hope that the Bureau would support it financially (Brinton to Boas, October 30, 1896:APS). Since Brinton had been president of the association in 1894, his reservations undoubtedly formed a substantial part of the conflict with Section H.

For both Brinton and Boas, conflict with the Bureau was long-standing. The primary issues were financial power, control over employment and publication outlets, and credit for research. In

1898, Brinton wrote to Boas (June 4:APS) that he could not consent to the Anthropological Society of Washington's proposal for the new journal if they retained four of nine members on the editorial committee and supplied the managing editor. He proposed a compromise of three members and annual election of the editor. "This is a condition so grasping in character that I shall not only decline to assent to it, but, if adopted by a majority of the committee, I shall have to enter a minority report against it." On June 13, he complained that "the new journal would be nothing but a continuation of the *American Anthropologist*, in name, management, and treatment." In spite of his objections, however, Brinton conceded financial realities and was prepared to compromise. Brinton attempted to argue that the American Association for the Advancement of Science committee, responsible for the formation of the new journal, wanted it to represent all branches of anthropology at a national level, and that he, as a past president, believed this was impossible if any local control were permitted.

In practice, of course, the Anthropological Society of Washington, closely affiliated with the Bureau, was the only organization with sufficient strength to exert such control. The numerical preponderance and superior organization of the Washington anthropologists was undeniable. Of the estimated 350 subscriptions to the new *American Anthropologist*, over two hundred were from the Washington group (Boas to Brinton, December, 1898:APS).

The initial editorial board was a compromise, consisting of Brinton, Boas, and Putnam as nonlocal members, and Baker, Dorsey, Holmes, Hodge, and Powell from Washington. Brinton complained to Boas (October 24, 1898:APS) that McGee at the Bureau was withholding information, particularly about the business arrangements. It appears that Brinton was considered a nuisance by the Bureau contingent at this time (personal communication, George Stocking). Certainly, Brinton's objection to control by Washington anthropology was personal in nature, and he did not have the practical commitment of Boas to developing alternative local frameworks and, ultimately, a national discipline of anthropology.

After the establishment of the new series, Brinton's contributions to the *American Anthropologist* became more frequent. He had published only five articles in the old series over a full decade. Between the establishment of the new journal and his death in 1899, Brinton made nine contributions. The conclusion is inescapable that the new journal, and indeed Washington anthropology itself, incorporated rather than vanquished its opponents. The *American Anthropologist* obituary of Brinton was blandly complimentary and ignored previous conflicts (although clearly associating Brinton with the old regime) (1899:764):

> Dr. Brinton was an active and versatile student of anthropology in all its aspects. His contributions to the science were many and important, his publications form a conspicuous part of the literature of American anthropology, while his editorial and professional work and his labors in the lecture field and in social organization aided materially in promoting and diffusing anthropology. . . . A frequent contributor to the *American Anthropologist* in its earlier form, Dr. Brinton was one of the foremost among the projectors and supporters of the journal in its new form and more extended scope.

There was, of course, considerable difference in the motives of Brinton and Boas in opposing the reorganization. Brinton disliked any form of control, preferred the American Association for the Advancement of Science as a coordinating body, and was more interested in ethnology than in ethnography (the focus of the Bureau). Brinton apparently failed to recognize that the future of American anthropology depended on increasing consolidation of institutional resources. He espoused the ideal of national organization, but opposed specific actions to implement it because of the relative strength of the Washington group. Boas, in contrast, shared with Powell and McGee the vision of a unified science of anthropology in America. He was willing to work within the framework of the Bureau to promote such developments. In fact, Boas was relatively independent of the Bureau. He was settled in New York and could put forth his American Ethnological Society as an institutional alternative to Washington anthropology. As the central figure of the second-largest faction, he gained greater control over the new journal than numbers alone would have justified. He was flexible enough to use the need for support from outside Washington to justify the national aspirations of the newly organized journal and to fit these factors into his own long-range plans. Brinton, already an old man in ill health, and without institutional backing, had no such plans. The reorganization of the *American Anthropologist* makes it clear that he was, in spite of his considerable influence, the last of the old guard.

Most histories of American anthropology, if they mention Brinton at all, take as his major claim to fame that he was technically the first university professor of anthropology in North America. He was appointed professor of Ethnology and Archaeology at the Academy of Natural Sciences of Philadelphia in 1884, a task which involved an annual series of public lectures in his field. In 1886, he became professor of archaeology and linguistics at the University of Pennsylvania. The appointment was an honorary one and did not carry salary. It was, in fact, an offshoot of the development of the University of Pennsylvania Museum, a public rather than an academic institution under the direction of Dr. William Pepper. Again, it was Brinton's name and reputation which made him useful to these schemes. Although Brinton appeared on paper to have very close ties to the running of the museum, he was never in a position to influence its operation or long-range development.

Between 1886 and his death in 1899, Brinton listed in the University of Pennsylvania Catalogue courses in American Indian philology; Algonquian, Nahuatl, Maya, and Kechua languages; linguistic families of North and South America; Maya and Aztec hieroglyphics; North American archaeology; and antiquities of the eastern United States. The catalogue noted that "The instruction in this group will be in large measure based upon the unusually rich collections of the University Museum, and will be arranged with reference to the preparation and aims of applicants." Unfortunately, this rich program existed only on paper. University listings of enrollment and student names indicate that Brinton's students consisted of a single nondegree candidate in 1894–1895.

However, Brinton did have some contact with students specializing in nonanthropological subjects. During at least the years of 1893–1894, all students seeking a Ph.D. in any language area had to attend lectures by Brinton on prehistoric picture writing and Mexican hieroglyphs and on primitive religion. After Brinton's death, he was theoretically replaced by Stewart Culin, then an employee of the University Museum, but Culin did not develop a teaching program either; this came only after 1910 under the direction of Frank Speck, whose ties were to Boasian anthropology (Darnell 1970).

However, in spite of the abortive nature of Brinton's actual teaching, he was intensely committed to the development of an academic framework for anthropology. His presidential address to the American Association for the Advancement of Science (1895:6) deplored the nearly universal opinion that education was unnecessary for anthropologists: "We erect stately museums, we purchase costly specimens, we send out costly expeditions; but where are the universities, the institutions of higher education, who train young men how to observe, how to collect and explore in this branch?" These were the words of a man who had watched the growth of a museum without a corresponding growth in educational facilities.

In 1892, Brinton had presented to the University of Pennsylvania a practical proposal for the teaching of anthropology which stressed his own teaching experience (at the Academy of Natural Sciences of Philadelphia and the university itself). Although the content is quite similar to the program in fact developed by Boas during the following decade, the university apparently gave no serious consideration to Brinton's proposals. He must have envisioned that this would be the case; the pamphlet was printed privately by Brinton, and his prospectus circulated to anthropologists outside Philadelphia. His message was to the future.

Boas, of course, was the first person to hold an institutional position which would enable him to develop an academic program. Indeed, his early efforts were also largely abortive; at Clark University, he granted the first American Ph.D. in anthropology to Alexander Francis Chamberlain, but did not stay to develop a teaching program there. Boasian anthropology, as we now understand it, developed only after Boas's first generation of students were practicing as anthropologists. Brinton, then, had the ideas, and went to some trouble to state them formally in an effort to encourage the development of university programs. In spite of all his efforts, however, he remained within the earlier institutional framework and his visions were left to younger men to bring into reality.

In sum, Brinton remains an isolated figure in the history of American anthropology. His theoretical work was done in the framework of an outdated evolutionism, and his presence at the end of an era of only semiprofessional anthropology kept him from having any real influence on the social organization of the twentieth century discipline. It is important to note, however, that Brinton, in spite of all the limitations enforced by his time, was closely involved in the crucial events and trends effecting the professionalization of anthropology. He stands, as it were, at a crossroads of paradigm shift, in the social organizational sense. His career, therefore, brings sharply into focus the changes which were taking place in the last years of the nineteenth century and which have done much to produce the anthropology we know today.

NOTES

[1]Much of the material for this paper is drawn from my unpublished master's thesis at the University of Pennsylvania. I have restricted myself here to comments on Brinton's role in the institutional changes in American anthropology at the end of the last century. I have cited documents from the American Philosophical Society (APS) and Bureau of American Ethnology at the National Anthropological Archives of the Smithsonian Institution (BAE).

[2]Brinton was mistaken about the date of founding of the American Ethnological Society.

LITERATURE CITED

1899   Obituary of Daniel Garrison Brinton. American Anthropologist 1:764.

Brinton, Daniel Garrison
1892   Anthropology as a Science and as a Branch of University Education. Philadelphia.
1895   The Aims of Anthropology. Proceedings of the American Association for the Advancement of Science 44:1–17.

Darnell, Regna
1967   Daniel Garrison Brinton: An Intellectual Biography. Unpublished M.A. thesis, University of Pennsylvania.
1969   The Development of American Anthropology 1880–1920: From Franz Boas to the Bureau of American Ethnology. Unpublished Ph.D. thesis, University of Pennsylvania.
1970   The Emergence of Academic Anthropology at the University of Pennsylvania. Journal of the History of the Behavioral Sciences.
1971   The Powell Classification of American Indian Languages. Papers in Linguistics 4(1).

Freeman, John Finley
1965   University of Anthropology: Early Departments in the United States. Kroeber Anthropological Society Papers 32:78–90.

Hodge, Frederick Webb
1931   Obituary of H. W. Henshaw. American Anthropologist 33:98–103.

Hymes, Dell
1962   On Studying the History of Anthropology. Kroeber Anthropological Society Papers 26:81–86.

Kroeber, Alfred L.
1960   Powell and Henshaw: An Episode in the History of Ethnolinguistics. Anthropological Linguistics 2:1–5.

Kuhn, Thomas
1962   The Structure of Scientific Revolutions. Chicago: Phoenix.

Wallace, Anthony F. C.
1961   Culture and Personality. New York: Random House.

APPENDIX I
PUBLICATION OUTLETS FOR D. BRINTON'S WORK

Proceedings of the American Philosophical Society (48), 1869 (2), 1870 (2), 1871 (1), 1873 (1), 1879 (1), 1880 (2), 1881 (2), 1884 (2), 1885 (4), 1886 (2), 1887 (4), 1888 (4), 1889 (1), 1890 (3), 1891 (1), 1892 (6), 1893 (2), 1894 (2), 1896 (3), 1897 (1), 1898 (2)

Proceedings of the American Association for the Advancement of Science (9), 1887 (2), 1888 (4), 1892 (2), 1893 (1)

Proceedings of the Academy of Natural Sciences of Philadelphia (5), 1884 (3), 1889 (1), 1897 (1)

Numismatic and Antiquarian Society of Philadelphia (5), 1883 (2), (P)1887 (1), (P)1891 (1), (P)1889 (1)

Philadelphia Oriental Club (2), 1890 (1), 1894 (1)

Science (19), 1884 (2), 1885 (4), 1887 (2), 1892 (7), 1893 (1), 1896 (1), 1897 (2)

American Anthropologist (12), 1888 (1), 1892 (1), 1894 (2), 1896 (1), 1897 (2), 1898 (3), (n.s.) 1899 (2)

American Journal of Folklore (3), 1888 (1), 1890 (1), 1892 (1)

American Antiquarian (11), 1881 (1), 1885 (3), 1886 (2), 1887 (1), 1894 (2), 1896 (1), 1897 (1)

Proceedings of the American Antiquarian Society (1), 1884 (1)

American Antiquarian and Oriental Journal (4), 1885 (2), 1886 (1), 1887 (1)

Historical Magazine (7), 1866 (3), 1867 (3), 1870 (1)

Bulletin of the Free Museum of Sciences and Arts, Philadelphia (5), 1897 (3), 1898 (1), 1899 (1)

Archiv fur Religions Wissenschaft, 1899

Annales del Museo Nacional de Mexico, 1886

Revue de Linguistique, 1888

Compte Rendue Congres International des Americanistes, 1890, 1891, 1894

Encyclopedia Brittanica: American Supplement, 1883, 1888

Iconographic Encyclopedia, 1886

Chambers Cyclopedia, 1890

Memoirs International Congress of Anthropology, 1894 (3)

Journal of the Anthropological Institute of Great Britain and Ireland, 1896

Folk-Lore Journal, London, 1883

Archaeologist, 1893, 1894
American Archaeologist, 1898 (2)
Contributions to American Ethnology, Geological Survey, 1882
Annual Reports of the Smithsonian Institution, 1866
Publications of the University of Pennsylvania: Series in Philology, Literature and Archaeology, 1894
Proceedings of the American Oriental Society, 1894
American Naturalist, 1881
American Bibliopolist, 1870
American Journal of Science and Arts, 1869
Lippincott's Magazine, 1868
Forum, 1893
Bureau of Education, 1892 (on Benjamin Franklin)
New Jersey Historical Society
The Magazine of History and Biography, 1885
Historical Society of Philadelphia, 1888
Century Magazine, 1898
Journal of Communication, 1896
Conservator, 1896, 1895
Poet-Lore, 1890, 1893 (3)
Werner's Voice Magazine, 1889 (19th Century Club of New York)
Penn Monthly, 1882 (2)
Medical News, 1896
Transactions of the College of Physicians of Philadelphia, 1892

Books:

The Florida Peninsula, 1859
Florida Guidebook, 1869
Myths of the New World, 1868, 1876, 1896
The Religious Sentiment, 1876
Essays of an Americanist, 1890
Races and Peoples, 1890
American Hero-Myths, 1882
Pursuit of Happiness, 1893
Religions of Primitive Peoples, 1897
Maria Candelaria, 1897
Giordano Bruno, 1890
The Basis of Social Relations, ed. Livingston Farrand, 1902

APPENDIX II
TOPICAL TABULATION OF BRINTON'S BIBLIOGRAPHY

General articles and works in Aboriginal American Languages:

Aboriginal American Authors and their Productions. 1883.
American Indian Languages and Why We should Study Them. 1885.
On Polysynthesis and Incorporation as Characteristics of American Languages. 1885.
The Philosophic Grammar of American Languages as set forth by Wilhelm von Humboldt. 1885.
The Conception of Love in Some American Languages. 1886.
American Aboriginal Poetry. 1887.
The Rate of Change in American Languages. 1887.
The Languages of Paleolithic Man. 1888.
Traits of Primitive Speech Illustrated from American Languages. 1888.
The American Race: A Linguistic Classification and Ethnographic Description of the Native Tribes of North and South America. 1891.
Characteristics of American Languages. 1894.
Indian Words in the Standard Dictionary. 1894.
On Certain Morphologic Traits in American Languages. 1894.
On Various Supposed Relations between the American and Asian Races. 1894.
The Present Status of American Linguistics. 1894.
Linguistique Americaine. 1888.

Mexican and Central American Languages:

A Notice of Some Manuscripts in Central American Languages. 1869.
The Phonetic Alphabet of Yucatan. 1870.
The Names of the Gods in the Kiche Myths, Central America. 1881.
The Books of Chilian Balam, the Prophetic and Historic Records of the Mayas of Yucatan. 1882.
The Graphic System and Ancient Records of the Mayas. 1882.
The Maya Chronicles. 1882.
The Gueguence: A Comedy-Ballet in the Nahuatl-Spanish Dialect of Nicaragua. 1883.

A Grammar of the Cakchiquel Language of Guatemala. 1884.

On the Language and Ethnological Position of the Xinca Indians of Guatemala. 1884.

The Annals of the Cakchiquels. 1885.

The Lineal Measures of the Semi-Civilized Nations of Mexico and Central America. 1885.

Notes on the Mangue. 1885.

On the Ikonomatic Method of Phonetic Writing. 1886.

The Phonetic Elements in the Graphic System of the Ancient Mayas and Mexicans. 1886.

The Study of the Nahuatl Language. 1886.

Ancient Nahuatl Poetry. 1887.

On the So-called Alagulac Language of Guatemala. 1887.

On the Chane-abal Tribe and Dialect of Chiapas. 1888.

On the Nahuatl Version of Sahagun's "Historia de la Nueva Espana." 1888.

On the Stone of the Giants. 1889.

On the Chontallis and Popolucas. 1890.

Rig Veda Americanus: Sacred Songs of the Ancient Mexicans. 1890.

Observations on the Chinantec Languages of Mexico and on the Mazatec Language and its Affinities. 1892.

Vocabularies from the Mosquito Coast. 1891.

The Written Language of the Ancient Mexicans. 1892.

On the Words Anahuac and Nahuatl. 1893.

Remarks on the Mexican Calendar System. 1893.

On the Relation of the Othomi and Tinne Languages. 1894.

A Primer of Mayan Hierglyphics. 1894.

What the Maya Inscriptions Tell About. 1894.

On the Matagalpan Linguistic Stock of Central America. 1895.

The Ethnic Affinities of the Guetares of Costa Rica. 1897.

Remarks on the Maya Group of Languages. 1869.

Los Libros de Chilan Balam. 1886.

Catalogue of the Berendt Linguistic Collection 1898.

North American Languages:

Notes on the Florida Peninsula, its Literary History, Indian Tribes and Antiquities. 1859.

The Shawnees and their Migrations. 1866.

The Natchez of Louisiana: An Offshoot of the Civilized Nations of Central
    America. 1867.
Contributions to a Grammar of the Muskokee Language. 1870.
Grammar of the Choctaw Language. 1870.
On the Language of the Natchez. 1873.
The Chief God of the Algonkins in his Character as Cheat and Liar. 1885.
The Lenape and their Legends. 1885.
The Taensa Grammar and Dictionary: A Deception Exposed. 1885.
The Taensa Grammar and Dictionary: A Reply to M. Lucien Adam. 1885.
On Certain Supposed Nanticoke Words, shown to be of African Origin.
    1887.
Lenape Conversations. 1888.
A Lenape-English Dictionary. 1888.
A Vocabulary of the Nanticoke Dialect. 1893.

South American and Antilles Languages:

Remarks on the MS. Arawack Vocabulary of Schultz. 1869.
The Arawack Language of Guiana in its Linguistic and Ethnological Rela-
    tions. 1871.
Notes on the Puquina Language of Peru. 1890.
Further Notes on the Betoya Dialects of South America. 1892.
Further Notes on Fuegian Languages. 1892.
Studies in South American Languages. 1892.
Some Words from the Andagueda Dialect of the Chococo Stock of South
    America. 1895.
Vocabulary of the Noanama Dialect of the Choco Stock. 1896.
The Linguistic Cartography of the Choco Region. 1898.
On Two Unclassified Recent Vocabularies from South America. 1898.
Indian Languages in South America. 1884.
The Hongote Language. 1892.

Linguistic Works Based on Grammar:

Remarks on the Nature of the Maya Group of Languages. 1869.
Contributions to a Grammar of the Muskokee Language. 1870.
Grammar of the Choctaw Language. 1870.
A Grammar of the Cakchiquel Language of Guatemala. 1884.

Notes on the Puquina Language of Peru. 1890.

The American Race: A Linguistic Classification and Ethnographic Description of the Native Tribes of North and South America. 1891.

Linguistic Works Based on Vocabulary:

Remarks on the Manuscript Arawack Vocabulary of Schultz. 1869.

The Arawack Language of Guiana in its Linguistic and Ethnological Relations. 1871.

On the Language of the Natchez. 1873.

Indian Languages in South America. 1884.

On Certain Supposed Nanticoke Words Shown to be of African Origin. 1887.

A Lenape-English Dictionary. 1888.

On the Chane-abal Tribe and Dialect of Chiapas. 1888.

Vocabularies from the Mosquito Coast. 1891.

Further Notes on Fuegian Languages. 1892.

A Vocabulary of the Nanticoke Dialect. 1893.

Some Words from the Andagueda Dialect of the Choco Stock of South America. 1895.

Vocabulary of the Noanama Dialect of the Choco Stock. 1896.

On Two Unclassified Recent Vocabularies from South America. 1898.

On the Language and Ethnological Position of the Xinca Indians of Guatemala. 1884.

Ethnologic Affinities by Unstated Criteria:

Notes on the Mangue. 1885.

On the So-called Alagulac Language of Guatemala. 1887.

Observations on the Chinantec Language of Mexico and on the Mazatec Language and its Affinities. 1892.

Studies in South American Languages. 1892.

On the Relation of the Othomi and Tinne Languages. 1894.

On the Matagalpan Linguistic Stock of Central America. 1895.

The Ethnic Affinities of the Guetares of Costa Rica. 1897.

The Linguistic Cartography of the Chaco Region. 1898.

Aboriginal American Literature:

The Books of Chilan Balam, the Prophetic and Historic Records of the
  Mayas of Yucatan. 1882.
The Maya Chronicles. 1882.
Aboriginal American Authors and their Productions, especially those in
  the Native Language. 1882.
The Gueguence: A Comedy-Ballet in the Nahuatl-Spanish Dialect of
  Nicaragua. 1883.
The Annals of the Cakchiquels. 1885.
The Lenape and their Legends. 1885.
Notes on Aboriginal Literature. 1885.
The Conception of Love in Some American Languages. 1886.
Los Libros de Chilan Balam. 1886.
American Aborginal Poetry. 1887.
Ancient Nahuatl Poetry. 1887.
Native American Poetry. 1890. (In Essays of an Americanist)
Rig Veda Americanus: Sacred Songs of the Ancient Mexicans. 1890
Primitive American Poetry. 1892.

Writing Systems:

The Graphic System and Ancient Records of the Mayas. 1882.
On the Ikonomatic Method of Phonetic Writing. 1886.
The Phonetic Elements of the Graphic System of the Mayas and Mexicans.
  1886.
On the "Stone of the Giants." 1889.
Inscriptions from Easter Island. 1891.
The Written Language of the Ancient Mexicans. 1892.
What the Maya Inscriptions Tell About. 1894.

International Language:

Report of the Committee Appointed to Examine into the Scientific Value
  of Volapuk. 1888.
The Aims and Traits of a World Language. 1889.
Supplementary Report of the Committee Appointed to Consider an Inter-
  national Language. 1890.
Spelling Reform: A Dream and a Folly. 1896.

Literary Efforts:

Facettes of Love: From Browning. 1888.
Giordano Bruno: Philosopher and Martyr. 1890.
The New Poetic Form as Shown in Browning. 1890.
Browning on Unconventional Relations. 1892.
The Epilogues of Browning: Their Artistic Significance. 1892.
Walt Whitman and Science. 1895.
Whitman's Sexual Imagery. 1896.
Maria Candelaria: A Historic Drama from American Aboriginal Life. 1897.

America as a Unit:

On Polysynthesis and Incorporation as Characteristics of American Languages. 1885.
A Review of the Data for the Study of the Prehistoric Chronology of America. 1887.
On the Alleged Mongolid Affinities of the American Race. 1888.
Essays of an Americanist. 1890.
The American Race: A Linguistic Classification and Ethnographic Description of the Native Tribes of North and South America. 1891.
Characteristics of American Languages. 1894.
On Certain Morphologic Traits in American Languages. 1894.
On Various Supposed Relations Between the American and Asian Races. 1894.
The Culture Status of the American Indian at the Period of his Discovery. 1898.

North American Ethnography:

Early Spanish Mining in Northern Georgia. 1866.
The Mound-Builders of the Mississippi Valley. 1866.
The Myths of Manibozho and Ioskeha. 1867.
A New Imposition. 1867.
A Guide Book of Florida and the South. 1869.
The National Legends of the Chahta-Muskokee Tribes. 1870.
The Probable Nationality of the Mound-Builders. 1881.

The Chief God of the Algonkins in his Character as a Cheat and Liar. 1885.
Iroquois and Eskimos. 1887.
Lenape Conversations. 1888.
Left-Handedness in North American Aboriginal Arts. 1896.
Native American Stringed Instruments. 1897.
The Potter's Wheel in America. 1897.
Notes on the Florida Peninsula, Its Literary History, Indian Tribes and
    Antiquities. 1859.
The Shawnees and their Migrations. 1866.
The Natchez of Louisiana: An Offshoot of the Civilized Nations of Central
    America. 1867.

North American Archaeology and Physical Anthropology:

Artificial Shell Deposits in the United States. 1866.
The Archaeology of Southern Florida. 1895.
Discussion of Ancient Key Dwellers' Remains on the Gulf Coast of Florida.
    1896.
American Archaeology. 1883.
Recent European Contributions to the Study of American Archaeology.
    1883.
Anthropology and Ethnology. 1886.
Prehistoric Archaeology. 1886.
On the Alleged Mongoloid Affinities of the American Race. 1888.
The African Race in America. 1890.
On Various Supposed Relations Between the American and Asian Races.
    1894.

Hoaxes Exposed:

A New Imposition. 1867.
The Taensa Grammar and Dictionary: A Deception Exposed. 1885.
The Taensa Grammar and Dictionary: A Reply to M. Lucien Adam. 1885.

Physiology:

On the Physiological Correlation of Certain Linguistic Radicals. 1894.
Variations of the Human Skeleton and their Causes. 1894.

The Relations of Race and Culture to Degenerations of the Reproductive
   Organs and Functions in Women. 1896.
The Measurement of Thought as Function. 1897.
The Factors of Heredity and Environment in Man. 1898.

Old World Races and Peoples:

The Ethnologic Affinities of the Ancient Etruscans. 1889.
The Cradle of the Semites. 1890.
On Etruscan and Libyan Names: A Comparative Study. 1890.
Races and Peoples: Lectures on the Science of Ethnography. 1890.
The Ancient Libyan Alphabet. 1892.
The Etruscan Ritual Book. 1892.
The Etrusco-Libyan Elements of the Song of the Arval Brethren. 1892.
European Origin of the Aryans. 1892.
European Origin of the White Race. 1892.
The Question of the Celts. 1892.
The Beginnings of Man and the Age of the Race. 1893.
The Alphabets of the Berbers. 1894.
The Proto-Historic Chronology of Western Asia. 1895.

Mythology and Primitive Symbolism:

The Myths of Manibozho and Ioskeha. 1867.
Myths of the New World: A Treatise on the Symbolism and Mythology
   of the Red Race of America. 1868, 1876, 1896.
The Religious Sentiment: Its Source and Aim. 1876.
The Names of the Gods in the Kiche Myths, Central America. 1881.
American Hero-Myths: A Study in the Native Religions of the Western
   Continent. 1882.
The Journey of the Soul: A Comparative Study from Aztec, Aryan and
   Egyptian Mythology. 1883.
The Ta Ki, the Svastika and the Cross in America. 1888.
The Origin of Sacred Numbers. 1894.
Religions of Primitive People. 1897.
The Origin of the Sacred Name Jahva. 1899.
The Basis of Social Relations: A Study in Ethnic Psychology. 1902.
The Chief God of the Algonkins, in his Character as a Cheat and Liar. 1885.
The Conception of Love in Some American Languages. 1886.

Folk-Lore:

The Folk-Lore of Yucatan. 1883.
Lenape Conversations. 1888.
Folk-Lore of the Bones. 1890.
Reminiscences of Pennsylvania Folk-Lore. 1892.
Nagualism: A Study in Native American Folk-Lore and History. 1894.
An Obstetrical Conjuration. 1894.
Popular Superstitions of Europe. 1898.

Use of Informants:

Contributions to a Grammar of the Muskokee Language. 1870.
On the Language of the Natchez. 1873.
Lenape Conversations. 1888.
A Lenape-English Dictionary. 1888.
Reminiscences of Pennsylvania Folk-Lore. 1892.

Obituaries:

Dr. Isaac Hays. 1879.
Dr. John Neill. 1880.
S. S. Haldeman. 1881.
Dr. Karl Hermann Berendt. 1884.
Philip H. Law. 1888.
George de Benneville Keim. 1894.
Dr. William Samuel Waithman Ruschenberger. 1895.
Henry Hazlehurst. 1896.
Dr. Harrison Allen. 1897.
Horatio Hale (2). 1897.
The Abbe Brasseur and his Labors. 1868.
Professor Blumentrill's Studies of the Philippines. 1899.

Brinton's Organization of his Own Work:

A Record of Study in Aboriginal American Languages. 1898.
Analytical Catalogue of Works and Scientific Articles. 1897.

Brintoniana: Three Volumes of Manuscript Material on American Indians. n.d.
Books on American Languages. n.d.

Summaries of Current Research;

Aboriginal American Authors and their Productions, Especially those in the Native Language. 1883.
American Archaeology. 1883.
Recent European Contributions to the Study of American Archaeology. 1883.
Notes on American Ethnology. 1885, 1886, 1887.
Anthropology and Ethnology. 1886.
Prehistoric Archaeology, 1886.
The Study of the Nahuatl Language. 1886.
Linguistique Americaine. 1888.
The International Congress of Americanists. 1891.
Benjamin Franklin and the University of Pennsylvania. 1892.
Current Notes on Anthropology. 1892–1899.
The Department of Archaeology. 1892.
Indian Words in the Standard Dictionary. 1894.
The Present Status of American Linguistics. 1894.
A Primer of Mayan Hieroglyphics. 1894.
Report on the Collections Exhibited at the Columbian Historical Exposition. 1895.
International Catalogue of Scientific Literature. 1898.

Works Based on Unpublished Materials:

The Ancient Phonetic Alphabet of Yucatan. 1870.
Grammar of the Choctaw Language. 1870.
The Folk-Lore of Yucatan. 1883.
On the Language and Ethnological Position of the Xinca Indians of Guatemala. 1884.
Notes on the Mangue. 1885.
On the So-called Alagulac Language of Guatemala. 1887.
On the Chane-abal Tribe and Dialect of Chiapas. 1888.
Vocabularies from the Mosquito Coast. 1891.

Further Notes on the Betoya Dialects of South America. 1892.
A Vocabulary of the Nanticoke Dialect. 1893.

Notices of Manuscript Materials:

A Notice of Some Manuscripts in Central American Languages. 1869.
Critical Remarks on the Editions of Diego de Landa's Writings. 1887.
On the Nahuatl Version of Sahagun's "Historia de la Nueva Espana."
   1888.
The Boturini-Aubin-Goupil Collection of Mexicana. 1893.
The Missing Authorities on Mayan Antiquities. 1897.
Catalogue of the Berendt Linguistic Collection. 1899.

Anthropology as a Science:

Anthropology and Ethnology. 1886.
Anthropology, as a Science and as a Branch of University Education in the
   United States. 1892.
The Nomenclature and Teaching of Anthropology. 1892.
Proposed Classification and International Nomenclature of the Anthro-
   pologic Sciences. 1892.
The Aims of Anthropology. 1895.
The Character and Aims of Scientific Investigation. 1895.

Definition of Terms:

The Society's Name. 1880.
The "Nation" as an Element in Anthropology 1894.
An Ethnologist's View of History. 1896.
Scientific Materialism. 1896.

Unclassified:

The Brinton Family. 1878
Essays of an Americanist. 1890.
Address Delivered on Columbus Day. 1892.
The Pursuit of Happiness. 1893.

6

Native American "Informants": The Contribution of Francis La Flesche

MARGOT LIBERTY

University of Pittsburgh

For many years it has been acknowledged that American Indian cultures, as subject matter, have played a unique role in shaping the development of American anthropology. The backyard scientific laboratory afforded by the expanding United States frontier offered different opportunities for research from those generally available in Europe. It is less often recognized that living representatives of these cultures played an extremely active role in preserving them.

Without them, American anthropology as we know it would never have taken shape. The native American informants who worked with outsiders at recording the traditions of their forebears for posterity often went on to become independent scholars; and even those who did not proved vitally important in compiling a priceless record. It seems fitting at a meeting devoted to the history of American anthropology to bring these people to mind: awareness is in fact rapidly growing (see Hertzberg 1971:305; Sanders 1973:236ff). We will consider some general background first and then the contribution of one man whose work was outstanding: Francis La Flesche of the Nebraska Omaha.

The range of Indian personalities represented by "informants" is as tremendous as the range of publications in which their work appears. By now, there are great literary figures: Ishi of the Yana of California (Kroeber 1961) and Don Talayesva of the Hopi (Simmons 1942), whose memoirs in *Sun Chief* have achieved undergraduate fame (fairly or otherwise) as a sort of Indian version of *Portnoy's Complaint*. There is Black Elk, the Oglala Sioux, whose recollections (Neihardt 1932) in a new paperback edition were endorsed a few years ago by *The Whole Earth Catalog*. I am told this set off an avalanche of orders which nearly broke down the University of Nebraska Press. Other subjects and books are nearly as famous: *Crashing Thunder* (Radin 1926, 1963), *Mountain Wolf Woman* (Lurie 1961), *Son of Old Man Hat* (Dyk 1938, 1967), and *Two Leggings* (Nabokov 1967) to name a few. They are all selling, even the works of a few imposters who need not be named here (consult Costo 1972:153–155 and the New York Times, March 11–25, 1972, for documentation of some of the controversy involved).

There is another whole group, however—less well known although at least as important. This includes Indians who worked as interpreters and/or research assistants, gathering information as well as providing it. Joseph Casagrande's book *In the Company of Man* (1960) is instructive here. Of six North American informants in a series of twenty sketches by anthropologists, five served as the major source: 1) the Eskimo, Ohnainook: 2) the Ojibwa, John Mink; 3) the Navajo, Little Schoolboy; 4) the Pueblo, Marcus Tofoya; and 5) the Seminole, Josie Billy (Carpenter, Casagrande,

Kluckhohn, Adair, and Sturtevant, respectively, in Casagrande 1960). The sixth, James Carpenter, was distinct, going ahead on his own to conduct independent investigations of Crow language and culture which he reported back to Robert Lowie for twenty years from his reservation home in Montana. This is the kind of involvement characteristic of Boas's assistant George Hunt, Grinnell's assistant George Bent, and a host of others. A survey of seventy-five anthropologists and historians in the summer of 1974, yielded a list of more than one hundred such persons as candidates for intellectual biographies, and the list is still growing (Sturtevant and Liberty 1974:6–9). Beyond these, a recent bibliography of life histories includes more than 150 titles about, if not in collaboration with, Indian sources (Langness 1965:54–82), and there is a new compilation (Hirschfelder 1973) summarizing the works of Indian and Eskimo authors.

Francis La Flesche (1857—1932) remains an outstanding member of this group. He belonged to a remarkable Omaha family: one memorialized by a special exhibit at the Nebraska Historical Society museum in Lincoln, and in recent works of biography and fiction (Green 1969, Wilson 1974). His father, Joseph La Flesche, (in the Omaha dialect, "Estamaza" or Iron Eye), though half French, was one of the last traditional Omaha chiefs (a post achieved in part through his adoption as a son by the famous chief, Big Elk). A daughter, Susette—better known as Bright Eyes—became nationally famous on an eastern tour seeking land allotment. Beautiful and articulate, she was credited—wrongly—with having inspired Longfellow's Minnehaha. Another daughter, Susan, became a physician—remarkable at that time for any woman, and doubly so for an Indian. Their brother Francis, however, claimed the greatest achievement by recording the cultural heritage of his people and that of the related Osage to the south.

La Flesche was born in 1857, three years after the Omaha reservation was established on the west bank of the Missouri River. His mother, too, was half white. Despite increasing numbers of settlers crowding in around them, the Omahas retained, for a time, much of their old culture. They had been savagely battered by epidemics (three in half a century) and in the 1850s numbered fewer than a thousand; but they continued to hunt buffalo for twenty years, camping in tepees each summer in traditional clan formation. Earth lodges remained in winter use, though Iron Eye discouraged them and built wooden houses in his own village, dubbed that of the "Make Believe White Men." Young Francis took part in the buffalo hunts, serving at fifteen as one of the runners sent to locate the herd, and covering on that occasion some one hundred miles in eighteen hours (Alexander 1933:328). During this same time he attended the Presbyterian Mission school above the Missouri River, an experience immortalized in his later book *The Middle Five.*

La Flesche had also been exposed to Omaha religion (though perhaps not all of it, as later described by Reo Fortune). He had acted the role of the Sacred Child in the Wawan ceremony, a peacemaking ritual in which he was profoundly moved by the music of several hundred massed voices (Fletcher and La Flesche 1911:386, 389). He was also impressed with the importance of the Sacred Pole, a major medicine object. His horses ran over and nearly upset its belabored keeper (who was carrying it along on his back during the summer migration.) A special offering set matters right, but La Flesche took particular interest in the Sacred Pole from then on, eventually enabling its transfer to the Peabody Museum. The story is dramatic. There was a meeting in September, 1888, between the Pole custodian, Yellow Smoke, and La Flesche, his father Iron Eye, and Alice Fletcher. Sacred traditions of the Pole were recited, and a solemn transfer ritual took place. Iron Eye (who had in the past opposed Pole-related reverance and ritual) became ill at once, and he died two weeks later in the same room (Fletcher and La Flesche 1911:224). The effect of this tragedy upon La Flesche is not known, but it must have been disturbing with other Omahas surely blaming him for his father's death.

Nearly ten years earlier (in 1879) he had gone East with his sister Susette and the Ponca chief Standing Bear to plead (among other things) for secure allotment of land to individuals; a journey arousing tremendous national interest (see Jackson 1881). For the most part, he remained in the East for the rest of his life, working as a copyist for the Office of Indian Affairs (1880-1910) and later as an ethnologist at the Smithsonian. He continued with the BAE for eighteen more years, retiring in 1929. He died in Nebraska three years later, at the age of seventy-five.

La Flesche's work was closely tied to that of Alice Fletcher, with whom he collaborated for forty years—until her death in 1923. They made a strange pair: the energetic "Lady from Boston" so determined to record Plains culture and to bring about individual land allotment (later recognized as a colossal mistake) and the earnest young Omaha whom she eventually adopted as a foster son (Green 1969:65ff; Lurie 1966:81–84). La Flesche's contribution was critical: through him, access was obtained to areas of myth and ritual which would never have been available to an outsider. Continuing to visit the reservation and through the aid of his father and other kinsmen, he gathered increasingly sensitive data: the ritual of the Sacred Tent of War in 1884, the Sacred Pole in 1888, eventually the secret societies. Only La Flesche's intimate personal knowledge of the Omaha language made such recording possible. In a day before ethnology used participant observation, the participation of such insiders as collectors of information was indispensable to preserve a record for the Nebraska Omahas' descendants, a record which elsewhere has been lost.

And the record was considerable. *The Omaha Tribe,* included in the 27th Annual Report of the BAE and published in 1911, contained 642 pages, more than half of which were devoted to the technical areas of kinship and religion. The rest ranged from history to political organization and warfare, economic life, music and recent reservation developments. Authorship was shared: Fletcher may have done more of the actual writing (Alexander 1933:399). But La Flesche was forging ahead on pursuits of his own. These included an autobiography of his early years, *The Middle Five;* and more importantly perhaps, enormous labor among a cognate Siouxan-speaking group, the Osage eventually published in more than 1600 pages of ethnography.

The Middle Five combined an Omaha version of Victorian prose with episodes and insights which are purely Indian. It describes La Flesche's school years in the mid-1800s at the Presbyterian Mission when he was between the ages of eight to twelve. Some of it reads like a cross between *Huckleberry Finn* and *Little Men*. For example, we are given this description of a fight (p 110):

> The Ponca made a determined resistance. I cannot very well relate what happened around me, for I was engaged in a lively bout with a impish looking little chap for whom I had taken a sudden and unreasonable spite. It was hard to get at him, for he was quick as a wildcat in his movements and he gave me a number of vicious blows . . .

But there are also passages of real emotional power, especially in the last chapter describing the death of his beloved friend, Brush, of some alien disease—probably TB. And the book stands as a classic vignette of the early days of missionary education, when the use of the native language was forbidden, and pressure for assimilation in all other ways was at its height.

La Flesche's Osage studies were more fundamental to the long-time anthropological record. They constitute a remarkably rich sample of Osage ceremonial life—one that has not yet been adequately analyzed. But the texts are there: 1600 pages, pubished serially in the 36th, 39th, 43rd and 45th Annual Reports of the BAE, under the general title *The Osage Tribe* (1915–1928). The material deals exclusively with ritual: The Rite of the Chiefs; Sayings of the Ancient Men; the Rite of Vigil; The Child Naming Rite; The Rite of Waxo'be. The material was collected in the Osage language, since La Flesche's native Omaha was close enough to permit its use.

His interest had been stimulated by the visit of an Osage delegation to Washington, some years after 1900. The delegation included a man named Saucy Calf; he and La Flesche discovered vast areas of shared intellectual interests. When asked if there was an Omaha Corn Song, La Flesche sang it. Saucy Calf encouraged La Flesche to pursue studies of the Osage at the reservation; he also visited his friend in Washington. Saucy Calf died in 1912 but his contribution to the effort was immense. The eventual reputation of the work as "the most complete single record of the ceremonies of any North American Indian people" is well deserved (Alexander 1933:329; La Flesche in 45th Annual Report 1928:530–536).

With this example in mind, we can move to some more general questions concerning the role of those Indian intellectuals who helped to shape American anthropology. We can distinguish, initially, the two types suggested above (although of course there are some overlaps): the classical "informants" or sources on one hand, and the more independent researchers on the other. What sort of background factors directed people toward these roles? Was marginality a factor? Certainly, many of the well-known Indians were exceptional in some way (cf. Barnett's *Innovation*)—by virtue of high intelligence if nothing else. Then, what about heredity? Mixed Indian and white ancestry appears to have been critical in many cases. The mixed blood interpreters deserve special study, having a place of their own in America history. Many went on to become active collectors of knowledge. Born of white fathers and Indian mothers, they generally remained predominantly Indian, often having unusual advantages in education. Exposure to different ways of life through membership in two societies seems to have been crucial in developing insight into cultural differences and the vital questioning process which led to so many anthropological discoveries. Fullbloods conversely may have remained more traditional. Perhaps they served more as sources (e.g. Ishi, Talayesva, and Black Elk), while the mixed bloods tended to become more independent and analytical as time went by (e.g. George Bent, George Hunt, and Francis La Flesche). It has been suggested, however, that this dichotomy, if it works anywhere, works best on the Plains, and even there it is far from perfect. My Cheyenne friend, John Stands In Timber, was certainly an independent researcher, and he was as full-blooded as they come.

For whatever reasons, it seems clear that too many of these people have received too little credit. Too many are mentioned briefly if at all in some author's preface, with only a note of thanks. It is time to give credit where credit is due.

Also, in passing, we might consider our own focus in recording material for the future. We have so often been obsessed with upstreaming—gathering material from the vanishing past—that we neglect the equally vanishing present. We seem to be supporting the adage that the only good Indian is a dead Indian. There have

been comments to this effect with reference to the forthcoming biographical volume of the new Smithsonian *Handbook of North
American Indians:* you have to be dead to get in. Some very worth-
while figures may not make it. More seriously, however, it seems
the La Flesches of the present—and there are some—should be encouraged to record their own life stories while there is time. (John
Stands In Timber wouldn't do it until he had finished his historical
material, and by that time he had gone to join the "good" Indians.)
The present counts as much as the past, nonetheless, as part of a
vital human record. In the words of a recent popular song, "These
Are the Good Old Days."

In closing, I would like to turn again to the story of Francis La
Flesche, who had difficulties with stereotypes. One of these concerned the acceptance for publication of his book, *The Middle Five.*
The manuscript was rejected twice with high praise of its literary
quality, accompanied by the complaint that it was not "Indian"
enough, but rather too typical of schoolchildren everywhere. Ironically, in stressing its common humanity, he had dedicated it "To
The Universal Boy" (Green 1969:189–191).

A second instance of such irony may be found in La Flesche's
obituary (Alexander 1933). It seems that, during his Bureau of
American Ethnology period, he was persuaded to pose one day for
some photographs. The results, showing him in standard white-
collar office attire, are preserved in the National Anthropological
Archives at the Smithsonian Institution. In the last of the series,
however, he is wrapped in a buffalo robe over his shirt and tie.

After his death in 1932, a portrait was needed to accompany the
obituary prepared by Hartley Burr Alexander for the *American Anthropologist.* The buffalo robe shot was selected, but apparently the
clash of cultures suggested therein was too great for the layout editor to bear. By some process—I am told that airbrushing was not a
common photographic technique in 1933—a unique job of cen-
sorship took place. All evidence of street clothes was removed from
beneath the buffalo robe. And we have a benignly smiling La
Flesche posed for posterity in a getup, which, had he seen would
surely have astonished him.

I am not sure of the moral of this story,—except perhaps that stereotypes of Indians are as bad as any other kind, and at least as prevalent (if not more so). An Indian can be a great scientist, as was La Flesche, while remaining Indian in other dimensions. The combinations are potentially infinite. And a man ought to be permitted to wear a buffalo robe over his street clothes in his obituary if there is any indication whatever that this is what he might have wanted.

LITERATURE CITED

Adair, John
    1960 A Pueblo G.I. *In* In the Company of Man, pp. 357–376. J. B. Casagrande, ed. New York: Harper & Row.

Alexander, Hartley B.
    1933 Francis La Flesche. American Anthropologist 35:328–331.

Barnett, Homer G.
    1954 Innovation: The Basis of Cultural Change. New York: McGraw-Hill.

Carpenter, Edmund
    1960 Ohnainewk, Eskimo Hunter *In* In the Company of Man, pp. 417–426. J. B. Casagrange, ed. New York: Harper & Row.

Casagrande, Joseph B.
    1960 John Mink, Ojibwa Informant. *In* In the Company of Man, pp. 467–488. J. B. Casagrange, ed. New York: Harper & Row.

Casagrande, Joseph B., ed.
    1960 In the Company of Man: Twenty Portraits by Anthropologists. New York: Harper & Row.

Costo, Rupert
    1972 Desecrating the Cheyenne. *In* The American Indian Reader: Education, Book 2 of a Series in Educational Perspectives, pp. 153–155. Jeannette Henry, ed. San Francisco: Indian Historian Press.

Dorsey, J. O.
   1884 Omaha Sociology. Annual Reports of the Bureau of American
       Ethnology 3:205–370.

Dyk, Walter
   1938 Son of Old Man Hat: A Navajo Autobiography. New York:
       Harcourt. Reprinted 1967 Lincoln, Neb.: University of Nebras-
       ka Press.

Fletcher, A. C., and Francis La Flesche
   1911 The Omaha Tribe. Annual Reports of the Bureau of American
       Ethnology 27:17–654. Reprinted 1967, Lincoln, Neb.: Uni-
       versity of Nebraska Press.

Fortune, Reo
   1932 Omaha Secret Societies. Columbia University Contributions to
       Anthropology, no. 14:1–193.

Green, Norma Kidd
   1969 Iron Eye's Family: The Children of Joseph La Flesche. Lincoln,
       Neb.: Johnsen.

Hertzberg, Hazel W.
   1971 The Search for an American Indian Identity: Modern Pan-
       Indian Movements. Syracuse, N.Y.: Syracuse University Press.

Hirschfelder, Arlene B.
   1973 American Indian and Eskimo Authors: A Comprehensive
       Bibliography. New York: Association on American Indian
       Affairs.

Jackson, Helen Hunt
   1881 A Century of Dishonor: A Sketch of the United States Govern-
       ment's Dealings with Some of the Indian Tribes. New York:
       Harper and Bros. Reprinted 1965 as A Century of Dishonor:
       The Early Crusade for Indian Reform. New York: Harper
       Torchbooks.

Kluckhohn, Clyde
   1960 A Navajo Politician, *In* In the Company of Man, pp. 439–466. J.
       B. Casagrande, ed. New York: Harper & Row.

Kroeber, Theodora
   1961 Ishi in Two Worlds: A Biography of the Last Wild Indian in
       North America. Berkeley and Los Angeles: University of Cali-
       fornia Press.

La Flesche, Francis
    1900 The Middle Five: Indian Boys at School. Boston: Small, Mayard and Co. Reprinted 1963 as The Middle Five: Indian Schoolboys of the Omaha Tribe. Madison. University of Wisconsin Press.
    1915-28 The Osage Tribe. Annual Reports of the Bureau of American Ethnology 36:35–604; 39:31–630; 43:23–164; 45:529–833.

Langness, L. L.
    1965 The Life History in Anthropological Science. New York: Holt, Rinehart and Winston.

Liberty, Margot, and William C. Sturtevant
    1974 Prospectus for a Collection of Studies on Anthropology by North American Indians. Mimeographed.

Lowie, Robert H.
    1960 My Crow Interpreter, *In* In the Company of Man. pp. 427–438. J. B. Casagrande, ed. New York: Harper & Row.

Lurie, Nancy O.
    1961 Mountain Wolf Woman, Sister of Crashing Thunder: The Autobiography of a Winnebago Woman. Ann Arbor, Mich.: University of Michigan Press.
    1966 The Lady From Boston and the Omaha Indians, American West 3:31–33, 81–85.

Nabokov, Peter
    1967 Two Leggings: The Making of a Crow Warrior. New York: Thomas Y. Crowell.

Neihardt, John G.
    1932 Black Elk Speaks: Being a Life Story of a Holy Man of the Oglala Sioux. New York: Morrow. Reprinted 1961, Lincoln, Neb.: University of Nebraska Press.

Radin, Paul, ed.
    1926 Crashing Thunder: The Autobiography of an American Indian. New York: Appleton. Reprinted 1963, New York: Dover.

Raymont, Henry
    1972 Doubt Cast on Authenticity of McGraw-Hill's "Memoirs of Red Fox." New York Times, March 10.

Sanders, Ronald
    1973 Literature of the Indian: A Critique. *In* The American Indian

Reader: Literature. Book 3 of a Series in Educational Per-
'spectives, pp. 219–244. Jeannette Henry, ed. San Francisco: Indian Historian Press.

Simmons, Leo W.
    1942 Sun Chief: The Autobiography of a Hopi Indian. New Haven,
          Conn.: Yale University Press.

Stands In Timber, John, and Margot Liberty
    1967 Cheyenne Memories. New Haven, Conn.: Yale University Press.

Sturtevant, William C.
    1960 A Seminole Medicine Maker. *In* In the Company of Man, pp.
          505–532. J. B. Casagrande, ed. New York: Harper & Row.

Wilson, Dorothy Clarke
    1974 Bright Eyes: The Story of Susette La Flesche, an Omaha In-
          dian. New York: McGraw-Hill.

7

Nineteenth Century Fieldwork, Archaeology, and Museum Studies: Their Role in the Four-Field Definition of American Anthropology.

JOHN R. COLE

Hartwick College

A recent book, *Reinventing Anthropology*, asks, if we had to do it all over again, would we do it the same way? Would we even do it at all? Dell Hymes (1972:3–4) answers:

No. What, after all, is this anthropology, that its absence
would be noticed or that cannot be done severally by its parts
or by other disciplines? If it is unique in its unifying perspective, where are its holistic, integrating works? Does
anyone write about "anthropology" as a whole except in the
smorgasbord of textbooks or as a committee? If it has a natural
unity, why does its makeup differ so much from one country
and national tradition to another, even from one department to
another? Who can read the program of the annual meetings of
the association and find in it the profile of a science? Would an
objective ethnographer, observing organized anthropology
today, not conclude that its structure reflects adaptation to a
past, not present, environment, that is essentially a survival?
That from the viewpoint of the next, last, generation of the
twentieth century, it will be found one of "the remains of crude
old culture which have passed into harmful superstition of
which it is a harsher, and at times even painful, office of ethnography to expose . . . and to mark, . . . out for destruction"
(Tylor 1871: vol. 2, p. 539).

There are many problems with this assessment, two of which this
paper will pursue. One is theoretical disagreement about what
anthropology is and should be. The other problem is historical: anthropology developed in a historical context that we do not have
now, so *of course* any "reinvention" would be somewhat different. I
would argue that these two problems are closely related, however,
our theory and history have been interconnected, and I will argue
that in the American case that relationship has been constructive
and profitable.

American anthropology differs from European most strikingly in
its holistic "four-field" approach. The most severe revisionist critics
of our discipline have periodically concentrated their attacks on this
concept, maintaining that the four fields are really unrelated, un-
manageable, or at least outmoded.

A criticism of lesser magnitude quibbles with the magic number
"four" suggesting that to cultural and physical anthropology, archaeology, and linguistics we add new specialties such as ethnohistory, kinesics, or human ecology. As long as revisions are addi-
tive there is no real challenge to the basic holistic definition of

American anthropology; there *is* a danger however, of losing track of basic elements if all new additions are treated as equals of the original four fields.

I suggest that anthropology has been a more fertile discipline in America than in Europe, and this is due largely to the association (occasionally forced!) of linguists, ethnographers, archaeologists, and physical anthropologists. Obviously this conclusion is debatable, but however one evaluates the present state of anthropology, a look at our discipline's origins is instructive. Criticisms that the four-field approach is *not* "self-evident" or "natural" miss the mark because they attack a straw man issue. God did not ordain a mystical four-in-one concept of anthropology, revealed to Americans but not to Europeans. *But it is an important theoretical statement.* The concept has been useful not because it is inherently more "natural" than the European approach. But it has worked well in a particular historical framework, and given the chance, it may work well in other frameworks, also.

Robert Murphy (1971:23–27) noted the relationship between theory and geographic areas of *ethnographic* anthropological fieldwork. In the formative years of the nineteenth century this relationship was more crucial than it is today, and our course was plotted long before Boas codified it in academia as an official four-field discipline. The relationship between practical fieldwork and our theoretical orientation in two areas was especially crucial in the original definition of an explicitly *American* anthropology. These areas of archaeology and museum exhibition and studies, are now treated by some anthropologists as secondary in specialized interests. (It should be noted that similar arguments apply to American linguistics, but that is beyond the topic of this paper.)

EARLY ARCHAEOLOGY

In Europe, archaeology developed earlier and better than in America. Its advances in technical expertise and theory had a strong initial impact on anthropology, especially the studies of cultural evolution which, for example, could use Thomsen's three-age system or artifact association with extinct fauna to give anthropological studies time-depth. Yet these common interests were offset by the accident of geography and the Enlightenment-based intellectual tradition of anthropological interest in "primitive" peoples—people who lived far from the arena which European archaeology investigated.

With the exception of Thomas Jefferson's (1788) famous but transitory foray into stratigraphic excavation of a burial mound in 1784, proficient field archaeology did not appear in the Americas until the 1840's. The midwestern explorations of Squier and David (1848), Mexican exploration by Stephens and Catherwood (1841–43), and the work of Caleb Atwater and a few other pioneers marked the beginnings of fieldwork as modern archaeologists might recognize it. But long before this there had been amateur or "armchair" archaeology by the same people who were interested in American Indians. The two subjects were taken for granted as being parts of the same "natural science" because their common geographic location, even if there were frequent flights of fantasy about Lost Tribes of Israel or "Moundbuilder races." Ethnographers and proto-archaeologists turned to the same field for their data. If not yet archaeologists, they were more than simple antiquarians because they were interested in the people behind the artifacts and in the general philosophical, if not strictly theoretical, issues of early natural science.

In Europe, the interest in explaining "thunderstones" fit into researches in historic and stratigraphic geology. Other artifacts could be placed within national *histories* (cf. Taylor 1967:9–19). In America, on the other hand, archaeology was recognized as the study of Indians—or perhaps "Mound Builders"—rather than truly unknown peoples such as the makers of thunderstones. Indians were outsiders—the subject of ethnography rather than history—but they were close at hand and available to rudimentary ethnographers or archaeologists who wished to interpret artifacts by ethnographic analogy. By way of contrast, it should be obvious that John Frere could not interview or observe local London suburbanites to learn the meaning of his Thames handaxes. Any ethnographic analogy had to refer to "stone age" peoples in a place like the New World. European artifacts were made by earlier Europeans, not neighboring but foreign Indians, so they had to fit into European history somehow, even if the history was occasionally geological.

The American setting for fieldwork was different in another way: Indians, however interesting to some people were by and large considered an undifferentiated military enemy. Hence, ethnography had immediate military and political uses, and by the same token, military operations and explorations were a source of secondhand ethnographic data. The Lewis and Clark Expedition, for example, was a combination of geographic exploration, military reconnaissance, and a search for natural scientific and ethnographic data.

Explorers, trappers, and missionaries who followed them continued this tradition at the behest of the War Department. While in government and long afterward Jefferson's Secretary of the Treasury, Albert Gallatin,[1] used his connections with Indian Commissioner Thomas McKenney and others to obtain anthropological information. He arranged to require trappers and other explorers to fill out questionnaires and file reports on "Indian customs, languages and prehistoric monuments" as a condition of their permits to enter Indian territories. Often this was mere vocabulary collecting (asking for the Seminole word for "moose," for example!) but much of the data were useful ethnohistoric descriptions. Some of this he used; he also arranged to have other scholars, including Rafinesque of Transylvania University, share in the proceeds of his secondhand fieldwork. The government was no doubt satisfied as well, because requiring cvilians to furnish information cost nothing, and some of it was potentially useful to the War Department.

It is important to note that "prehistoric monuments" were treated as a routine part of this nascent ethnography. They were not of military use, perhaps, but the War Department treated archaeological sites as part of the same body of data,—a "peaceful" by-product, of interest to Gallatin in his effort to trace the origin of Indians to Siberia! After Gallatin's death in 1849 this tradition of rudimentary government concern with archaeology as a clear part of ethnography continued—notably in the operation of the Smithsonian Institution.

Anthropology, then, had quasi-governmental support and usefulness in this country, and archaeology was actually in the forefront of "Indian studies" in some ways—the first Smithsonian "Contribution to Knowledge" was Squier and Davis's (1848) archaeological survey. Since Indians were "natural history," more literally historical data such as archaeological artifacts, information, and speculation fit readily into the picture along with morphemes, religion, and subsistence practices. Later, the Bureau of American Ethnology, despite its name, readily incorporated a concern for archaeology, although Powell frowned on *"mere"* archaeology devoid of "ethnological" uses (Darnell 1969:37–38).

EARLY MUSEUMS AND THE CULTURE AREA CONCEPT

Another major influence on later American anthropology was the nineteenth century ethnological museum, which mingled ethnography and archaeology from the first as the above reference to the Smithsonian would suggest, although the National Museum itself was not founded until 1881. Almost by definition, museums house "things"—material objects. Better than European collections, American museums were drawn to an incipient culture area approach, even when it was not intentional, by their exhibition of Indian materials, historic or prehistoric, in the same buildings. Once again, the field of study helped determine anthropological results or definitions. Before the Civil War collections seem to have been private, essentially antiquarian affairs rather than museums in a modern sense, but even then historic and prehistoric material was *intellectually* mingled. The catholic concerns of Gallatin and Morgan, for example, included the sorts of material things which would later be displayed in formal museums.

If a European museum exhibited both ethnographic and archaeological materials, a choice had to be made: either house local archaeological and remote ethnographic material, or make the major theoretical innovation of seeking out archaeological artifacts from the distant culture area represented by the museum's ethnographic collections. This latter approach would have required 1) a concept of culture area which did not really bloom until late in the nineteenth century; 2) an understanding of *archaeology* in terms of these same culture areas; 3) a sophisticated (and expensive) interdisciplinary approach to data gathering rather than the usual commercial or private "accession" route via dealers and collectors; and 4) a total revolution in artifact display, replacing the grossly comparative "arrowheads of the world" cabinets with a "tool kit," or "cultural unit" or "culture area" approach.

Despite this limited amount of theoretical insight or sophistication American museums, once they got under way, solved *some* of these problems simply by housing display objects from the same general area, whether archaeological or ethnographic. Displays could be a meaningless, random hodgepodge, but within the clutter lay an implicit theoretical statement: Indian "things," past and present, are a common subject matter. Minor museums and private displays such as roadside "tourist traps" still exhibit this incipient culture area idea in their unplanned, eclectic lumping together of whatever is locally available.

It should be restressed that museums collected items of "material culture." In both hemispheres they provided a potential basis for the anthropological study of techno-environmental materialism. Museums collected material data in anthropology or ethnology, but only America had a *purely* material branch of anthropology—archaeology. In Europe, archaeology could remain somewhat more set apart from ethnology, and material ethnological data could be dealt with in terms of the burgeoning ethnographic research that went beyond the museum collections. Informants' explanations of artifacts along with language, myths, kinship, and so on, could be included. The extent to which museums influenced anthropological theory—or the very concept of anthropology—was thus slightly different where archaeology played a lesser, or separate, role. Of course, American anthroplolgy did *not* follow a uniformly more materialist course than European, despite its potential. Still, American museums were better suited to Tylor's definition of anthropology as a discipline placing people's works co-equal with their beliefs (Harris, n.d.), because of the inclusion of the uncompromisingly materialistic realm of archaeology.

When Clark Wissler wrote his book *The American Indian,* he openly acknowledged the debt he owed to museum work in formulating his culture area theory. "(The book) is in the main a by-product of the author's activities as a museum curator in which capacity he has sought to objectify and systematize the essential facts relating to North America" (Wissler 1917:v, quoted in Darnell 1969:458). Wissler, of course, was essentially a "museum man," but one who was generally in the Boasian camp, making his situation somewhat exceptional, especially in later years.

FROM DE FACTO TO "OFFICIAL" HOLISM

Franz Boas began *his* career as a museum man. After his field-work in Baffinland he worked at the Berlin Museum which sent him to North America in 1886 to collect "ethnological" specimens. It is important to note that he was simultaneously collecting anthropological information for E. B. Tylor, a man whose concept of anthropology embodied what would later take root in America under Boas' aegis as the "four-field approach," even as Tylor's definition withered in Britain and Europe.

When Boas first visited the Northwest Coast, he was dealing mostly with material culture. The museum wanted *things.* If only because of his European background, his concept of archaeology was perhaps more historical than evolutionary—filling in a progression between A and Z in accretional, particularistic steps—but whatever minimal early interest he had in archaeology must have fit in nicely with his interest in ethnographic material culture. He and American archaeologists investigated the history and interpretation of *things.* So on a practical level, his museum work reinforced in his mind the clear unity of cultural items, historic or prehistoric, as a general field of research.

Boas was not unique or first in recognizing the value of material culture. After all, it was the major reason for the creation of ethnological museums. But "ethnology" was a *rival* of anthropology at first, being historical rather than comparative by one definition (Eggan 1968:119). Boas's experience working as an anthropologist for Tylor and an ethnologist for the Berlin Museum, while dealing with identical Northwest Coast data, must have reinforced the idea that the two approaches should be reconciled.

Boas was also influenced by the beginnings of the culture area idea advanced by Ratzel, Bastian, and others—not the least because of his own training in geography. When he arranged museum displays in Berlin and later at the Field Museum and American Museum, he instituted an explicit culture area approach which had as many ramifications for anthropology as for museology. The idea was also quickly and naturally applied to archaeological exhibits. Instead of "axes of the world" or whatever, more or less complete materials began to be brought together in displays of "*cultures* of the world," historic and prehistoric. The role of his museum background in formulating his concept of anthropology has often been slighted, and even less attention has been paid to the effect of his anthropological material culture emphasis on archaeology. (His own work in archaeology was limited, although not nonexistent, as popular belief seems to hold.)

Unlike their European contemporaries, American ethnographers such as Schoolcraft, Powell, Long, Mooney, and Morgan could do field work at home, right alongside archaeologists. They could also do *more* fieldwork, since the common field was economically close at hand. Boas's influence was most important to the extent it institutionalized this practical commanality of interest. He appeared just as anthropology was entering a "professionalization period," or Penniman's "Constructive Period" (1952:20–21). Capitalizing on a fairly chaotic, uncentralized American scene in which various aspects of what today is anthropology were scattered in various museums, government agencies, and miscellaneous uni-

versity departments, Boas was able to define the discipline along
the lines advocated by Tylor. He assembled a four-field program out
of pre-existing American raw materials, and exploiting a university
base of operations; he and his students were in a position to train all
or most future professionals in an age when such professionalization came into vogue. Museums did not produce similar student-
missionaries, and their limited niche was filled to capacity, anyway,
unlike the virgin terrritory of university academia for which the new
elite of Ph.D.'s were trained. Similar professionalization occurred in
Europe, but the relative scarcity of university positions there,
combined with already existent historical or classical orientations
(as discussed earlier), served to segregate archaeology from anthropology even further as departmental dividing lines rigidified.

It is not surprising that the old guard anthropologists in America
did not appreciate being displaced. Considering Boas's museum
background, however, it is a bit ironic. The university setting
proved a more fertile ground where anthropology could expand, but
perhaps the personal schisms between Boas and the Field Museum,
the American Museum, and later the Heye Museum (Cole, n.d.),
have obscured his museum roots. The nonacademic contributions to
Boas's definition of anthropology have also been obscured through
powers struggles such as the flap over his denunciation of
"Scientists as Spies" (Boas 1919). In this dispute, he and his AES
associates were opposed by Washington, archaeology, and museum
forces including Kidder, Fewkes, Morley, Saville, Dixon, Spinden,
Judd and Lothrop (Darnell 1969:483; Stocking 1868:273ff.). Yet the
museum provided one of the major sources of Boas's age-area
concept and the culture area approach which is the forerunner of
modern cultural ecology.

The same dispute may have obscured the leading role of earlier
archaeology in American anthropology, since archaeologists were
prominent among the anti-Boasians in museum circles. We still feel
the repercussions of that 1919 dispute (and the issues it
symptomized) in which the more empirical branches of anthropology tended to be allied against the Boasian ethnographers. The
Boasians ultimately triumphed in the power struggle over who
would define the discipline. But although Boas would be appalled at

being classified as unempirical, this early feud between "culture" and "empiricism" advocates laid a certain groundwork for later developments in which archaeology, physical anthropology, and linguistics at least *seemed* to grow more and more empirical in contrast with most ethnology. To some extent the Boasian victory for a holistic definition of a discipline, which would not exclude cultural anthropology, had the unintended effect of downgrading *non*-cultural anthropology in some people's minds. This was *not* the "Boasian program," by any means, but continuing the four-field approach required a rebuilding process to replace the now partially exiled museum crowd, and this perhaps has not been completely successful.

Like his lifelong interest in museums, his staunch support of archeaology as part of the four-field concept seems to have suffered as a result of his recurring feuds with museums, where archaeologists continued to be entrenched. For example, after Saville left the Columbia anthropology department, they did not always have a resident archaeologist until Strong's arrival (despite a "Loubat Chair in American Archaeology" waiting to be filled). It should be noted that Saville himself had been among the anti-Boas votes in 1919. And at Berkeley, Kroeber did not provide systematic training in archaeology until the appointment of Heizer and, later, John Rowe (Steward 1973:39–40).

Archaeology seems to have been a backwater area in the Boasian program for a time, and with a few exceptions such as Kidder, Morley, and Judd, the gap was not filled by scholars from museums or other, non-Boasian, strongholds (Uhle at Berkeley and Fewkes and Holmes at Harvard were the only professionals Boas respected at the turn of the century, and they were not among his disciples) (Darnell 1969:240). Certainly, there were and are important Boas-trained archaeologists, beginning with Kroeber (although he was more self-trained in archaeology) and Manuel Gamio, but archaeology was the one branch of anthropology which continued for a time to be dominated by non-Boasians. Its inhibited growth into a professionalized institutional format is exemplified by the fact that the Society for American Archaeology was not founded until the 1930s, long after the other three fields were well established with what, in retrospect, might be called lobbying organizations within the discipline. Archaeology remained outside the Boasian circle, and it would ultimately come to be outside the *Anthropological* circle because of the degree to which the Boasian program came to be equated with anthropology in general.

Why Boas and not Putnam, Brinton, or someone else should have been so successful at capitalizing on the academic "niche" is far beyind the subject of this paper. His unquestioned personal ability was certainly an important factor, but I would suggest a more comprehensive reason may lie in his advocacy of the four-field approach. Here, his innovations drew heavily on a combination of the American fieldwork tradition and the extent to which that tradition had already developed in conjunction with museum work. When that cohesion deteriorated in practice for a time, despite Boas's continued advocacy of an anthropological archaeology, dissension undermined this aspect of holism in the minds of later students. Weakening, or failing to nurture adequately, one of the links weakened the entire four-field concept in later years as archaeology tried to catch up with the rest of anthropology, borrowing its theory while it struggled for a proper foothold in academia. To a degree Boas seems to have let part of his original strength slip away by not solidly defining the place of archaeology in his program after his falling out with museum people. I have attempted to show how his original program was uniquely suited to the American scene, largely because of the commanality of interests between ethnographers and archaeologists who, from the earliest days of the AES, could study "Indian customs and ruins" as one coherent subject. Losing track of that coherency, even partially, was counterproductive.

CONCLUSIONS

Hymes (1972:3-4) is correct when he writes that anthropology has different definitions in different countries, but instead of being evidence that it is therefore chaotic or undefinable, this is evidence of different processes at work when anthropology was being invented. This paper has tried to describe a few of the factors in the *American* invention which I think have been useful and yes, *superior*, whether accidental or not.

The *relative* lack (not the total lack Hymes claims) of holistic, integrative, studies is indeed lamentable, but this can be attributed to theoretical—or antitheoretical—schools within anthropology rather than to the independent issue of the value of the four-field approach. In fact, I would place much of the blame on exclusionists who have tried to *narrow* the holistic approach by concentrating on myth analyses or value system studies which I submit are less productive avenues for generalization than are the trails blazed by Morgan, Tylor, and Boas (despite his own supposed antitheoretical bent). Evolutionism, for example, is reasserting itself in anthropology in the work of White, Fried, Harris, Steward, Service, Lanning, Adams, and many others. Whether one agrees with them or not, they are to varying degrees practicing an anthropology which builds on nineteenth century holism of the American model I have been discussing. Perhaps there have simply been too many diversions from a basically sound integrative, four-field anthropology wherein archaeology, historical linguistics, and physical anthropology, for example, can give time depth to cultural evolutionism which too often has been the province of a more or less synchronic ethnography.

Today American anthropologists' interests *do* range far beyond those of the nineteenth century. Perhaps this does call for a redefinition of our discipline. But before we "reinvent" anthropology or abolish it, I suggest that we take a closer look at the reasons we have been relatively successful and at the same time document our failings. We may have outgrown many of the historical specifics this paper has touched upon, but have we outgrown the problems and issues with which those specifics originally dealt? It is possible that current attacks on holism in anthropology, while more sophisticated, are spiritual descendants of the 1919 anti-Boasians and the Galton Society who sought to define anthropology as a biological discipline, excluding culture (Stocking 1968:289–290). Now to exclude biology, archaeology, material, or "empirical" subjects in general may be equally shortsighted.

NOTES

[1]This and other material relating to Albert Gallatin is based on manuscripts in the Albert Gallatin Papers Collection of the New York Historical Society—which Gallatin founded, incidentally. The collection is catalogued and microfilmed except for the "unimportant" papers—which includes his papers relating to Indians and ethnology! I thank the Society for letting me examine this material.

I also thank John V. Murra, Doug Brintnall, Shirley Gorenstein, Elaine Neudecker, Brad Ross, and Marvin Harris for useful comments. Needless to say, they may not agree with the *results,* for which I am culpable!

LITERATURE CITED

Boas, Franz
    1919   Scientists as Spies. The Nation 109.

Cole, John R.
    n.d.   The Political Life of Franz Boas. Columbia University. MS.

Darnell, Regna
    1969   The Development of American Anthropology 1879-1920: From the Bureau of American Ethnology to Franz Boas. Ph.D. thesis, University of Pennsylvania.

Eggan, Fred
    1968   One Hundred Years of Ethnology and Social Anthropology. *In One Hundred Years of Anthropology,* pp. 119–149. J. O. Brew, ed. Cambridge: Harvard University Press.

Harris, Marvin
1970 The History and Ideological Significance of the Separation of Social and Cultural Anthropology. Columbia University. Memeographed.

Hymes, Dell, Ed.
1972 Reinventing Anthropology. New York: Pantheon.

Jefferson, Thomas
1788 Notes on the State of Virginia. Philadelphia.

Murphy, Robert F.
1971 The Dialectics of Social Life. New York: Basic Books.

Penniman, T. K.
1952 A Hundred Years of Anthropology. London.

Squier, E. G., and E. H. Davis
1848 Ancient Monuments of the Mississippi Valley. Smithsonian Contribution to Knowledge. no. 1.

Stephens, J. L.
1843 Incidents of Travel in Yucatan. 2 vols. New York.

Steward, Julian
1973 Alfred Kroeber. New York: Columbia University Press.

Stocking, George W., Jr.
1968 Race, Culture, and Evolution. Glencoe, Ill. Free Press.

Taylor, Walter W.
1967 A Study of Archaeology. Carbondale, Ill. Southern Illinois University Press.

Tylor, E. G.
1871 Primitive culture. London: J. Murray.

Wissler, Clark
1917 The American Indian: An Introduction to the Anthropology of the New World. New York: Douglas C. McMurtrie.

8

The American Ethnological Society: The Columbia Phase, 1906–1946

ALEXANDER LESSER

Professor Emeritus, Hofstra University

The American Ethnological Society, the oldest anthropological society, was founded in New York in 1842 and remained a New York organization through more than 100 years of its history. The Columbia phase—actually the Columbia-American Museum of Natural History phase—began around the turn of the century.

At the time, anthropology was expanding at Columbia University and the American Museum, and an increasingly professional membership of the Society reorganized and activated itself as a scientific association. Anthropologists at the university and the

126

museum were the moving forces behind the redevelopment, among whom Franz Boas, from 1896 to 1905 a member of the staff of both institutions, was a leading influence. An effort was made from the beginning of this twentieth century period to maintain strong relations between the museum and the university; Boas was convinced that anthropological work, and especially the training of anthropologists, required the coordinated effort if not the integration of a university anthropology department with an anthropological museum. In addition to such direct relations, the American Ethnological Society and the Section of Anthropology and Psychology of the New York Academy of Sciences, headquartered at the museum, proviced a mechanism for professional and public relationship. Active professionals in the section, like Clark Wissler and Robert H. Lowie, were also active in the American Ethnological Society.

Prior to 1911, the activities of the AES and the New York Academy section on anthropology were not regularized, although several joint sessions were held between 1907 and 1911. Thereafter, with few exceptions for many years, meetings of the AES were held jointly with the Academy Section at the American Museum of Natural History. The annual schedule of the AES became stabilized at seven meetings during the year; on the fourth Monday of September, October, November, January, February, March, and April. The January meeting became an annual organizational affair during which the year was reviewed, budgets approved, and new officers elected. At a later time, AES and section meetings alternated.

Dr. Robert H. Lowie's records of activities and sessions over the years as secretary of the section, and as secretary of the AES (until he accepted a post at the University of California in 1921) are rich evidence of the manner in which the Society became a meeting ground for all those in the New York area interested in anthropology. Lowie attempted to summarize the scientific presentations at AES meetings as well as the discussions that followed. Before 1916 when the Society remained a membership association, until its incorporation that year as the American Ethnological Society, Inc., and for some years thereafter, Lowie recorded such papers and discussions as: Boas's "New Evidence on the Instability of Human Types," Nels Nelson's outline of "The Southwest Problem," the Tylor Memorial Meeting of 1917, Elsie Clews Parsons's initial attempt that same year to distinguish pre-Spanish and post-Spanish features in several pueblos, and A. A. Goldenweiser's analysis of "The Problem of Origins." In this last case, in 1919, Lowie summarized the discussion, which included Franz Boas's first public statement, to my knowledge, on a distinction between biological evolution, which he accepted, and the orthogenetic character of classical cultural evolution with its unilinear doctrines, which he did not.

In so far as possible, Lowie also tried to record the names of those present. From these lists we get a strong impression of the intimate character of the meetings and the small but expanding circle of men and women who seemed aware that they were shaping and molding the fundamentals of modern anthropology. In the early period these include: Boas, Goddard, Goldenweiser, Haeberlin, Kroeber, Lowie, Parsons, Sullivan, Spinden, Spier, Wissler. It is noteworthy that in 1919 William F. Ogburn, Columbia sociologist, was elected to AES membership.

From the remarks already made it should be apparent that the American *Ethnological* Society, which became so acutely aware of its name in the past quarter-century, was first and foremost in its Columbia-American Museum phase an *anthropological* association. Its presentations and discussions drew on the whole field of general anthropology and its branches. When it incorporated in 1916, it retained its statement of purpose of earlier years: "To promote inquiries into the origin, progress, and characteristics of the races of man; by publishing and distributing documents; by arranging scientific meetings and public lectures; and by other means adapted to the ends for which this corporation is organized."

Despite the New York incorporation of the AES and the adoption of provisions that its principal office and the area of its principal operations were to be Manhattan, the Society saw itself from the beginning as more than local. Three of the incorporators, Boas, Goddard, and Kroeber, and a good many members and fellows, were not residents of New York City, and members who moved to other parts of the United States were eligible to retain membership and participate actively when in New York. Moreover, corresponding members outside the United States further indicate the Society's view that it was not only national, but in some ways international.

All who belonged to the AES automatically became members of the American Anthropological Association. The *American Anthropologist,* new series founded as a national professional journal in 1902, became the journal of the American Ethnological Society as well.

The professional development of anthropology in the United States was young, and the need for specialties and branches within anthropology that became so decisive later, was not felt by either the AAA or the AES in the early years of their joint activities.

The status of the American Ethnological Society during its Columbia period is indicated by the variety of events it participated in or initiated. In February, 1917, within two months of Edward B. Tylor's death, the AES held a Tylor memorial meeting. Wissler, Lowie, and Goldenweiser discussed Tylor's evolutionary principles, his treatment of material culture, his historical reconstruction methods, and his doctrine of animism. Spier, Frachtenberg, Spinden, and Goddard added comments in discussion. Dr. Boas, who planned to speak on "Tylor's Influence" was unable to attend.

In 1920, the AES joined the Anthropology-Psychology Section of the New York Academy of Sciences in a memorial meeting for Wilhelm Wundt, who had died that year. Professor Cattell offered "personal memories of Wundt", Prof. Morris R. Cohen discussed Wundt as Philosopher; Goldenweiser spoke of "Wundt's Contributions to Folk Psychology"; and Professor Woodworth talked informally on Wundt as a promoter of psychological laboratory work.

In 1922, the AES cosponsored a memorial meeting for W. H. R. Rivers, English psychologist and anthropologist, who had visited this country only two years earlier and had addressed a joint meeting of the AES and the Academy Anthropology-Psychology Section at Columbia University under the chairmanship of Prof. R. S. Woodworth. Unhappily, in his 1920 talk "Ethnology: Its Aims and Needs", Dr. Rivers had associated himself with Elliot Smith and what he described as the new English diffusionist school. At the

1922 memorial meeting, Goldenweiser discussed Rivers's contributions to ethnology; Professor Hollingworth talked on his contributions to experimental psychology; and Professor Ogburn summarized Rivers's contributions for psychoanalytic science.

On November 14, 1942, the AES held a major meeting and evening dinner for the centenary of the American Ethnological Society. This event, a notable success, perhaps signalled the imminent end of the Columbia period of the AES, which will be discussed.

Among outstanding presentations by the AES, selected examples might include Dr. Franz Boas's general public lecture at the American Museum of Natural History on January 24, 1910: "The Changes in the Physical Characteristics of the Immigrants to the U.S.", a report on his epoch-making study of the head form of immigrant children which disproved the traditional conviction that cephalic index was strictly hereditary, uninfluenced by environmental change.

On January 25, 1909, the New York Academy of Sciences sponsored a lecture by Prof. Albrecht Penck, on "The Antiquity of Man" and invited the AES as guests.

On March 26, 1923, the AES cosponsored a symposium at Columbia University on "Race Problems in America".

Among AES reports are Boas's 1910–1912 statements on the establishment and first year of the International School of American Archaeology in Mexico; reports in 1926 and 1930 on the 22nd and 24th International Congresses of Americanists—and a special presentation by Rudiger Bilden on "Race Mixture in Brazil". In several years of special research Mr. Bilden was perhaps more responsible than any other person for opening the field of race relations in Brazil to modern study.

The changing and expanding character of anthropology in America is interwoven with the history of AES publication. In the Columbia period AES publication began with the announcement in 1906 of a proposed "series of publications which is to contain authentic material collected among native tribes of America", the volumes to appear at irregular intervals. The announcement continued:

Notwithstanding the large amount of work that has been done in American ethnology, comparatively little material has been collected regarding the customs, beliefs, and ideas of the natives, in their own words. Most of our collections have been obtained indirectly through the assistance of interpreters, or are discussions of information collected from individuals more or less familiar with English or with the trade jargon. Knowledge possessed by the Indians is of great importance as well to the ethnologist as to the student of the early history of the American Continent. For this reason authentic records of information given by the Indians seem to be of prime importance for a thorough study of these subjects. The American Ethnological Society, in beginning its series of publications, is desirous of collecting and preserving for future use such records, and it is hoped that this undertaking will meet with the support of the public.

The Publications of the American Ethnological Society were launched under the editorship of Franz Boas, whose lifelong commitment to records in the original native language is well known. Two volumes were announced in press: Wm. Jones's *Fox Texts* and Edward Sapir's *The Upper Chinook;* three were in preparation: R. B. Dixon's *Maidu Myths,* Franz Boas's *Tsimshian Myths,* and R. B. Dixon's *Shasta Myths.* Two more were proposed: Livingston Farrand's *Alsea Indians* and H. H. St. Clair's *Coos Texts.* By 1942, the publications numbered nineteen volumes.

During the Columbia period of the AES, I was asked to speak particularly about the years in which I took part. I was at Columbia doing graduate work from 1925 until I completed my doctorate and dissertation in 1929. Thereafter, I was associated with Columbia anthropology while engaged in several years of research. I began teaching at Columbia in 1934, an activity that ended in 1939. Although I was party to AES activities during my graduate years, it was not until the year I began teaching, 1934, that I was asked to take the position of secretary-treasurer on the AES board. I continued in this dual position until 1938, and as secretary alone through 1939. Thereafter I became co-editor of the mongraphs, as well as vice-president and director, for single terms of office. The tricks memory plays are curious. The four years of major activity as secretary-treasurer seem in retrospect much longer.

Boas continued as editor of the AES publications throughout my time at Columbia. During my time on the AES Board, the others who were active were: Elsie Clews Parsons, Ruth Benedict, Clark Wissler, and Gladys Reichard. The programs continued as they had with reports of ethnological field research and archaeological excavations, plus special lectures and talks. For example, Richard Thurnwald talked on "Problems of Acculturation in Africa"; Dr. Edward Sapir discussed "The Concepts of Pattern and Function in Cultural Anthropology"; Ruth Underhill reported on her Papago research; Ruth Bunzel on Zuni; Ella Deloria on the Teton Dakota. Some new subjects were beginning to appear: the study of primitive music, led by George Herzog and primitive law, led by Prof. Karl Llewellyn of Columbia University. Gunter Wagner's *Yuchi Texts* was published in 1932; Ella Deloria's *Dakota Texts* in 1933–1934; and Bunzel's *Zuni Texts* in 1935. Other linguistic publications were in process.

Most of the linguistic publications required subsidy. The membership total was 144 in 1933, but only about twenty-six volumes of a new publication—apart from distribution to members—were being bought. Income, apart from grants and savings withdrawn, was a total of $1200 in 1932–1933, of which more than $700 had to be paid to the AAA for the *Anthropologists* sent to AES members.

It was my view at the time, undoubtedly shared by others, that the AES could not flourish unless its membership and income increased. As volumes of the Publications were issued between members and libraries, less than 160 copies were distributed and the rest held in storage for future sale. Obviously, some effort to sell more of the undistributed volumes was needed. Similarly, the low dues for fellowship (six dollars) was maintained for too long, allowing the AES only one dollar after the AAA was paid for the *Anthropologist,* as against the later membership rate of ten dollars, eventually reduced to nine dollars.

Apart from the financial aspect of AES affairs, there was the substantive or scientific side. Anthropology had grown by leaps and bounds everywhere in the country. The crying need, especially in relation to dissertations, was for places to publish middle-sized ethnological studies, of about 200–250 pages. Most Ph.D.s were subsidizing publication of their own dissertations in the *American Anthropologist,* the Memoirs of the AAA, or elsewhere. It was my conviction, also shared by others, that the AES could help in the field of publication but, of course, only if its available funds could be increased.

With board approval, I made a special effort during the next two years to market more of the publications by offering libraries the entire series at a substantial discount. Many sets were sold, and the libraries which bought the sets became subscribers to new volumes issued. At the same time special efforts were made to gain new members and fellows.

The results were satisfactory; membership was 187 in 1934, 213 in 1935, 233 in 1936, and 270 in 1937. In 1937, for the first time, the members, paying the higher dues, outnumbered the fellows. The sales of back volumes of the publications, principally in sets, were substantial, and increased the probable sale of new volumes, apart from membership distribution.

On the basis of substantially increased current funds and increasing income, it was possible for the editor to propose that a publication, volume seventeen, *Caddoan Texts* by Gene Weltfish, be financed without subsidy from current funds.

Finally, a proposal was made in 1936 for executive council approval that a new series of monographs of the American Ethnological Society be established. Monographs in ethnology were to be issued annually and publications of linguistic texts issued biannually. This was approved and in 1938 a board of editors for the monographs was established composed initially of Dr. Wissler as chairman, Dr. Hallowell, and Dr. Lesser. A notice was published in the *AA* and *American Antiquity,* and in 1939 the *Anthropologist* published the AES notice for manuscripts to be published in the monograph series, giving details as to subject, size, and condition of the manuscript.

Thus the monographs of the American Ethnological Society were born. The first monographs were published in 1940, and by 1942, at the time of the Centenary AED meeting, six were in print. This series launched the AES in a broad and expanding field of ethnological publication.

The Centenary Meeting of 1942 was a scientific and organizational success. The broad subject of the afternoon contributions was acculturation: in Indonesia (Raymond Kennedy), and in Latin America (Julian Steward). Ruth Benedict gave her famous paper on "Two Patterns of Indian Acculturation," and Clyde Kluckhohn offered his concept of "covert culture" and its relation to administrative problems. William Duncan Strong was chairman, and about 400 attended the afternoon session at the American Museum of Natural History.

In the evening, Dr. Harry L. Shapiro, president of the AES in 1942, chaired a dinner commemorating the history of the Society. Albert Gallatin, great-grandson of the founder of AES spoke and Dr. Clark Wissler talked about Albert Gallatin as the original founder and its early days. Dr. Franz Boas summed up the meeting when he, to quote Marian Smith: "placed the Society within the general framework of its anthropological setting, especially in regard to other scientific organizations and their efforts toward publishing anthropological materials."

The AES centenary meeting was a highlight, perhaps the climax, of the AES Columbia period, but it also seems in retrospect to have marked the end of an era. Franz Boas, the founding spirit of its redevelopment in the twentieth century, and central figure in its newly forty years of activity in New York linking Columbia University and the American Museum, died in December, 1942, some five weeks after the centenary.

The AES remained New York-centered through 1950, but in 1949, Dr. Esther Goldfrank, AES president, speaking at the AAA meetings in Toronto, broached the AES dilemma of whether to be regional, functional, or national. By 1956 members of the executive board were being drawn from the nation rather than locally. For example, Dorothy Keur, President, was in New York, while Allan Holmberg, vice-president, was at Cornell; Willard Rhodes, acting secretary, was at Columbia University; and Verne F. Ray, an AES ex-president and then editor, was at the University of Washington in Seattle. By that year all AES publishing operations and the entire stock of back publications were at the University of Washington Press in Seattle.

˙Since then, the AES has taken on its peripatetic existence, drawing itself, officers, members, and interested anthropologists together for a spring meeting and a fall meeting; and these meetings may be located wherever the membership and board decides.

Taking a broad view, the transformation of the AES from a New York organization from its founding through the Columbia period, into a national organization with only transient homes and offices, is understandable in view of the development, expansion, and dispersion of anthropology in America. Fifty or sixty years ago, New York was the primary center of American anthropology. Such a center needed an AES whose role was to provide for meetings of all those interested in anthropology, to exchange ideas, and promote the development of the field. Today there are many centers and many institutions, and none is as central for American anthropology as New York was years ago. The informal and intimate meetings and discussions of that small central group of leading anthropologists of years ago, have been replaced by larger and larger gatherings with more impersonal and bureaucratic structures. The AES as one of the smaller functional groups can still provide something of the intimacy and personal relationships which once dominated all meetings of anthropologists.

*

THE ROLE OF
ROBERT REDFIELD

*

9

Discussion: American Ethnology: The Role of Redfield

Discussants: June M. Collins, Chairperson, Everett C. Hughes,
James B. Griffin, Margaret Mead

June M. Collins: We have a distinguished guest with us today,
Dr. Everett C. Hughes of Boston College. He was for many years a
colleague and close associate of Robert Redfield's at the University
of Chicago.

Everett Hughes, Boston College: I am enjoying the discussion
very much. I agree with the statements of what went on, but need to
carry the story back a little further. You couldn't be at the University of Chicago at that time (1925) without being a pragmatist. The

principles were easy to know: in a given case your being who you were, wondering about what the consequences will be.

It was a school devoted to William James through George Herbert Mead. It was also the university of John Dewey and Robert Redfield. Robert E. Park was also there. As a youth Park ran away from home and went to Minnesota to study. When his father heard of it he said, "Why don't you go back East to a real university? Go to Ann Arbor." So Park went, and there became a close associate of John Dewey. Later he studied with William James at Harvard.

Park had been a newspaper man; he even thought of solving the world's problems by establishing a newspaper to be called "Idea News." As a journalist, he was a meticulous describer. The first time he was sent out on a murder case he came back with a story about the scene of the murder and even spoke about a piece of pie in the restaurant where it took place. Park's editor later said: "How many drops of blood showed? Had it turned black yet?" And he got his precise description from Park. (Redfield also possessed this incredible talent for precise descriptions.) People think of Park's ecology as being firmly rooted in cities, but back around 1910 he also read the new botany publications that dealt with plant communities. If you read his later work about world ecology and the confrontations of countries for space, land, and resources, you would see that his study of the city was simply a reaction to what others were studying at Chicago when he came there. All this was deeply part of Redfield's background. Park's real interest was world ecology: the competition of the races for the earth's surface.

Redfield and I were in the same class the first fall I turned up at the University of Chicago. He was married to Margaret Park before that date. Much has been made of the smoothness of his career in anthropology. Remember this man was brought up by an aristocratic Danish mother. His father, he used to say, was "a real go-getting Chicago lawyer, who had inherited a nice place in the country." Redfield had studied law; when he was through with it, his father-in-law told him to try newspaper work.

Redfield and I worked together on term papers for the three years we were there. He was a meticulous, hard worker and very fast. One summer, many years later, when were up in Michigan, Park came over and tapped on our window. He said, "I have got something to think through, and Redfield is too damn fast. I keep trying to think things over." It was true.

For our term papers I read the German and he read the French; later on I could beat him at the French. We were all reading human geography at that time, and the university had a very lively human geography department. Practically all the French books were in human geography, a new science that could be used in the new program.

Park said to all of us one day, "Now sociology is getting to be statistics. We need it, but we also need more anthropology and social psychology; let the rest go." Then we had ecology which dealt with man and geography.

We also questioned the idea of the primitive as the most important object of study, and Redfield was "into" that. What would he do? He concluded that Mexico was a good place to study. Park thought everyone else would to through the in-between societies. They were going to be in so called civilization, while we would want to kncw what had gone on before and how it happened.

Redfield went down to Tepoztlán and studied the distinction between what we would call the demos and the public. Bob Redfield was an exceedingly urban man, yet he could not stand life in Chicago except around the university. He did not like cities. He never went to a baseball game, yet we played baseball in his own yard in the country. Nonetheless, his concern was with the real demos most of his life.

We both got our degrees in the spring of 1928 before anthropology and sociology were separated. Of course, he went into anthropology, but we were still very close. For years he and I had the same students in our courses, no matter from which department they came; although he was in the anthropology department and I in the sociology.

James B. Griffin, Director, University of Michigan Museum of Anthropology: I had attributed some part of Redfield's precision of definition, his emphasis upon clarity of expression, to his legal training. I began graduate school at Chicago in the fall of 1928, which was Redfield's first year as an assistant professor there. Fred Eggan and I had been going through undergraduate school together; he was teaching psychology and other social sciences at Wentworth Military Academy near Kansas City, while I was training to be a junior executive for the Standard Oil Company, where I achieved a dislike for unions and the behavior of large corporations. Fred and I decided to go back into anthropology together, but Fred continued to teach in the year of 1928 and 1929 while I started at Chicago because I had taken only two courses as an undergraduate. I can remember Cole telling us there were more jobs for Ph.D.s than there were Ph.D.s in 1928. So Fred said, "Now, take courses from Cole and Sapir. I don't know much about this young man, Redfield, so take the courses from Cole and Sapir." I did as he advised the first couple of quarters. Then I took some courses from Redfield, whom I found a superior teacher because he was much better organized and clearer in his presentation. He was a somewhat formidable appearing individual before a class. Occasionally he would break down or hesitate in those introductory lectures that all professors struggle through. You are not always as good in these early lectures as you think you are going to be. I remember one time when he was explaining something about Australian kinship that he reached a point when it was obvious to him, not to the class, that he had gone wrong. I could practically see the wheels reversing, going back as he retraced his steps and then came out again correctly. This was an impressive performance for a person to give. While Redfield had a somewhat abrupt manner, a rapid tongue, a very rapid mind, and an intolerance of shabbiness, he was also a very warm human being. Now you didn't find that out, perhaps, unless you played tennis with him early in the morning. You can learn a great deal about a person by how he behaves in sports. We had attained some degree of mutual respect although he was, I think, always a bit puzzled about archaeology and why otherwise apparently intelligent people were attracted to it. He had an experience in archaeology in 1926, I believe, at the Seip mound in Ohio where he, along with Krogman and Setzler, perhaps saw Henry Shetrone buried by a cave-in of a face of the mound. That may have turned him away from archaeology. I think he never sympathized much with a number of the young archaeology students at Chicago who were there through Cole's program.

Redfield directed my master's thesis and did me a great favor in helping criticize my work, and guiding me through that program. I remember one seminar I visited in 1931–1932 after Mr. Brown ([Radcliffe-Brown]) had appeared and let us know that nothing good had ever been done in the United States in anthropology and that nothing good would ever be done unless it followed the Brown pattern. Kroeber stopped through and talked at one of the seminars and then came under attack from Alfred Reginald Radcliffe-Brown, who really sneered at Kroeber's interest in historical studies. He finally turned to him and said, "Why do you do this sort of thing?" Kroeber answered, "Because I enjoy it." Things like this are not found in histories of anthropology.

Redfield did not know German well, and in his attempts to understand the ideas of some of the other thinkers on social theory, he was somewhat frustrated. During a seminar in 1929–1930, while he was studying Bastian, he had a student named George Karl Herman August Neumann, who was a native German speaker. He asked Neumann, "Would you please report on Bastian?" Well, George worked and worked and worked and finally came in with many pages for his class statement on Bastian, but his report was not very clear. Redfield finally said, in exasperation, "But George, what is it he was trying to do?" George said, "I really don't know," which irritated Redfield a bit, but it also pleased him to find out that Bastian was difficult even for a native German to understand.

In 1953 Redfield gave seminars in Uppsala, Sweden. I was in Stockholm at this time and met a man named Esteruud who was a professional expert on folk cultures (as they call them in Sweden). He was taking the course and asked me to go with him Monday evening to attend. I did, but arrived a bit late. As I followed Esteruud in, Redfield looked up to see why he was being disturbed—his feeling about punctuality was that it was an obligation to be kept—and his face showed his astonishment. Afterwards Esteruud proposed that the Redfields and he and I and our wives go to the peasant folk museums in central Sweden during the weekend. We started off on a Friday afternoon because there were a great many folk museums.

On Sunday, while coming back into Stockholm after seeing many museums, we drove through a large park belonging to a former noble family that held the last of the museums, and a shot rang out. Esteruud turned around and said, "Pheasants!" Redfield in the back seat said, "Did you say 'peasants'?" Well, by that time the nonspecialists in Swedish folk culture were all ready to see Swedish peasants shot.

June M. Collins: Any other comments?

Margaret Mead, American Museum of Natural History: I think something ought to be said for the benefit of the very few young people here about one part of Redfield's work that came under a great deal of discussion. This occurred after Oscar Lewis went back and studied Tepoztlán. Oscar was very upset that Redfield hadn't been interested in murder and other problems. He went to work and read the newspapers to discover how many murders had been committed that Redfield hadn't noticed while he had been there. The original draft he wrote, was, I think, much more critical than the final draft, but it still was highly contentious and critical of Redfield. It implied the kind of criticism that graduate students particularly enjoy, indicating that Redfield didn't know what was going on. In comparison, it provides a most interesting example of the difference in perception and selection of materials between two ethnographers. Redfield was interested in harmony; he was interested in what made things go well. Oscar, as everybody knows, was interested in what made things go badly. As a result, those two studies which are very interesting and very informative, are excellent statements about the temperaments of those two men.

I remember one other that occurred around 1939 while first coming into Redfield's office in Chicago. I heard him pick up a phone and say, "This is Robert Redfield," and my first reaction was that was the most arrrogant statement I had heard in my life. He was a combination of arrogance and humility; you know they go together, but not like superiority in the sense of inferiority which also go together. He had this kind of patrician arrogance that could afford to show humility. He could say, "This is Robert Redfield." I was used to professors at Columbia who would say, "This is Dr. So-and-So."

I also remember an incident that took place between Redfield and my youngest sister, whose daughter, Margaret Rosten, is here from Rhode Island and is going into anthropology. My sister was his assistant when he became dean of the Division of the Social Sciences.

He followed a man named Bob Schlesinger who was a very sloppy character. He had been a foundation secretary and was now at the university where my younger sister worked and ran the office. In the middle of her turn as secretary there, the deanship shifted to Redfield. As an example of how well Redfield knew himself, he described the office as working beautifully as long as it was Schlesinger and Pat. He said, "Pat and I are chafing each other and hiding from each other behind pillars because we are both so precise and we are both so insistent that things should be done right."

I would also like to comment on one very brief meeting with Redfield that was very dramatic. That was in London, when he came back from India. I had just seen the first run of Alan Lomax's film about the hobbyhorse dance in Cornwall, called Oss, Oss, Wee Oss, made by the English Folk Dance and Song Society. I had never really grasped before what a folk society was, in the sense of what survivals in a folk society were about. There is a mask in this film that could have come right off the Sepik River and there are survivals of feudal behavior from the episode where they go and pick boughs on the squire's land all the way down to an organized opposition; organized by the temperance group which organized another mask that could have come from New Guinea, only, of course, the money would go for temperance rather than getting drunk. I had just seen this when I had breakfast with Redfield who was on his way back from India. I said, "I really know a lot more about what you have been talking about all your life than I have ever known before. I have never really seen a folk society." And he said, "I have just come back from seeing my first primitive society." And it was the Pathans, as I remember, that he was talking about.

10

The Hedgehog and the Fox in Robert Redfield's Work and Career*

CHARLES LESLIE

New York University

Isaiah Berlin began a famous essay on Tolstoy by quoting a fragment of Greek poetry, "The fox knows many things, but the hedgehog knows one big thing." To Sir Isaiah this suggested a division of

*I am grateful to a number of people who commented on earlier versions of this essay, and have made changes in it suggested by the following commentators: Ralph Beals, John Bennett, Edward Bruner, Matt Cartmill, Fred Eggan, Paula Brown Glick, John Janzen, Charles and Rosemary Kaut, Robert Kemper, Jerrold Levy, Owen Lynch, June Nash, Manning Nash, Martin Orans, T. N. Pandey, James Redfield, Margaret Park Redfield, Milton Singer, George Stocking, Constance Sutton, Neil Tappen, and Sol Tax.

thinkers and writers into two categories. On one side were those "who relate everything to a single central vision, one system less or more coherent or articulate, in terms of which they understand, think and feel." These were the hedgehogs, whereas the foxes were

> those who pursue many ends, often unrelated and even contradictory, connected, if at all, only in some *de facto* way . . . their thought is scattered or diffused, moving on many levels, seizing upon the essence of a vast variety of experience and objects for what they are in themselves (Berlin 1966:1).

So defined, Robert Redfield's life and thought were clearly those of a hedgehog. He had one wife, one university, one career. His life was anything but mercurial or foxy. His thought from first to last was distinguished by a continuity of outlook that is justifiably called Redfieldian. His books developed and explored "a single central vision," a stylistically and intellectually unified view of mankind. Yet, Redfield was a hedgehog without loyalty to his species, for he observed the limitations of hedgehogs and the virtues of foxes. His work had a single line of development, but he asserted that a multiplicity of approaches was necessary to comprehend human affairs.

The hedgehog and fox distinction resembles one that Redfield used in distinguishing between science and history. Science was a selective, abstract way of comprehending things, while history reported the world as it presented itself to us, describing the concatenation of circumstances that composed events to comprehend their particular character. The distinction was important for Redfield's understanding of anthropology and of his own contributions to it. His first article, published in 1926, used the distinction to analyze the development and current state of the discipline, and thrity years later, near the end of his life, it was a central concept in his Huxley memorial lecture.

The first paper was titled "Anthropology, A Natural Science?" and the Huxley lecture was called "Societies and Cultures as Natural Systems." They both advocated a natural science orientation in social and cultural anthropology. Their tone was not polemical—Redfield never wrote in a polemical manner—but the

1926 essay was a critique of Boasian particularism, and in 1956 his Huxley lecture implicitly refuted an argument Evans-Pritchard had recently advanced.

Evans-Pritchard had asserted that the natural science tradition in social anthropology was wrongheaded and unproductive because societies were moral rather than natural systems (Evans-Pritchard 1962:13–28). The Huxley lecture was also a critique of the work then dominant in social anthropology that described and compared communities as if they formed a series of discrete unchanging systems in functional equilibrium. Cultures were treated as "primitive isolates," and described in the present tense so that they provided fixed specimens for comparison: the Trobriand Islanders, the Nuer, the Azande, and so on. The limitations of this approach to human variation did not mean that the study of societies and cultures as natural systems should be abandoned. Acknowledging the achievements of structural and functional ethnology, Redfield described it as a passing stage in the development of anthropology. He saw it being displaced by research on social and cultural change that required "for its typology a recognition of corresponding forms in the histories of communities within a civilization" (1962:137). His own work in peasant communities had long anticipated this new direction in anthropology, but he described the variety of research by other scholars that was currently bringing it about.

Redfield welcomed this new direction in the tradition of scientific humanism that distinguished everything he wrote. This tradition was, according to Evans-Pritchard, a pernicious inheritance in the social sciences from the eighteenth century Enlightenment, yet even he recommended work that resembled the kinds of research Redfield advocated. They both called for generalizing historical analyses, and Redfield would have approved Evans-Pritchard's description of these analyses as "really empirical and, in the true sense of the word, scientific" (1962:26). Redfield's scientific humanism was congruent with this goal, but some part of Evans-Pritchard was repelled by such a secular and pragmatic world view. To Evans-Pritchard the hedgehog in Redfield must have looked self-satisfied, even smug and narrow minded, for all his pretty phrases. To Redfield, Evans-Pritchard appeared to be a man of defective character who, despite his genius, was a confused intellect.

Redfield wrote the paper that was published in 1926 while he was a graduate student. The question in the title, "Anthropology, a Natural Science?" arose because the discipline

> grew up around a body of materials and not a defined method. For this reason its relation to history and to natural science did not at once become clear . . . anthropological method has been both that of history and that of a natural science (1962:4).

Redfield's purpose was to strengthen the natural science component in anthropology. He argued that since Boas and others had demonstrated the fallacies of nineteenth century evolutionism, anthropological research had become "primarily history"—a kind of history that limited itself to data collection and analyses at low levels of abstraction. Yet he noted and praised the work of Kroeber, Sapir, Wissler, and Rivers for contributing to "a nomothetic science of human behavior." He wanted anthropologists to turn from the particularistic, museum oriented assemblage of information to study processes of cultural change as they occured in modern communities.

In this early paper Redfield did not mention the works of Malinowski and Radcliffe-Brown. In the mid-1920s they became the leading advocates of nomothetic goals for ethnology, and their brands of functionalism were to inspire new work that joined the scientific approaches of Durkheim and other theorists with empirical field research. Redfield had completed only one year of graduate study when he wrote the article and was not yet familiar with their ideas. A few years later, when he published his Ph.D. dissertation on Tepoztlán, he cited Radcliffe-Brown and Malinowski in arguing that for scientific purposes the historical approach to ethnology was less satisfactory than direct observation. He wrote:

> If the interest of the student lies in an investigation of social processes in general terms, it would seem a more direct procedure to study such processes as they occur, rather than to content one's self with comparing historical sequences so laboriously determined by the historical methods of the ethnologist. . . . If one is interested in studying what happens

rather than what happened, one moves more directly if one
studies it as it happens (1930:12).

Nevertheless, Redfield's work stood apart from the mainstream of
work by his contemporaries. Their most influential books were inte-
grated accounts of autonomous societies: Radcliffe-Brown and
Malinowski on the Andaman and Trobriand Islanders, Ruth
Benedict's descriptions of American Indian and Dobuan societies,
Margaret Mead's South Pacific studies, or the monographs of
Evans-Pritchard, Meyer Fortes, and Raymond Firth on African and
Polynesian communities. From 1920 to 1950, while these and other
functional and configurational analyses described the homeostatic
processes of structural equilibrium, Redfield was concerned with
processes of cultural and social change. In 1935 he coauthored with
Ralph Linton and Melville Herskovits a memorandum on acculturation. However, most acculturation studies used a procedure that
Redfield had little confidence in, one of sorting out indigenous items
of culture and showing how borrowed items were selected and reinterpreted to fit into an integrated pattern of indigenous culture.

Redfield's work stood apart because he came to the traditions of
Maine, Tonnies, Simmel, Durkheim, Weber, and other theoretical
sources of modern thought through Robert Park and the "Chicago
school" of sociology, rather than through the functionalist approaches of Radcliffe-Brown and Malinowski. The processes that interested him, and that he considered to be at the center of the social
sciences, were the transformations of mind and spirit that occur in
civilizations. His conception of these processes evolved through empirical research that began with the simple study of a peasant community in Morelos, advanced to the controlled comparison of communities in Yucatán, proceeded to the broad evolutionary analysis
of *The Primitive World and Its Transformations,* and concluded by
exploring concepts that would enhance the complementarity of humanistic and scientific studies of Asian civilizations. The nomothetic drive of all this work, its consistent focus on the humanity
of its subject, and its processual, evolutionary perspective, justify
calling it the work of a hedgehog—of a man engaged in a consistent,
continuously developing and highly articulated scientific enterprise.

THE HEDGEHOG OF NORMAL SCIENCE AND THE FOX OF NAIVE REALISM

Redfield conceived of his work as a continuing educational process, and when he analyzed this process he described a dialectic between experiences of the world and concepts for thinking about it. He pictured the mind moving back and forth between ideas and lived reality. Ideas were used to separate, order, and interpret different aspects or parts of the world. In contrast, lived reality was dense with immediate perceptions of the odors, sounds, textures, and temperatures of things. It was holistic and unreflective. In Redfield's epistemology experiences were concrete and jammed with implication, while concepts were sparse and abstract in the sense that they selected from reality a few elements for attention. Of course, experience was always mediated by ideas; it was never raw. But Redfield was a naive realist, for he believed the world to be out there on the simple experiential ground that we stub our toes on it, and that whatever cultural traditions mediated ordinary experiences, most human experience corresponded roughly to reality. He conceived the scientific enterprise to be a systematic examination of ideas in relation to reality. In the social sciences this entailed a dialogue between different "forms of thought" or conceptual models (Redfield 1955:passim).

If we use a term that Thomas Kuhn has made fashionable, we can say that Redfield conceived anthropology to be a dialogue of paradigms. He thought that the dialogue itself created a scientific community. Kuhn has the opposite belief, for he maintains that a scientific community arises when competing paradigms are eliminated so that "the number of schools is greatly reduced, ordinarily to one" (1970:178). Kuhn has used the concept of a scientific paradigm to denote different things (Masterman 1970), and people who borrow the concept often compound his ambiguities with new meanings and confusions of their own, but what I have called a dialogue of paradigms could only occur in a situation that Kuhn later referred to as a community that lacked "mature science," yet shared a "disciplinary matrix" (1970:182–187).

In contrast to this notion that a mature scientific community is based on a single paradigm, Redfield maintained that the intellectual structure for scientific studies of mankind was necessarily pluralistic. He did not argue that pluralism was necessary because cultural systems were separate from nature, and thus varied in an arbitrary manner. In his view, cultures were natural systems, but what mattered to us about them ultimately rested in our experience. Assuming this epistemology, he reasoned that every set of ideas selected some aspects of cultural reality and neglected others. Since each set of ideas employed some modes for ordering and interpreting phenomena and neglected others, *all* conceptual approaches to human experiences were partial and incomplete views of them. Scientific work sought to improve the analytic power of particular paradigms, to invent new ones, and to discover the advantages and limitations of different paradigms by comparing their utility for understanding human life (Redfield 1955:passim).

The contrary notion, that theoretical consensus is a prerequisite for work to achieve scientific status, dominates contemporary anthropology and is reinforced by the fashion of Thomas Kuhn's ideas. Anthropologists who accept this notion may try to establish the scientific character of their work by declaring that colleagues who use different paradigms "are not really anthropologists." They would limit the discipline to their own "school." Or, when paradigms that differ from their own are used by other social scientists, they dismiss whole disciplines as "not really scientific." This dogmatism is the opposite of what Redfield stood for. His manner in the classroom and in all that he did made him a model of openness and generosity of vision.

Another tactic of scholars who seek a closed theoretical structure is to proclaim that an essentially rhetorical shift in vocabulary constitutes "a new theoretical breakthrough." They assume that the supposedly new and better theory makes work based on alternative paradigms obsolete. Again, Redfield was a model to students and colleagues, for an effort to force the appearance of consensus without its substance was conspicuously absent from his work, and his ironic manner subverted pretentiousness. In academic encounters he was serious but ready to be amused; he knew exactly what had been said, yet he might be puzzled about just what it meant, and he could be astonished. His demeanor was always correct, but no one could miss the fact that he had an eye for folly.

This description of Redfield's manner anticipates the concluding section of my paper, so let us return to the argument of the present section. I have described Redfield's view of his own work, asserting that he was a naive realist who saw a pluralistic dialogue of paradigms as a necessary aspect of the scientific study of mankind. This model of science differs from the one that Kuhn derived from the histories of astronomy, physics, and other natural sciences. In that model, such a dialogue would indicate a "preparadigm" condition in which the activities of scientists would be "something less than science." (Kuhn 1970:13). The dominance of a single paradigm made "normal science" possible, according to Kuhn. The successful paradigm solved one or more initial problems in a manner that promised further successes.

> Normal science consists in the actualization of that promise, an actualization achieved by extending the knowledge of these facts that the paradigm displays as particularly revealing, by increasing the extent of the match between those facts and the paradigm's predictions, and by further articulation of the paradigm itself. Few people who are not actually practitioners of a mature science realize how much mop-up work of this sort a paradigm leaves to be done. . . . Mopping-up operations are what engage most scientists throughout their careers. They constitute what I am here calling normal science. . . . No part of the aim of normal science is to call forth new sorts of phenomena. . . . Nor do scientists normally aim to invent new theories . . . normal-scientific research is directed to the articulation of those phenomena and theories that the paradigm already supplies (Kuhn 1970:24).

I quote this description of normal science at some length because Redfield worked in this way. He explored the implications of a paradigm in the existing body of social thought by seeing how it could be used to analyze new data on Mexican and Guatemalan communities, and, finally, how it might be used to comprehend various studies of Asian civilizations. That paradigm contrasted primitive

and civilized societies, *Gemeinschaft* and *Gessellschaft*, the societies of status and of contract, and of mechanical and organic
solidarity. It defined the transitions from one to the other major
form of society as sets of interrelated changes in technical and
moral orders. Redfield's scientific contributions are not to be
compared to an innovator of new paradigms—to a Marx of a Freud.
Nor did he act as the advocate of a methodology such as
behaviorism or functionalism. He was not the self-conscious
adherent of a master—a Weberian or Durkheimian. He was not a
system builder, like the great American hedgehog, Talcott Parsons.
If he had been any of these things he would have worked in the
partisan style of a "school." Instead, he worked in an ecumenical
and pragmatic manner, drawing upon the common sources of
modern sociology—from Simmel, Durkheim, and others—and
learning from anthropologists whose research differed from his own.
When Oscar Lewis or George Foster criticized his formulations he
did not contest with them, but used what he could in new efforts to
educate himself. His education proceeded as does "normal science."
It was a puzzlesolving enquiry that used a preexisting paradigm to
extend our knowledge of facts that the paradigm helped reveal, and
inventing new concepts to clarify the logic of the paradigm itself.

Redfield saw the tradition in which he worked as only one way of
doing anthropology, and anthropology as only one of many traditions for studying human reality. Those traditions, gathered in a
modern university, formed a realm of discourse involving voices
with different analytic styles and conceptual frameworks. Within
the social sciences and within his own discipline, Redfield thought
the diversity an advantage, and meant to contribute to it rather
than to reduce it to a single dominant paradigm. Thus, he did not
propose that analyses of the folk-urban continuum displace other
ways of analyzing cultural change, and he did not think that
research on the social organization of great and little traditions
should displace other ways of studying civilizations.

It may seem paradoxical that Redfield practiced normal science
but did not espouse a single paradigm for his discipline. Normal
scientists work like hedgehogs within "one system less or more
coherent," and one expects them to change into polemicists when
confronted by advocates of another system. Redfield, on the

contrary, eschewed polemic argument. This fact is essential to his perspective, and is perhaps related to his legal training. He earned a law degree and practiced briefly (and unhappily) before turning to anthropology. The dialogue of paradigms he encouraged in the study of man was a Socratic inquiry rather than a proceeding of adversaries, and he characteristically used irony to demystify the rhetoric of adversaries. For example, he once chaired a meeting of anthropologists where bitter wrangles occurred on the platform and with members of the audience. Redfield refrained from the argument, and began his summary approximately as follows, "From the preceding discussion, one can only be impressed by the magnificient unity of our discipline" (Tappen 1975).

Nevertheless, the impress of legal thinking on his mind predisposed Redfield to work in the manner of normal science when he became an anthropologist. Legal thinking assumes a body of law; its puzzlesolving enterprise is to determine the principles relevant to a case, and to establish their utility for interpreting the facts. Like work in normal science within a paradigm, legal work seeks to clarify ambiguities within the body of law, and in the relationships between concepts and facts. The pleasure in reading Redfield's work is often like that of reading a well reasoned judicial decision.

To describe Redfield's work as "normal science" does not deny that he was original. During the 1920s, when anthropologists studied tribal societies as "primitive isolates," and sociologists limited their research to their own society, Redfield's description of the Mexican Indian town of Tepoztlán initiated community studies of peasant societies in Latin America. Among anthropologists the idea of holistic, functional, social description based on participant observation was championed by Malinowski, but since Redfield got it from the urban sociologists at the University of Chicago he began his study of Tepoztlán by locating it with reference to city life. He distinguished three levels or types of culture, all of which appeared in the town: the folk culture of the local community, the popular culture of national institutions and the mass media, and the sophisticated culture of urban society. He and his wife worked as ethnographers recording folklore and customary practices as they observed them in 1926 and 1927, but his monograph emphasized the study of "changes occurring in that folk culture due to spread of city ways" (1930:13). Wissler provided his model, and in the manner of anthropology during the 1920s, he thought of his analysis as a "diffusion study" (1930:11, 217-223). Yet it differed from other diffusion studies in that the distribution of culture traits was conceived by Redfield as a map of communication networks and relationships that was itself changing.

Redfield described a two class system in Tepoztlán, with *los correctos* in the center of the town representing city ways to villagers, their influence growing thinner as one moved to the periphery of the community. When threatened by the revolutionary violence of the period, they fled to Mexico City or Cuernavaca, while other townspeople joined the contending forces or took refuge in the mountains. Using a concept that Redfield later employed, *los correctos* were a "hinge group" between the community and the city. They were "an intelligentsia who live in two worlds, in two cultures, the city and the folk, and are correspondingly restless and often unhappy" (1930:209).

In the map image of diffusionism, *los correctos* were on the frontier of urban cultural influence, transforming the material conditions of life and the mentality of townspeople. This changing mentality particularly interested Redfield, who described a new self-consciousness, a "sensitiveness, pride, and zeal for reform," along with patterns of thought that surrendered supernaturalism to "a general tendency to solve problems by means wherein the mechanisms involved are understood" (1930:222–223).

The study of Tepoztlán was in the style of the time. Instead of the old-fashioned discursive ethnography, it was holistic, functional, problem oriented social anthropology. Its concern for urbanization processes was new to anthropology, and only came to be recognized as a special field within the discipline many years later with the appearance of "urban anthropology." It was work on a modest scale: the Redfields spent eight months in Mexico and less than three months living together in the town. The book itself was written as a Ph.D. dissertation, and it was brief—one-third the length, for example, of Elsie Clews Parson's discursive account of Mitla, another Mexican Indian town. Despite its modest scale, however, it served well as a prelude to the ambitious project that culminated ten years later with publication of *The Folk Culture of Yucatán.*

INNOVATIONS WITHIN A PARADIGM

Compared to other major research in social anthropology during the 1930s, Redield's project in Yucatan was innovative in the way that it developed and combined the following elements:

1. The controlled comparison of four communities that differed from each other in size, heterogenity, and degree of isolation from cosmopolitan society.
2. The coordinated research on these communities by three husband and wife teams.
3. The use of a formal model of urban and folk societies as an analytic device.
    a. To define multiple criteria for social and cultural change.
    b. To designate the kinds of empirical observations that would measure degrees of change.
    c. To generate hypotheses about the causal relationships between different kinds and degrees of change, particularly the way that social change effects and is effected by cultural change.

Redfield's model of the folk-urban continuum was suggested by Robert Park, and based upon ideas in Max Weber's work. It was a "heuristic device" for comparing societies. Such devices do not themselves describe real societies, and are not, therefore, true or false. Redfield did not use an ideal-type construct to classify events or societies in what he would have called "pigeonholes." He avoided typological thinking, and used the construct to generate questions about, and to analyze relationships between complex variables as they were observed in real communities.

Redfield's analytic, of nontypological, use of an ideal-type construct has been difficult for some scholars to understand. It is helpful to substitute the word "model" for "ideal-type," but anthroplolgists have also misunderstood the analytic use of models—for example, in debates about formal and substantive approaches to economic systems or to comparative law. Thus, Oscar Lewis, George Foster, and some other Latin Americanists garbled Redfield's analysis of a folk-urban continuum, or failed altogether to grasp its significance. In their view, Redfield was a "romantic" who distorted reality to fit his idyllic conception of folk societies. Their garbled version of a "romantic" Redfield has become a stock figure in the anthropological literature.

Romanticism is properly understood in relation to its contrast with classicism. When one looks again at Redfield's work, his perspective might just as well be described as classical. The choice of one or the other term depends upon what one wants to emphasize within his work, or what other work his is compared to. For example, the contrast between a romantic and a classic view is clear when one compares Redfield's books on Mexico to those by Oscar Lewis. Lewis's emphasis on connivance, violence, hatred, suspicion, promiscuity, betrayal, suffering, and death is verismo only in an operatic, or romantic sense. By comparison, the classicism of Redfield's ethnography resides in balanced reporting, and in the symmetry of his analyses, which are the work of a restrained, ironic sensibility.

George Foster and his students have asserted that Redfield's model of folk society neglected conflict, and thus led to descriptions of bucolic harmony in communities that in fact were racked by envy, scheming, and distrust. Foster missed the point that the model designated variables on a continuum between contrasting kinds of societies, and was thus a tool designed precisely to study conflict and differentiation in real communities. Before Redfield formulated the model he had observed differences between *los correctos* and *los tontos* in Tepoztlán, and he used the model to describe community, ethnic, and class variations in Yucatan. Its heuristic value was to suggest ways of analyzing recurrent processes of commercialization, individualization, and securalization by

comparing communities with varying structures and relationships
to the outside world. In a later restudy of one of these communities
Redfield analyzed factional disputes at length in what would now be
called "local level politics" (Redfield 1950, Swartz 1968). Ultimately, however, the differences that underlie Foster's misinterpre-
tation of Redfield's work are those between a "liberal" and a "conservative" conception of culture and human nature. Redfield's
liberalism caused him to describe the communities he studied with a
sympathetic confidence in human rationality and good will, despite
their tribulations, while Foster's conservative outlook, offended by
such optimism, gives priority instead to rascality and the vicious
circles that frustrate progress. In Mexico Redfield studied the vicissitudes of progress, but in his ethnography the pain was balanced
by an affirmation that progress does occur, and hope that it will be
bearable.

The point that needs to be made is that Redfield and his colleagues in the Yucatán project compared a city to a town, a village,
and a tribal hamlet. They did not try to document the ethnography
and history of the peninsula, but instead sought to bring a systematic body of evidence to bear upon the contrast between
mechanical and organic solidarity, *Gesellschaft* and *Gemeinschaft*,
and related concepts that form one of the fundamental paradigms of
modern social thought. Redfield plotted the networks of communication within and between communities, but his interest in diffusion
was subordinated to an analysis of the causal nexus in which different degrees of secularization, commercialization, and cultural
disorganization affected social relationships and world views.

After the second world war Redfield returned to Yucatán to restudy the village of Chan Kom. The interval between his first visit
to Chan Kom in 1931 and this field trip had been 17 years, and with
his wife and youngest son, he spent only six weeks in the community. The small book he wrote about this research is a social history of the way Maya Indian farmers on the frontier of Yucatecan
society decided to found a town, adopting ideas of progress and institutions of the larger society. *A Village that Chose Progress* was a
modest book, like the earlier study of Tepoztlán. The community
was much smaller than Tepoztlán—several hundred people rather

than several thousand—and Redfield had collaborated with Alfonso Villa-Rojas in his early study so that he knew Chan Kom better and longer than he had known Tepoztlán.

The Folk Culture of Yucatán had been a scientific work; the new book on Chan Kom was an historical study of simple people in a remote community who set out to improve their lot in the world. The narrative form worked as an allegory of civilizational processes—a tale in which the social forces that Redfield's science had sought to comprehend were played out in the life of one village. He ended the story on a characteristically "classic" note:

> The people of Chan Kom are, then, a people who have no choice but to go forward with technology, with a declining religious faith and moral conviction, into a dangerous world. They are a people who must and will come to identify their interests with those of people far away, outside the traditional circle of their loyalties and political responsibilities. As such, they should have the sympathy of readers of these pages (1950:178).

Following this second study of Chan Kom, Redfield and his wife planned to work in China. When revolution made this impossible they turned to South Asian studies as part of a large-scale project on the comparative study of civilizations. Milton Singer's essay in the present volume describes this period and the social background of Redfield's thought, emphasizing its continuity with the perspective and research I have described.

WHAT REDFIELD STOOD FOR

Style is the ultimate morality of mind, according to Alfred North Whitehead, and this was certainly true of Robert Redfield. Without calling attention to itself—that is, without being stylish, Redfield's style was noticeable. Our access to it now is in what he wrote. His prose has a distinctive cadence. It sounds as he sounded, for he spoke in sentences and paragraphs, and wrote without great difficulty or the need to drastically revise what he had once set down.

Redfield was at home with ideas, and so he wrote elegantly, or with a graceful economy unusual among American academics. Reading his books or essays one feels the presence of a powerful mind and a generous spirit. These qualities impressed colleagues and students so that he was a legendary figure at the University of Chicago. I want to describe this legendary Redfield.

So that our enterprise will not degenerate from the outset into a eulogy we should begin with an unfriendly observer. Margaret Mead, who has an excellent memory and strong first impressions, said that when she first encountered Redfield she thought he was the most arrogant person she had ever met. Other people were also offended by Redfield's seeming arrogance. His self-assurance and rapid grasp of situations, ironic demeanor, and impatient mind that seemed to get to the point more quickly than anyone else, were signs of arrogance to people who felt that they might be condescended to. Margaret Mead had heard from Ruth Benedict about the arrogance of the Chicago anthropologists when she met Redfield (Mead 1974:50-52). Another observer might have been enchanted by these same manners, and characterize them as "brilliant," or "aristocratic." Both terms were used from time to time to describe Redfield.

In the loose sense in which the term is often used, Redfield was "aristocratic." His daughter Lisa did not use the term, but she described the quality that provoked others to use it when she said that her father knew the boundaries of his ego; he was not confused or ambivalent about where he stopped and other people began. He was certain about what he was, and valued himself. In field research, she said, he was not the sort of anthropologist who wanted to get drunk with the Indians and pretend that he was one of them. In this sense, then, he was a man apart, "an aristocrat." He was that way, too, with students and colleagues, so that if they were insecure about themselves they might feel that he was aloof, and would fear trespassing on his time.

Students and colleagues rarely engaged in chit chat with Redfield. What Malinowski called phatic communion (simple conversation in which what is said doesn't matter, but the act of conversing affirms a social bond), Redfield reserved for his family and a few family friends. Even they were sometimes awed by his "brilliance," or, at least, took it into account in their relations with him. He and his father-in-law, Robert Park, were strongly attached to each other, but Everett Hughes tells how Park asked him to go for a walk one summer morning when their families were vacationing together, explaining that he wanted to talk through some ideas that he was formulating, and would have asked Redfield but he was too fast for him, and would see through the problems before Park could accurately define them.

Edward Bruner was a graduate assistant in the department of anthropology in the mid-1950s, but when he gave a house-warming to celebrate moving into a new apartment he invited everyone, students and faculty, except Redfield. Bruner says that he is not sure why he did this, but it seems clear to me that he did not want to intrude on Redfield's privacy, or to make him feel that he should come to an affair he would not enjoy.

Making fun of Redfield's manner and legend, the students once enacted a skit at a party in which they also satirized other professors. In the skit a student timidly knocked at Redfield's door. He arose from his desk and with flourishing gestures welcomed the student into the office. When they were seated he asked, "My good man, what is your name?" The frightened youth could not remember. Redfield interrupted his tongue-tied efforts by jumping from his chair and ushering him out, proclaiming, "You *do* have a name, therefore you have a Human Nature." Outside the door again, the bewildered student exclaimed, "God, what insight!" (Bruner 1970).

The legendary Redfield was political—his example affected others, and he enjoyed power. But here the failure to distinguish a gentry tradition, to which Redfield belonged, from an aristocratic tradition, would be fatal. Rather than aristocratic, Redfield was middle class; he was descended from property owning people who worked to earn their livings. James Redfield emphasized this distinction in describing his father, who was the son of a lawyer and himself had practiced law. Other ancestors had been scientists, doctors, and civil servants, so that Redfield was raised with a strong sense of family worthiness and tradition. James described him as representing a kind of American gentry . . . this stratum in American life has been relatively unrecognised—many would see us as a nation of pioneers, entrepreneurs, plutocratics, propertyless immigrants, estate-holders, sharecroppers. My father was none of these things; he was an establishment figure par excellence exactly in that he represented a stratum which, throughout the history of the country, has maintained a functioning establishment which has served to mediate the conflicts between the opposing interests of a nation in rapid economic development and social change (Redfield 1975).

Other people that Redfield might have been compared to at the University of Chicago may have been as talented as he was, and their work as significant and perhaps even more influential than his work, yet in his field of activity he was "a great man"—a professor, a dean, a department chairman, a president of the American Anthropological Association, a member of distinguished boards and committees, and so on. And, like other "great men," he did not get there without wanting to. He was ambitious and competitive. But, to many people at least, he stood for something other than himself, the offices he held, and the particular work that he accomplished. How shall we describe what the legendary Redfield stood for?

In the gentry tradition of American society, he was a gentleman. He especially disliked bad manners, pretentiousness, and sham. He was and he seemed to be a liberal—one who exemplified an undogmatic quest for knowledge. He was, similarly, a democrat who in his manner made democracy inspiring, rather than the mediocre performance of a "common man." Knowing the boundaries of his own ego, he seemed aloof, but valuing himself, he valued others.

Among people who customarily practice phatic communion, being listened to can be a disconcerting experience. As a reflex, one then listens to himself, and is overcome with his own foolishness. But it can be a refreshing, even a revelatory experience. Though it would not occur to many people to put it this way, the legendary Redfield was a listener. Rosemary Firth said that when she accompanied her husband on his first appointment as a visiting professor to the University of Chicago, her life was changed by realizing that Redfield actually listened to her. Because he valued what she had to say, she gained a new sense that what she said was worth valuing. Redfield was praised as "a good teacher," and, aside from the fact that he lectured well, the key to his effect on students was that he heard what they said. A student might feel like a genius or an idiot when Redfield summarized what he had said, but either way, he was instructed in an unusual manner by having been listened to.

Even people who were put off by Redfield's manner thought that he could be counted on in matters of principle. He was known as a civil libertarian—not one who made the defense of liberties a bitter and revengeful opposition to injustice, but one who thought that most wickedness was due to Ignorance, the behavior of Fools. The legendary Redfield stood for our ideals of the Enlightenment, and it is therefore appropriate to capitalize these terms in the eighteenth century manner.

Redfield's personal manner created an aesthetic field in whatever he did. He was a tenderhearted individual who could be moved to tears at a wedding or other sentimental event, and his toughness was in his wit. Amused by the world's foibles, he delighted in a good wine, the latest New Yorker, and other minor pleasures of "the good life." That phrase is a key to the moral suasion and strength that outsiders felt in Redfield's character. He used the phrase with high seriousness in various essays and lectures, but his manners spelled out meanings of the good life when he did ordinary things. In 1953, for example, he typed a hurried note on a scrap of office paper to acknowledge having received my first batch of field notes from Mexico. They were in the form of a diary, which he must have found appallingly personal, for his manner elevated the situation and he wrote:

> I suppose that every considered act of communication—a novel, an ethnographic report, a personal journal, the *Confessions*— is made possible by a bargain struck. For something given up, a power to form is granted. When a man has made the bargain and accepted the consequences, he can work. He has chosen the form, and is content with the bargain.

The legendary Redfield was a seamless man. If there was a division between the legend and the man it was not visible; not even, I think, to his family. When he was alive his conduct made the science of man seem both scientific and humane. He seemed to prove in his person that reason and good will could be used to improve the circumstances of life, and that the power to use them depended upon a bargain struck. His example remains in the style as well as the content of his work.

LITERATURE CITED

Berlin, Isaiah
  1966 The Hedgehog and the Fox: An Essay on Tolstoy's View of History. New York: Simon and Schuster.

Bruner, Edward
  1970 Personal Communication.

Evans-Pritchard, E. E.
  1962 Essays in Social Anthropology. London: Faber & Faber.

Kuhn, Thomas S.
  1970 The Structure of Scientific Revolutions. 2d ed., enlarged. Chicago: University of Chicago Press.

Masterman, Margaret
  1970 The Nature of a Paradigm. *In* Criticism and the Growth of Knowledge, Cambridge: Cambridge University Press. pp. 59–89. Imre Lakatos and Alan Musgrave, eds.

Mead, Margaret
  1974 Ruth Benedict. New York: Columbia University Press.

Redfield, James
  1975 Personal Communication.

Redfield, Robert
  1930 Tepoztlán, a Mexican Village: A Study of Folk Life. Chicago: University of Chicago Press.
  1941 The Folk Culture of Yucatán. Chicago: University of Chicago Press.

1950   A Village that Chose Progress: Chan Kom Revisited. Chicago: University of Chicago Press.

1955   The Little Community: Viewpoints for the Study of a Human Whole. Chicago: University of Chicago Press.

1962   Human Nature and the Study of Society. Margaret P. Redfield, ed. (Papers, vol. 1) Chicago: University of Chicago Press.

Swartz, Marc J. Ed.

1968   Local-level Politics: Social and Cultural Perspectives. Chicago: Aldine.

Tappen, Neil

1975   Personal Communication.

11

Robert Redfield, The Yucatán Project, and I

ASAEL T. HANSEN

University of Alabama

What follows is intended to tell about Redfield during the stage of his career when he interacted with me most frequently as an anthropologist, a supervisor of my labors, a fellow field worker, and as a person. It is true that he did have great impact on me. But what he did to and for me is irrelevant, except insofar as these experiences may help all of us to understand him better. The Yucatán Project occupies the central location in the title. It is not, however, the center of our attention. When it is discussed, the motive is to reveal Redfield, not to probe this already much-probed project. It was my privilege, periodically, to see him grapple with the Yucatán undertaking that he designed from 1931 until he released the manuscript of *The Folk Culture of Yucatán* to the printer ten years later. Parallel observations by Alfonso Villa Rojas cover a slightly longer time.

INTRODUCTION TO REDFIELD AND TO THE PROJECT

Over the years many persons have asked me, "How did you happen to get involved in the Yucatán Project?" The critical word is *happen.*

I have to begin either with the project or with me. The project wins. Redfield did his field work in Tepoztlán from November, 1926, to July, 1927. Professional recognition came rapidly. The Carnegie Institution of Washington appointed him a research associate in 1930. Alfred V. Kidder, head of the institution's division of historical research, invited him to set up what was then called a sociological study. It is my understanding that, within reasonable budgetary limitations, Redfield could write his own ticket. He chose to field test what became known as the folk-urban continuum—bracketed at each end by "ideal types," pure constructs of the human mind which can never exist as tangible realities.

For a few months in 1930, he inspected Yucatán and concluded that the social-cultural landscape would serve as a suitable test site. He even picked a peasant village, Chan Kom, in the maize-without-hennequen zone, and started gathering data with the aid of Alfonso Villa Rojas—then the local school teacher.

Before Redfield returned to Chicago, the main outlines of the research design were becoming clear. There would have to be an investigation of a tribal village, a town, and the capital city, Merida (Later I shall second-guess why he omitted haciendas. According to my best recollections that community type was never seriously considered to be an appropriate component of his folk-urban field test.)

Staffing the project concerned him greatly as I learned gradually when we began to become acquainted. Chan Kom was early taken care of—he and Villa would do it. Everything else was open when he came back to Chicago in the summer of 1930.

He did have a prime candidate he hoped to interest in Merida—a luminary among the urban sociologists that the University of Chicago had been producing for a few years. Alas, a nice grant to explore the sociology of fashion in Paris reduced this scholar's interest in Merida to zero.

About this point, my name came under consideration. In 1928 Ralph Linton left the Field Museum to profess anthropology at the University of Wisconsin. I had been there as a sociology graduate student for two years. After a brief exposure to Linton, the light dawned. I had been yearning to major in anthropology since I was a sophomore, in the early twenties in Utah, nobody seemed to have heard of the discipline. Planning to major in a subject one does not even know exists is very difficult.

I gobbled Linton's courses and seminars, chatted with him informally for many hours, and served as his first graduate assistant. By June, 1930, the volume of my graduate credits in sociology and anthropology was about equal.

Instead of teaching summer school at Wisconsin in 1930, Linton chose to work at the Field Museum. That same summer, the time had come for me to devote my full energy to writing my Ph.D. dissertation in sociology under Kimball Young.

As occurs among colleagues in the same city, Redfield and Linton found occasion to talk shop. Included in their conversations were Redfield's questions on his staffing problems in Merida. As reported to me informally by Linton in the course of a weekend in Madison, Redfield had come to believe that the person he wanted for Merida was a sociologist accustomed to dealing with populous cities and regions, but who had enough experience with ethnographers and ethnologists to understand their viewpoint. Linton indicated that he had mentioned my name favorably and wondered if I would be interested. My overt answer was a definite yes; inwardly, I jumped with joy.

My recollections are that I had two interviews with Redfield. The second included my wife, who had also taken all of Linton's courses and seminars. Linton reported that he was requestioned about me, and Kimball Young said that he had spent more than an hour with Redfield reviewing my Wisconsin performance.

In mid-July I had to accept a teaching job, comitting me to be on duty in September. A year after the 1929 crash, openings were getting scarce. My action was all right with Redfield. It would give me a chance to complete my Ph.D. (which I did), and he would have more time to ponder and refine the project. Besides, Mrs. Hansen and I could pay a few urgent debts and build a thin financial cushion for changing countries and climates.

In August, 1930, the magic letter arrived saying that I had an appointment to participate in the Yucatán Project effective the following August. Earlier I had agreed to a two year contract (later extended) for my wife and me plus modest but ample field expenses. A shocking change, however, had been made. The salary had been raised to $2500 on the grounds that Mrs. Hansen's background seemed certain to contribute to the investigation. Rather than putting her on the payroll, "our" salary would be increased a bit. Without making explicit inquiries, I have always given credit for the idea to Redfield though my later acquaintance with Alfred Kidder leads me to believe that he would have approved readily.

PRELIMINARY INTRODUCTION

August, 1931, came. We spent four days in Chicago and many hours with the Redfields at their country place. The rest of the time we "borrowed" the Redfields' then empty apartment near the University of Chicago which they kept for winter use.

Redfield and I exchanged second thoughts about the whole project but mostly talked about Merida. Uppermost in my mind was the question of how to collect and organize material on a regional metropolis having a population of almost 100,000 so that the results would be comparable with data gathered in a country town of 1200 (Dzitas), a peasant village of 250 (Chan Kom), and a still unknown tribal village. His answer was excellent and I put it down in the form of an approximate quotation, "I don't know. If I were to undertake the task myself, my ideas are rather vague as to how I would proceed. After all, it has not been done before. You know what the problem is; you go to Merida and learn all you can about that city. Maybe after awhile you will see solutions that you can't imagine now. We'll keep in touch and I'll help in any way I can."

The "approximate quotation" comes out as a sort of speech. Its content is true but the words and phrases were said in smaller units in more than one conversation.

My contacts with Redfield were pleasanter in 1931 than in 1930. On the earlier date, I was under inspection—rarely a relaxing situation. In 1931 he still overwhelmed me with his great knowledge, and his formality (or seeming formality) kept me tenser than was my custom. But we had some informative talks when I relaxed. When we parted I admired him immensely, feared him a bit (which I tried to hide), and trusted him to be fair and honest in all things.

I left Chicago concerned about the study that faced me, but not terribly worried. I would make out somehow. Elation was probably my predominant mood through New Orleans and across the Gulf of Mexico on a combined freight-passenger ship, the *Munplace*. I was fulfilling my dream of doing fieldwork in another culture. Such innocence!

REAL INTRODUCTION

My degree of culture shock was awful, painful to recall after more than forty years. My inadequate Spanish was useless. I decided that Spanish speakers did not have words; they simple produced streams of vocalizations that somehow conveyed meanings among them. Eventually I could hear words; but this was only one problem: where to begin? What to do? Census materials were safe and easy, but they had little information that would show the internal structure of the city. The electric company provided me with good maps. On buses and on foot I got a sense of the layout of the community: subcommunities, land use, house types, the daily flow of people.

The dwelling that American friends had helped us locate and lease was in a middle class area. Most of the householders did not know each other. We got on moderately easy speaking terms with three families more or less by accident. My idea of obtaining data on at least one spatial piece of Merida would have involved intrusions into the private lives of our neighbors. Actually, after eight months we did have enough information to characterize the area (it was not a neighborhood) so that it did have some utility later.

My reports to Redfield were thin. I became increasingly discouraged and so did he. His request, about March, 1932, for a statement of my proposed plans of action, resulted, after hard days and nights, in an impressive looking document that was not a very feasible guide for my future efforts. Doubtless, he recognized it for what it was: a desperate effort on my part to put something on paper even though it might be quite unrealistic. It would show that I was thinking hard.

REPRIEVE

In very late June or early July, 1932, Alfred Kidder came to Merida and invited Mrs. Hansen and me to dinner. After initial pleasantries, he told us he was engaged in his annual cleanup job. He explained that two or three archaeologists in Guatemala kept discovering that a few more days on the site would give them just the kind of information they needed. Two archaeologists at Chichen Itza felt they just had to continue for another week or so. He firmly notified all of them to put the sites in order and leave for home on specific dates, and to write up what they had learned. He concluded, "I am convinced that archaeologists can stay in the field too long, that in due time they reach a point of diminishing productivity. Every season I have to send some persistent diggers home to think and write."

He went on, "Redfield and I have decided that you have been in

Merida too long already. You need to get away for a month. Talk with Redfield; he wants to see you. Confer with anyone else you think may be of help. But look at Merida from a distance for a month."

I expressed the opinion that I had not learned enough to earn a vacation. His response was the kindest reprimand that I can imagine, "Maybe Redfield and I should decide that. We have already spent a good deal of money on you. We want you to succeed, to do the job we hired you to do. And we believe a month away from here and plenty of conferring with Redfield would increase your chances of success."

Kidder next reported that there was enough money to pay for our trip to Chicago, but he would not be sure until he had been in his office in Washington for a few hours. He was flying there the next day and would telephone Redfield as soon as he had the facts.

A wire from Redfield two days later told us to head for Chicago as soon as arrangements could be completed. This meant giving up our lease and finding a place to store our household goods (many of them inherited from the Redfields who had acquired them during their 1930 sojourn in Merida). Already my plans for next year called for living in a markedly different area of the city.

Our departure from Merida was an eager retreat. The *Munplace,* a dumpy freight-passenger ship, looked like a luxury liner. Chicago was beautiful. We spent a few days with friends on a lake outside of Duluth, Minnesota, living it up in the wondrous coolness so far from midsummer Merida. When our hosts asked for food preferences our answer would be, "Good beef if you have it, but really anything but chicken." (Chicken is the easiest way to get protein in Merida.)

Most of our time however, we spent in Chicago talking with the Redfields. I failed to inquire exactly how he fulfilled his university obligations. Anyway he arranged for relaxed long-continued conversations. He asked me as many questions as I did him while we tried to figure how the Merida study could be done so as to make its maximum contribution to the Yucatán Project.

One night we had a very special session, certainly very special for me. In all of our previous talks, I had hidden the full depth of my discouragement and my ultimate foreboding of defeat. I repeated how hard I had tried, and said that I really felt that I was letting my part of the project down, and declared that apparently I was undertaking a task that was just plain beyond my capacity to carry out.

"Asael, let me tell you what happened to me. The trip into Tepoztlán was long and tiresome. Greta (Mrs. Redfield) and I took turns carrying the baby. Lisa was old enough to ride in a saddle bag all right. It was toward evening when we arrived. On an earlier trip I had arranged for a house. We had a simple supper and prepared sleeping arrangements. I helped tuck people in. Probably all but Greta were asleep when I decided I needed to ponder. I climbed part way up the mountain, sat on a rock, and thought as the lights below went out. I asked myself, "Why had I done it?—over and over. Why did I bring a wife and two children into this isolated community? The more I asked, the lower I felt. I got so far down as to wonder if I should have been allowed the privileges and responsibilities of parenthood. Asael, I don't think you could ever have felt as low as I did. Maybe you will not have to.''

I have never written this reconstructed conversation before. I have told it to maybe a half-dozen students who felt caught in an impasse during a thesis or dissertation.

I am quite sure that I related the interchange to Mrs. Hansen. Its full impact on me has been my secret till now.

As I turned Redfield's self-revelation over in my mind, my earliest thought was, "My God, he's really human." But this was a superficial observation. Actually, I already knew he was human. There had been plenty of evidence already in my experience to assure me of that with him. Second thoughts were more somber and realistic. Maybe he suffered self-doubts more accutely then most other men because he was so intelligent and sensitive. This idea led me to admire and respect him even more.

One point was clear to me on the background of the material just reported. When the *reprieve* ended and I headed for Yucatán, I quietly told myself that I would do a reputable study of Merida or die in the effort. The resolve was not announced; you are the first to know.

FIRMER FOOTING

The subhead is meant to convey that gradually during the second year the sense of utter floundering that had characterized the first year abated. Episodes would speed or slow the process. Still, by midyear I like Merida, which, twelve months before, I had mostly hated. My Spanish was still not good, but it became fairly efficient and comfortable. Completing my research assignment still troubled me. Yet the routes to learning the multitude of things I needed to know were becoming clearer. There was plenty of rough going ahead, but I had a sense of forward momentum.

Getting my bearings was aided by a decision arrived at before the *reprieve*. It seemed to me early in my thinking that it would be important to know if rural migrants from Yucatán formed spatially segregated colonies in Merida, or if it was the migrants from some segments of the hinterland. The answer would cast light on the regional culture and on the basic relations between country people and city people in Yucatán. I asked in every way I could devise if rural colonies existed within or on the fringes of Merida. The reply was always negative. Migrants, I was told, hunt housing where they can find it and reside in a mixed setting with old time *meridanos* and migrants from everywhere.

Then, several persons suggested a rough test. After the 1910 revolution began, migration to Merida speeded up. Troubles with the federal government, particularly after 1914, hastened the movement from communities to the west of Merida. The most convenient means of transport was a narrow gauge railway, owned by a hacienda, which carried passengers as well as freight. Its terminus was in the western part of the city at "The Corner of the Dove" (La Esquina de la Paloma). The consensus was that, if a discernable grouping or colony exists anywhere, it would be in the area surrounding la Paloma.

It was a working class area. Luckily a house, just a little more ample than the average, had just been reconditioned by the owner. For five dollars a month we had a good living-working base within two blocks of the corner of the Paloma. After a few weeks of inquiry, mostly casual, it was plain that rural migrants from the west unloaded themselves and their belongings at the Paloma and then spread through the city.

To be doubly sure, I hired a schoolteacher to run a simple house-to-house survey in a small area across the city from the Paloma. The section was older and a little poorer. The results as to rural-urban background were substantially the same.

During the *reprieve* Redfield and I had selected several relatively narrow topics for me to concentrate on. In January, 1933, he planned to join me as a co-fieldworker. While he investigated the town of Dzitas, we could have occasional conversations on Merida or any other phase of the project.

CO-FIELDWORKERS

The Redfield expedition consisted of Robert, his wife, Greta, and their infant daughter Johanna. We met the ship, the *Munplace,* at the port of Progreso. In a serious discussion like this, maybe their tedious delays in entering Mexico should be omitted. But they show a side of Redfield that may not be well known. Remember, it was the Great Depression. Thousands of legal Mexican migrants in the United States lost their jobs, got on relief, and were deported back to Mexico. It was legal, but Mexicans did not like it. So, if the difficulty of the entrance of United States citizens into Mexico was increased, it is understandable. Moreover, in 1933, U.S. Immigration Offices were doing what they could to reduce the amount of "moral turpitude" among international travellers.

Redfield knew about travelling and assumed he had all of his papers in order. At the Immigration Station, an early question, "But where, sir, is your marriage license?" He could only explain that it was at home in Chicago and that he and Mrs. Redfield had crossed many international boundaries without it. Official: "But your country is taking the lead in this matter. It is our duty . . ." By this time Mrs. Redfield had joined the conversation. Both parents assured the official that Johanna was their legitimate daughter and that they had two legitimate children with relatives and attending school in Chicago. Eventually the official was satisfied that their admission as tourists would not seriously deteriorate the moral fiber of Mexico.

Then there was the matter of the collapsible playpen as they went through customs. All of their other baggage was all right. "But this is furniture and you must pay duty," the official pointed out. Redfield explained patiently that three babies had used it and that Mexican duty had already been paid on it twice. "Do you have the receipts?" the official inquired. "No," replied Redfield, "We find it inconvenient to keep receipts so long, but I shall be pleased to pay again so that your records will be clear."

Throughout the exaggerated officialese, neither his patience nor his formality wavered. He had known officialese before. After not much more than twice as long as it should have taken, he was inside of Yucatán.

They stayed with us that night, after some protest because we had to squeeze a bit in our smallish house near the Paloma. But there were plenty of hammock hooks, and we thought we could ease the transition of Johanna to Yucatan better than a hotel could.

At five a.m. the next morning, the only departure hour, they left on the narrow gauge railway for Dzitas and Chichen Itza. The Carnegie headquarters could house them comfortably until Redfield could get a house in Dzitas.

The house was ready in record time. It was easy to find contacts in the town who knew of an empty residence. A platoon of workers moved in to clean up and do minor rearrangements. Perhaps the most drastic innovation was a simple enclosed outdoor dry sanitary facility, built according to the standards of Yucatán's public health department. Everybody else (or practically everybody) used the open yard or patio.

While the house was being fixed up for the family, Redfield was organizing something else. He rented another small dwelling for an office and photographic studio, plus a room for developing film and making prints. Dzitas had had no photographer previously;

suddenly they had one. And Redfield had a locally comprehensible role in the community while he pursued the less understandable role of ethnographer. His photographic fees were modest, so that he would break even—not counting his time.

The office gave him a place to work night and day, without disturbing the daughter. Much of what he learned of the community, he found out in conversations that he or his wife conducted anywhere there were people. Men, however, went to his office on occasion to discuss matters that took more time and maybe needed some privacy. These were "interviews" in contrast to the casual visits here and there.

During the discussion period after the Worcester presentation, Hale Smith of Florida State, a Chicago Ph.D., asked a good question. He recalled that at Chicago, Redfield was famous for his formality. A student had to request an appointment in advance and submit a written agenda. The items would be considered quickly, intensely, and precisely. When the final item had been treated, the student departed promptly and another student entered. Smith continued, "I have often wondered how he did fieldwork among peasants in Yucatan where being late for appointments (or even forgetting them) is normal; where the state of each family must be discussed; where the weather calls for more or less extended comment; where an event in public affairs or some plain gossip needs consideration—all of this before the original topic for the get-together is mentioned."

The answer I sought to give in Worcester, which was more or less all right, I shall amend. Redfield knew perfectly well when he was at the University of Chicago and when he was in back country Yucatán. He was fully aware of the vast culture differences between the two. I alluded to his great patience as he was being "processed" for entering Mexico. In Dzitas I was present during one of his interviews. The interviewee was greeted, invited to sit down, and asked about his health. The questioning was clear but not direct and never abrupt. Initial phrases were sprinkled with "it is said" or "I have been told" or "Don Fulano seems to hold", and so on—followed by "What do you think?" or "How does it look to you?" The man appeared comfortable and to be enjoying the talk. I

could see information piling up, all freely given. At no point did I
note evidence of the awful sign, "What does this man from the
United States want me to say?"

Redfield and I had different fieldwork styles; each of us visited
casually and interviewed. He did more of the latter than I did. The
only interview I saw him do led me to applaud his skill.

On a few occasions Redfield criticized me for spending too much
time on Merida history both on the scanty written history and on
the richer oral history "of the days of our grandparents." He would
go so far once in awhile as to say, "What I would really like would
be simultaneous infinitely detailed snapshots of the four communities. Then we would make folk-urban comparisons of truly con-
temporaneous societies and cultures."

We never settled the argument (if there really was one). I kept
probing Merida's past, trying not "to spend too much time." In retrospect, I wonder why the subject came up. In *The Folk Culture of
Yucatán*, there is a two or three generation history of each community. And this history enters into almost every topically organized presentation. Heritage is the clearest exception. The history on which that chapter is based happened so long ago and is so
inadequately documented that the current facts were given and the
actual history assumed.

During our co-field work experience, we had a semicrisis. Early in
March, 1933, he came to Merida to see me. He had quite a batch of
notes on Dzitas to share with me. But the *nugget* was a two-page,
single-spaced working paper that he had beaten out on his much-
beat-up portable Corona two days before. (The machine if it sur-
vives should be in a museum.) The nugget was a statement on where
we stood; what fieldwork remained to be done; how soon and how
we could get to the writing stage. He handed me the two pages
which I read with great care. It did not surprise me that, omitting
Tusik, (still to be started on) the biggest fieldwork gap existed in
Merida. I felt mildly unhappy but a good deal of fieldwork time for
me was already in the budget. So I knew there was a lot of hard
work ahead. Still, I felt no sense of alarm.

I did, however, have a serious question. "Robert," I asked, "how
long did it take you to compose those two pages?" His first re-

sponse brought up an overdue point, "Call me Bob if you don't mind—from now on." I agreed happily; I'd been wanting to do so for weeks if not months.

Then I returned to my question, "Bob, how long did it take you to compose these two pages?"

His reply: "Oh, I don't know. Since I knew I was coming to Merida to see you, it occurred to me that it would be a good idea to review our situation and take a good look at what lies ahead. A couple of days ago I wrote it. How much time did I spend? A half hour, maybe 45 minutes."

Hansen: "This discourages me."

Redfield: "That's terrible. I didn't bounce and careen for five hours over that narrow gauge railway to discourage you! What's wrong?"

Hansen: "Nothing is really wrong. The statement is excellent. It tells us where we are and lays on the line what's ahead. There is much for me to learn about Merida. But week by week, as my data accumulate, more data is added with a little less effort than before. The city, I begin to believe, will be pretty well represented among the four communities when this study is finally done."

"What discourages me is something else. I have been with this project long enough so that I could have written a document closely parallel to the two pages you brought. But my version, done so that it would satisfy me, would have consumed two or three days of hard and dedicated labor. And you did it in a half hour or forty-five minutes!"

Redfield: I feel better now. Let's leave it that I have done much more of this kind of writing than you have. It pleases me that you are confident that you could have produced a comparable document in two or three days. Some people could not do it ever."

We parted with full good will, each of us to concentrate on our share of the tasks sketched in the two-page nugget.

Early in April 1933, Redfield concluded that his information on Dzitas, the town component of the overall investigation, was sufficient. Looking forward to his eventual discussion of Holy Day to Holiday, he spent a few days in Tizimin (a city or almost a city) which had by far the most elaborate patron saint fiesta in the peninsula.

In the midst of the final stages of their packing to leave Dzitas, Easter came. Urgent packing tasks were put aside so that the infant daughter, Johanna, could have a proper and adequate Easter egg hunt. When the story was relayed to me two or three days later, my admiration for the Redfields intensified.

The Redfields joined us in our smallish house near the corner of la Paloma without question on their way out. Besides eating, sleeping, and arranging for their departure, important project business was done. Leonor Cetina, the Hansen's number one maid, advisor on protocol, and source of information on many topics, had attended and supported the fiesta of Chicxulub regularly for several years. Much of the information on the Chicxulub fiesta was gathered as we ate Leonor's delicious food—though I did send a supplementary statement on Chicxulub when *The Folk Culture of Yucatán* was being composed.

The Redfields' departure on the Munplace from the coast of Yucatán proceeded simply. No questions were raised regarding the possibility that they had been living in sin without a certificate of matrimony. The thrice-dutied playpen was put aboard without incident.

CHICAGO EXILE

August, 1933 came time for our "escape" from fieldwork in Merida. Another *reprieve?* God no! We disoccupied our smallish house near la Paloma reluctantly. Our neighbors recommended that we just close it up, protected by an inexpensive guard so it would be ready for us on our return. We could give no sensible explanation as to why we had to abandon this house and find another residence elsewhere in the city when we came back. We did assure them, however, that we would visit them, a promise we fulfilled.

The year before, in August 1932, two lonely gringos passed through Progreso with the impressions already sketched. The difference one year made is believeable only by those who have had meaningful cross-cultural field experience.

In August, 1933, thirty people saw us board the *Munplace* and sought repeated reassurances that we would return. The Munplace, a luxury liner the year before, was a smelly freight-passenger ship. When we got there, Chicago looked like itself—not beautiful. In general, the rediscovery of the United States was immensely unexciting.

The 1933 plans for Chicago represented no reprieve in any way. We were to stay in that city until early January—grappling with such knowledge as we had of Merida and beginning to write. Even trying to get an apartment for four months turned out to be a major trauma. After much inquiring and more walking, we managed to lease a peanut-sized furnished apartment for the going price of a substantial mansion in Merida. Mrs. Hansen and I both became homesick for Yucatán. Why anyone would try to survive in Chicago was almost incomprehensible.

Redfield, as usual, was right. Once a person has come to terms with a fieldwork situation, life is beautiful. Everyday one learns new things from people who are pleased to instruct a sympathetic or empathetic foreigner about his culture. Productive fieldwork could go on joyfully forever. But fieldwork becomes useful ethnography and ethnology only when it is clearly written and reposes on the shelves of libraries.

This point is unarguable. As soon as I had a flat surface to work on, I began to organize my accumulated notes.

I had not been working long when Redfield had an idea, "Already you have enough information from talking and walking and reading and maplooking to do a paper at the Christmas meeting of the American Sociological Society (as it was called then) on the ecology of Merida." He further suggested, "It should introduce the Chicago urban ecologists to some information they have been overlooking."

He made arrangements to get me on the program. After some conferences with him, I wrote the article "The Ecology of a Latin

American City". Maybe it is one of the earliest publications in what is now urban anthropology.

FRANTIC MERIDA FINALE

We landed in Progreso early in January, 1934. During our absence, I had kept in touch with Leonor Cetina, our multipurpose aide, and she had communicated our plans to our favorite taximan. (A few millionaires, near millionaires, and, of course, politicians, owned private automotive vehicles in 1934.) Probably fifty persons were on the dock to greet us, having arrived by bus after our favorite taxi was full.

In Merida we dropped our baggage in our hotel room a little before noon and reentered the hostelry about midnight. The hours in between we were busy catching up on the lives of our many friends. In four months innumerable vital events had occurred. There were no regular meals; we just ate all day. It was a wonderful homecoming. Cold and windy Chicago seemed a million miles away.

Even before the happiness subsided, I could feel the shadow of the end of the Merida study. What we learned in 1934 would constitute the body of our material on the city and on the state of Yucatán as well. We chose a house with good bus connections to the center of the community. Government records concerned us more than in either of the other years. Still, the best data on medicine, magic and details of family life were garnered that last year. Information flowed in easily. Keeping up with our notes was an increasing and endless burden.

The whole year was sort of frantic, but the last four months stand out in my mind. Every day was full and eventually I lived by hours. I kept thinking of more items of information which might be useful, and everything was easier to get than early in the study.

My wife had departed in September for a job which would tide us over while I looked for work. Time finally forced me to quit studying Merida and to pack. Folding my linen suits I remember vividly. Tears almost came as I wondered if I would ever wear them again.

Another unerasable memory: my wife met me at the train in Chicago about December twentieth. She had borrowed an overcoat because it was minus six degrees, Fahrenheit. To both of us Merida seemed a glorious memory.

WRITING THE FOLK CULTURE OF YUCATÁN

Redfield spells out his collaboration with Alfonson Villa and me in the preparation of *The Folk Culture of Yucatán*. A few further details regarding my preparation would seem to be appropriate. I speak not at all for my friend and colleague, Villa.

Redfield sent me the complete manuscript for inspection and comment. I read it as carefully as did he or any editor. Most of it was complete. If I said anything, it was to wonder about a phrase or question some area of emphasis. Other sections would tell of Tusik, Chan Kom, and Dzitas. Them something like: "And in Merida . . .?"

All of these gaps I managed to fill in, just how I do not recall. At the time I was teaching fifteen hours per week at Miami University (Ohio). My guess is that Sundays made it possible.

On an earlier occasion Redfield had informed, or warned, me that he was famous or infamous for being a ferocious editor. The point came up when I submitted a chapter of the monograph on Merida which I was never able to finish. In about forty pages (double spaced), he had raised two minor questions in marginal comments. It was his way of saying that he thought my manuscript was good.

When the book came out in August, 1941, an early copy reached me. In Redfield's handwriting inside the front cover there appears "To Asael, who wrote part and made all possible. From Bob."

I like to think that it was more than a polite verbal gesture.

POSTSCRIPTS

From the time I first met him, Redfield impressed me as being an adult. I was delighted. In the world in which I grew up, finding an adult model was difficult. I knew I couldn't be Redfield; I did not even want to be like him. But here was a man whom I could use to design my own style of adulthood—which I did.

I saw him infrequently after 1940, though I telephoned and tried to get together with him whenever I was in Chicago.

About 1940, I ceased to fear him or to notice his ingrained formality. We could relax together easily.

I was in Chicago very soon after he ceased to be a dean. I congratulated him heartily on his demotion to professor. He ws doing the Dzitas study when he was asked to become a dean. We talked about it then. Both of us regretted that there had to be deans and agreed that professors constituted the best manpower pool for recruiting them. He made some comments on how difficult it is to get out of a deanship in a proper way once you are one.

In 1953, I attended the meeting of the Society for Applied Anthropology in Chicago. I wrote Redfield, hoping that he would have time to talk with me. The Merida monograph was still weighing on my conscience.

When I reached the department of anthropology at Chicago, there was a message saying he was ill and at his country place north of Chicago. I was suppose to call his number. I did.

For two days, Redfield and I talked. A few years before, I had had a massive coronary. The Chicago trip was my first so far from home. Redfield was suffering from bronchitis which usually lasted three days. Anyway, we were both mildly ill, which allowed us ample conversation time. We discussed everything, with much rethinking of what we had done together. It was a good *adult* interchange. I treasured it.

When I learned that he was terminally ill, I shared sadness with hundreds of friends and kin. But as I reviewed our lives as they touched periodically, our *adult* talk became more important. We separated permanently knowing and respecting each other.

NOTES

[1]In April, 1974, when I participated in the AES session on Redfield, I was in the department of anthropology at the University of Alabama, scheduled for retirement at the end of the next month.

My current affiliation (since December 1974) is with the Southeastern Regional Center (based in Merida) of the National Institute of Anthropology and History of Mexico. (The organizations are done in English; the Spanish versions sound better to me.)

[2]My report was done orally, the only way I could take being included on the program. The academic year 1973–1974 left no leeway; my wife since 1928 died suddenly in November and my prospective retirement loomed ahead like partial death until the opportunity to return to Yucatán became a possibility. Nurturing that possibility required some time. Meanwhile, I carried a full load at the University of Alabama.

[3]Eventually, transcripts of my taped oral remarks reached me through the good offices of Carol Franz who provided the recorder of June Collins who did the transcription, and of John Murray who went to some trouble to get the transcripts into my hand. At the AES meeting in Detroit, Arden King functioned as an important courier.

[4]The written statement is not an "edition" of the tapes in any usual sense. My talk wandered around and through the topic. The transcriptions furnished information for me to compose in a more orderly report—with the oral flavor retained insofar as seemed feasible.

12

Robert Redfield's Development of a Social Anthropology of Civilizations*

MILTON SINGER

University of Chicago

Table of Contents

*For valuable comments and criticism of a first draft of this paper I am indebted to Fred Eggan, Charles Leslie, John V. Murra, Margaret Redfield, James Redfield, Helen Singer, Edward Spicer, and Sol Tax. I am also grateful to Everett Hughes and David Riesman for some personal reminiscences.

1. SCIENCE AND HUMANISM IN THE STUDY OF CIVILIZATIONS

" . . . I think that social anthropology is about again to command a deep historical perspective" Redfield concluded in his Huxley memorial lecture delivered in 1956 and published in 1955. This conclusion was not intended to express a personal millenial prophecy but rather to register a carefully considered observation on recent developments in social anthropology and in the allied fields of archaeology, history, and ethnology. Redfield saw these developments as having occurred during two periods and about to enter a third. In the first period, led by Tylor, culture was studied as a global totality without much attention to the plurality of societies and cultures as integrated natural systems. The discipline at this period was both historical and generalizing, especially with respect to the order of the evolution of different stages of culture.

In the second period, from about 1900 to 1950, social anthropology came to recognize the discrete and integrated organization of societies and cultures as natural systems, studied first hand some of the simpler ones intensively, and compared them in a side-by-side timeless equivalence to arrive at generalizations about the nature of society and of culture.

From about 1950 on, social anthropology begins to return to the historical perspective, muted in the second period, by comparing the ways in which the simpler societies and cultures depend upon the larger systems of national states and civilizations. Such studies connect social anthropology with the histories of civilization. They do not, however, turn social anthropologists into historians or archaeologists, for a social anthropology of civilizations remains generic and comparative, and is based on a reduced set of facts, usually directly observed, and schematized according to explicit, analytic concepts. A social anthropology of civilizations draws on archaeology and history as it does on ethnology, ethnography, and cultural anthropology, but it represents an emerging and distinctive synthesis from the first two periods, a synthesis that develops anthropology in a new direction.

The questions to be discussed in this paper are where Redfield's own work fits into his three-fold periodization in the development of social anthropology, and what is the nature of his contribution to this development. It is well known, of course, that he looked with favor on the return to a more historically oriented anthropology. The major thesis of the Huxley lecture leaves no doubt on this point:

> The comparisons of simultaneous equivalent social or cultural whole systems come to demand qualification and development to take account of the compound, historically recognizable, larger systems of which they are parts [Redfield 1962:130].

It would, however, be unjustified to infer from this thesis that Redfield rejected his pre-1950 studies in Tepoztlán and Yucatán as belonging to an obsolete second period of ahistorical side-by-side comparison of separate communities. And it would be equally erroneous to conclude that his post-1950 work introduces a new and radical departure from his earlier theory of a folk-urban continuum.

A careful reading of Redfield's published and unpublished papers would probably provide the correct answers to the questions posed. Although disinclined to use the first person singular or to emphasize his own contributions, he generally did place his own work, if only in passing reference, in relation to that of others. I happen to be fairly well acquainted with these references, but I should like to discuss the relation of his earlier theories to his later ones, not primarily in terms of a careful *explication des textes*, but rather in terms of the somewhat broader context of the ongoing research which both stimulated the theoretical formulations and was in turn stimulated by them. Institutional and social contexts also seem to be to have played an important part, and I shall refer to some of these.

Nineteen-fifty is probably as good a dividing line between Redfield's earlier and later work as one could find. Before this time his work is guided largely by the natural science model that he finds coming to dominate the social anthropology of the first half of the twentieth century, while his emphases on a more humanistic approach and on history begin to be expressed in the late 1940s and early 1950s.

The keynote statement, calling on social scientists and anthropologists to look to the humanist neighbors on their left as well as to the natural scientists on their right, was sounded in a series of lectures delivered at the University of Frankfurt in 1949. Several of these lectures were published separately in the United States, "The Art of Social Science" in 1948; "Social Science among the Humanities" in 1950; and "Social Science in Our Society" in 1950 (Redfield 1962:32).

Some of the same issues were restated for professional anthropologists in Redfield's paper on the "Relations of Anthropology to the Social Sciences and the Humanities," presented to the Wenner-Gren Conference on *Anthropology Today* held in New York in 1952 and for a British audience in his Huxley memorial lecture in 1956.

The general social background against which these new theoretical orientations were being formulated and discussed were the Second World War and the problems of postwar reconstruction and international organization. Redfield participated actively during this period in the Joint Committee on Latin American Studies, the American Council on Learned Societies, the Social Science Research Council, the Committee to Frame a World Constitution, and other professional organizations. While serving in these organizations he came into direct contact with many problems associated with the war and its aftermath, but he did not necessarily devote his energies to these practical problems or accept some of the fashionable panaceas which were being proposed. Instead he preferred to use his service in these organizations as an opportunity to learn about the practical problems and to consider how the social sciences and the universities could be of some help in solving them. As the dean of the Division of the Social Sciences of the University of Chicago (from 1934 to 1946) he was also faced with many problems of administrative and intellectual reorganization within his own university.

It is my belief that Redfield's interest in a comparative study of civilizations was stimulated and crystallized in the social and institutional context of the Second World War and the immediate postwar period. I also believe that the crystallization of his interest in the comparative study of civilizations intensified and focussed his humanistic tendencies. Before this crystallization, Redfield had independent interests in history; in human nature; in cognitive, moral, and esthetic standards; in mentality and states of mind; and in the subjective factors in anthropological methods of observation and interpretation. But not until he turned his attention to the problems of characterizing and comparing civilizations did these humanistic interests coalesce with one another and with his previous anthropological work to generate the important and fruitful conception of a social anthropology of civilizations.

In the remainder of the paper I will at first indicate how some social and institutional contexts stimulated Redfield's thinking in the direction of a social anthropology of civilizations, and then I shall discuss the influence of this conception on anthropological research. In spite of the significant changes introduced in his later thinking, I hope to show that these were not so much radical departures from his folk-urban continuum theory as they were extensions of that theory.

2. INSTITUTIONAL CONTEXTS: AREA STUDIES AND THE STUDY OF CULTURE IN GENERAL EDUCATION

In a paper presented at a conference of representatives of university and social science research organizations to consider proposals for postwar area studies, held at the offices of the Social Science Research Council on April 29–30, 1944, Redfield expressed some doubts with his usual crispness.

> I suggest that we discuss how we are to organize area programs in peacetime only after we are sure why we are to do so. The ends of universities are not the same as the ends of the wartime area programs. The ends of a university are education and research. The ends of the wartime area programs are training and more training.

Conceding that the military area programs had developed methods, particularly in language instruction, for communicating useful information about a particular region to businessmen and social scientists who planned a career in that region, he thought such area programs would be hard to justify for students not planning to work in just that part of the world.

Redfield was not dogmatically opposed to area programs. He saw merit in them as a means to devise a fresh plan for general education. This plan takes "a complex subject matter—the customs, institutions, language and literature of a country—and treats this subject matter as the natural whole that it is, bringing to bear upon it the illumination provided by the established disciplines." Such a program may communicate modes of thought and ways of life different from our own, and it would do so through the medium of that other land's language. This kind of communication, he believed, is an important element in a general education, because it gives the ability to look at one's own culture with the fresh perspective given by acquaintance with another traditional way of life. For his authority, he appeals to the words of John Stuart Mill:

> Without knowing the language of a people, we never really know their thoughts, their feeling and their type of character; and unless we do possess this knowledge, of some other people than ourselves, we remain, to the hour of our death, with our intellects only half expanded . . . since we cannot divest ourselves of preconceived notions, there is no means of eliminating their

influence but by frequently using the differently colored glasses of other people; and those of other nations, as the most different, are the best.

An area program can then provide some of the elements of a general education—acquaintance with an alien culture and its language through an integration of the social sciences and the humanities. But it cannot give all of a general education, for it would omit the biological and physical sciences. Redfield also raises the question of whether the literature and scholarship that exists is adequate to construct a general education program for an alien culture comparable to what is available for European and American studies. He thought it would take a long time and much research to build up those scholarly materials on non-Western cultures needed to discuss the enduring and significant problems. In the meantime it is probably important that the organization of teaching in regional terms "waits upon research in the societies of parts of the world other than western Europe and the United States."

> When we have carried on long and intensive study of the economics, government, sociology, anthropology, history, and arts of Russia, China, India, and Latin America, and have brought these different disciplines into considered relation to one another with reference to each of these regions, then we shall have in our understanding of these other parts of the world a basis for general education comparable with what is provided by our knowledge of Western Europe and some of its offshoots. We shall also have one or more excellent sets of different colored glasses through which to see and correct our preconceived notions. What the study of primitive societies now contributes to education will then be attainable through study of important world civilizations with the aid of the specialized disciplines.

Redfield did not think that such knowledge of the world civilizations was to be had in 1944. He found some beginnings of it in the study of history and religions of the ancient Orient, and in some specialized social science studies of Russia and Asia. But the integrated scholarly study of the great civilizations, developing a scholarship comparable to that on western Europe, would take the work of generations to produce:

> One university or another might well seriously make an effort in that direction with an Institute of Far Eastern Studies, or Russian Studies, or Latin American Studies. Such an enterprise would look to the long future, and would be content to develop a few first-rate scholars dealing with one aspect or another of the region chosen, and talking often with each other about their work. Such an enterprise would combine the study of books and texts with field study of the people living in the area today. The organization would include both representatives of the humanities and social scientists. For the conception which would give unity to the effort would be not so much the spatial fact that China or Russia or Latin America is one part of the earth's surface, as the fact of culture. These students would all be concerned with a traditional way of life that had maintained a distinguishing character over a long time, to great consequence for mankind. A literate people expresses its traditional way of life in what is written; and every people expresses it in institutions and customs and everyday behavior. Ultimately the conception of culture as a naturally developed round of life and the conception of culture as enlightenment through mental and moral training, go back to the same reality; a people with a way of life that is or can be the subject of reflective study. The regional program in research may take the form of long study of the great world cultures.

This plea for an interdisciplinary scholarly study of the world's cultures, little and great, is probably Redfield's first statement of his conception of a social anthropology of civilizations. It did not, however, immediately lead to the creation of the scholarly programs and institutes he envisaged, either at Chicago or elsewhere. Where new area programs were introduced, they continued to emphasize short-run practical problems and were organized by geographical region and discipline rather than by culture and civilization.

Perhaps the first group to respond favorably to Redfield's conception was the social science faculty of the College of the University of Chicago. During and immediately after the Second World War this faculty was expanded and was charged with the responsibility of re-organizing a three-year sequence of courses for undergraduates. The first year was revised to concentrate on great issues in the development of American democracy; the second year was to deal with general sociological, anthropological, and psychological theories about society; and the third was to concentrate on selected policy problems with the help of political economy, political science, political sociology, and political philosophy (Singer 1951).

Redfield occasionally taught in these courses and was frequently consulted about them. In 1946–47 he was given the administrative responsibility of chairing the entire program, directing its reorganization, and moderating some of the sharp differences of opinion among the faculty as to best direction of future development. It was in this institutional context that he wrote his essay "The Study of Culture in General Education" (1947).

In this essay Redfield returns to the 1944 conception of an integrated study of Non-Western civilizations but now develops it far more positively as a possible contribution of the social sciences to general education. His main proposal is that, in addition to a historical study of our own society and its values and the analysis of contemporary policy problems, a third element should be included: "An intensive acquaintance with the fact of integrated culture and the fact of human nature and the development upon this acquaintance of a basic generalizing knowledge of society and human nature with some primary scientific concepts for the description and further understanding of that subject matter" (1962:117).

Redfield compared the understanding of peoples and cultures other than our own to coming to know another person as a persisting integration of dispositions to behave—"unique, complex, self-consistent," and he felt that it takes much time to come to know them just as it takes much time to know a personality well. To be of educational value, the understanding of an unfamiliar culture must reach the point where an educated individual "begins to think how he would act in given situations if that other culture were his own," where he recognizes that the institutions and ideas of the other culture provide goals, motives, and meaning to those who live in terms of it; and where he comes to see on closer acquaintance that beneath the enigmatic or repugnant mask of the alien culture, there are men and women quite like one's own people, who share a common humanity.

For Americans in particular, Redfield believed the educational experience of learning about more consistent and harmonious cultures was especially needed. "The culture of the people of the United States is an entity much less well defined than the cultures of most of the peoples of history and the world today. In this sense contemporary Americans need acquaintance with a well-integrated culture because they have never had any" (1962:114).

The choice of a culture to study was not, in Redfield's opinion, as important as the amount of time given to the study and the materials used. The most surprising of his recommendations is that one culture, preferably a literate one such as the Chinese, be studied continuously and intensively from the first through the fourteenth years of school. Until the tenth year the primary teaching materials would consist of personal documents—autobiographies, letters, good fiction about the society, accounts of personal relations between Americans and members of the foreign group. He gives as illustrations, Turi's *Book of Lapland,* the Chinese novel *All Men are Brothers, The Egoist, Fathers and Sons,* Plutarch's *Lives.* Abstract and systematic concepts of culture and society would not be introduced until the tenth year, when they can be referred to the source materials in which people express themselves in their own words.

Redfield obviously was thinking of the debate going on in the college at the time between those who wanted students to read the classic social theorists and those who wanted more empirical and personal documents included. He recommended a compromise:

> My impression is that the young college people I know who, as part of their general education, read Locke and Bentham and Sumner, become aware of the fact that assumptions as to human nature underlie the views of these writers. But I also have the impression that they are unprepared to judge these assumptions and that some acquaintance with human nature as a scientific subject matter would make their reading of these works more enlightening to them (1962:116–117).

Redfield's bold proposal of a fourteen year study of another culture or civilization envisioned a unified administrative power to plan the curriculum from the elementary and secondary schools through the first two years of college as a whole. Such an administrative structure did not exist at Chicago at the time. Although there was some discussion of the desirability of combining the university's laboratory schools with the first two years of the college, this did not come to pass. As an alumnus of both the University of Chicago Laboratory Schools and the college, and one whose children were following in his footsteps, Redfield no doubt had the local institutional setting in mind when he developed his ideas for a study of culture and human nature in general education. The proposal attracted the attention and interest of some members of the faculty in both the laboratory schools and the college. When I succeeded Redfield in 1947 as chairman of the college social sciences staff and program, I circulated a manuscript copy of "The Study of Culture in General Education" among the staff. It was discussed by the faculty of the second-year social science course ("Soc. Sci. 2"), who were at that time considering a major revision of the course under the direction of David Riesman. The revision turned the course into a broadly conceived "culture and personality" course. Although the course focussed on the social consequences of industrialization in Europe and the United States, the approach was holistic and cultural. Ruth Benedict's *Patterns of Culture* and some of Margaret Mead's South Pacific studies were read for comparative perspectives.

The strong interest of some members of the college social sciences faculty in the study of culture and human nature became a matter of record when a group of this faculty proposed to Redfield about 1950 a federated project for "the Interdisciplinary Study of Culture and Social Character," with some special reference to American culture. The immediate occasion for the proposal was the prospect that the university might receive a grant of funds from the recently organized Ford Foundation for the support of cultural studies under Redfield's direction. The proposal was cordially received. Redfield said he would report the enterprise as "a separate ring within the main tent," but did not yet know how or when the interests of the university in the field were to be presented to the foundation. In the end the college proposal was not funded either by the Ford Foundation or by other sources, although some of the individual projects eventually found independent support.

3. HOW TO COMPARE CIVILIZATIONS: CULTURE PATTERNS, SELF-IMAGE, ETHOS, AND WORLD VIEW

Robert Redfield devoted the last decade of his life (1949-1958) to studying and advancing the dialogue of civilizations. Practically all of his time and activities were in the service of this goal—his travel to China, Europe, and India; his teaching, thinking, and writing. The organizational channel for these activities was a project on intercultural studies based at the University of Chicago and supported by the Fort Foundation from 1951 to 1961. Robert Hutchins's strong personal interest in the project was for Redfield an important source of personal inspiration and encouragement. I was associated with Redfield and the project as a junior colleague and an associate director. When Redfield asked me to join the project I was teaching in the social sciences program of the "Hutchins College" at the University of Chicago. As a result of my association with Redfield I was converted professionally to anthropology and to the comparative study of civilizations. Through more intensive Indian studies and three trips to India I personally joined in a small way the dialogue of civilizations between the United States and India.

For Redfield the major practical goal of the Ford project was to advance the common understanding that the peoples of the world have of one another by bringing their "great traditions" and cultures into greater comparability at the level of systematic thought and scholarly research. He saw a hope in this of "modifying in some degree the separateness with which the study of Western civilization has been carried on, and of supplementing, through a more central vision, the efforts made in UNESCO and elsewhere to develop a world community of ideas."

Seeing the "cold war" with the Soviet Union of the 1950s pushing the United States toward the brink, Redfield emphasized that "mutual security depends on mutual understanding and for understanding you have to have a conversation" (1962:233). His practical advice was to walk quietly and to carry an intercultural hearing aid and radar.

> At home and abroad to talk and then to listen, to listen with the help of reason and then reasonably to talk, is to strengthen us just where we can be so much stronger than the Soviets. It is to build the community of free minds, "the civilization of the dialogue" (1962:240).

The relevance of anthropology and other scholarly disciplines for carrying on the art of the "great conversation" and enlarging thereby the company of the free mind is that "the perception of both difference and likeness is a necessary basis for a conversation between two individuals or between two nations. To talk as free men each must in effect say: 'You have a different view from mine, but we are both reasonable and human creatures, and I should like to know what your view is.' That this ideal is not usually realized in life does not make its influence on us any less" (1962:240).

The "great conversation" between nations and civilizations requires, then, a widespread knowledge of the differences and similarities among different civilizations and of the common humanity underlying them. Redfield saw that such knowledge was not abundant and would need to be developed, systematized, and disseminated. He defined the scholarly task as one of developing concepts and methods for characterizing and comparing civilizations.

By 1951, when the University of Chicago received the first Ford grant for the support of intercultural studies under Redfield's direction, he had already become convinced that a long-run cooperative effort among many scholars working in different disciplines was needed to build a body of comprehensive and systematic knowledge for understanding and comparing the world's living civilizations. Only through such an interdisciplinary approach, he believed, was there a likelihood of modifying to some degree the separateness with which the field was then studied. Not only the theoretical intellectual problems, but the immediate practical problems in the field of international and intercultural relations needed the new approach. Our joint foreward to *Studies in Chinese Thought,* which introduced the monograph series on the "Comparative Studies of Cultures and Civilizations," challenged the scholarly community to join the common effort of accumulating and refining the study of particular civilizations and particular historical periods, and helping develop valid methods for the generic characterization and comparison of cultures and civilizations.

A jacket paragraph which Redfield and I drafted to announce the project's monograph series also emphasized the cooperative and interdisciplinary spirit of the undertaking:

> This is a series of monographs under the general editorship of Robert Redfield and Milton Singer which has been accepted by the *American Anthropologist* as a Special Memoir Series. The series has been designed to make available to a broader public the results of some recent work in the field of intercultural studies. This work represents the fruit of interdisciplinary cooperation among outstanding scholars and scientists in the United States and abroad. The subject matter of the monographs will cover these broad problem areas: The methodology of comparative studies, the characterization and interrelations of the world's major civilizations, and original research which has broad cross-cultural significance. There will be about ten monographs completed within the next two years. Support for publication as well as for the seminars, conferences, and field research which have been the chief source of the monographs, has been provided by a grant from the Ford Foundation. [Sol Tax, who was then editor of the *American Anthropologist,* negotiated the arrangement for the memoirs and also worked out an agreement for simultaneous publication of some of the monographs by the University of Chicago Press.]

While many scholars were skeptical of such a broad interdisciplinary approach at the time, we were able to enlist the cooperation of some leading specialists on Oriental civilizations, for example, Arthur Wright and John Fairbank on Chinese civilization,

Gustave von Grunebaum on Islamic Civilization, W. Norman Brown, Daniel Ingalls V. Raghavan, and M. N. Srinivas on Indian Civilization.[2] In addition, some linguists, anthropologists, historians, philosophers, and sociologists were willing to discuss with us in seminars, conferences, and symposia, or informally, the relations of their own research to the project, even when they did not always agree with our approach. The continuing "Comparison of Cultures" seminar which we held at the University of Chicago became an important forum for building a common universe of discourse among scholars interested in the comparative study of civilizations. We did not expect to arrive at a single unified science of civilizations, but aimed to construct a set of coordinates by which to order and evaluate existing studies, develop some new and valid methods for characterizing and comparing civilizations, and build a framework of concepts and hypotheses to guide future research. We also hoped that the publication of the monograph series, including a culminating volume by the directors, would make the activities and results of the project known to a wider public and thereby enlarge the dialogue of civilizations.

In the first two years of the project, from October 1951 to October 1953, we concentrated on learning about the work of others, on enlisting the cooperation of various kinds of specialists, and on systematically reviewing and testing basic concepts and methods that seemed useful for a comparative study of civilizations. One of my initial assignments in the comparison of cultures seminar was to review and appraise the studies of national character with reference to their use of the concepts of "basic personality," "ethos," "total cultural pattern," and related concepts (I had started this project in the college and developed it, at Redfield's suggestion and with the encouragement of Fred and Dorothy Eggan, in the comparison of cultures seminar).

In the summer of 1952, while on a study trip to European centers, I drafted a preliminary report on the results of this review in an eighty-page paper on "Total Culture Patterns." The paper, which included references to the work of European scholars I had recently met as well as expanded versions of my presentations to the comparison of cultures seminar, was reproduced in Chicago and circulated to members of the seminar and to some friends of the project. Alfred L. Kroeber, who took a personal interest in the project, returned his copy of the paper with many valuable comments written in a small fine hand on the margins, a practice he continued with subsequent papers. Portions of the "Total Culture Patterns" paper were later revised and published separately under the inspiration of Redfield's search for comparative methods and concepts in the study of civilizations (Singer 1953; 1960; 1961; 1964b; 1967a; 1967b; 1968; Kroeber 1963[2]: foreword).

A major portion of the "Total Culture Patterns" paper, consisting of fifty pages on five models of cultural interpretation and explanation (logical, symbolic, esthetic, functional, and causal), was never published, although Redfield included a brief summary of it in his paper for the 1952 Wenner-Gren conference on "Relations of Anthropology to the Social Sciences and the Humanities" (1953,a).

Redfield himself took responsibility for reviewing and developing world view studies in the comparison of cultures seminar. Redfield's conception of world view is reminiscent of Malinowkski's at the end of *Argonauts of the Western Pacific:* "to grasp the native view of *his* relation to *his* world." But he goes beyond Malinowski in two respects: (1) In explicitly relating his conception of the insider's characteristic outlook on everything to other "thought forms" which the anthropologist has available for describing and comparing cultures, and (2) In tracing the structural changes in world view in relation to the influence of urban centers and the growth of civilization. In the fifth chapter of *The Folk Culture of Yucatan,* Redfield sketched the Maya villagers' world view in the context of the folk-urban continuum. He did not, however, become especially impressed with the importance of listening to the "native philosophers" and *"their* order, *their* categories, their emphasis upon this part rather than that" until he started to think about civilizations (see Redfield 1955a: ch. 6).

The broad range of Redfield's interest in world view was first expressed in his paper on "The Primitive World View" which was published in the *Proceedings of the American Philosophical Society,* 96 (1952), pp. 30-36 and then republished in a revised and expanded version as chapter 4, "Primitive World View and Civilization," of

The Primitive World and Its Transformations. He was particularly stimulated at this time by Marcel Griaule's (1965) published conversations with the blind Dogon philosopher, and by the lectures on *The Intellectual Adventure of Ancient Man* which had been given at Chicago by specialists in ancient Near Eastern civilizations. He found evidence in these works for the reflective systematization of world views into a cosmology, and he suggested that with the development of cosmologies in civilization, the organic interrelations of Man, Nature, and God in the primitive world view were "fractured." Whitehead's *Adventure of Ideas* also influenced his interpretation of this transformation in primitive world view.

In his paper on "Thinker and Intellectual in Primitive Society," written in 1957 and published in 1960 in the volume in honor of Paul Radin *(Culture in History,* edited by Stanley Diamond), Redfield was led by further analysis of the Griaule studies of the Dogon to a conception of "culture-society, as a body of knowledge more or less pyramidal, more or less multilineal," the understanding and cultivation of which is differentially distributed among different members of a society according to their different degrees of training and learning. Redfield had by this time already formulated his conception of "the social organization of tradition" and had sketched its application to Islamic, Chinese, and Indian Civilizations (Redfield 1955b, 1956a). He saw their "great traditions" as a developing specialization and systematization of the archaic world views of early civilizations as well as of those of tribal and peasant cultures. For this reason he encouraged and supervised field research on Meso-American world views by E. Michel Mendelson (1957; 1958), Charles Leslie (1960), and Calixta Guiteras-Holmes (1961).

The "Afterword" to *Perils of the Soul,* written by Sol Tax, includes correspondence between Redfield and Guiteras-Holmes as well as a memorandum Redfield sent to Mendelson (and later to Guiteras-Holmes) on what kind of information to collect about world view and how to record it. Mendelson had come from France, along with Claude Tardits and Eric de Dampière, to study with Redfield. They made us acquainted with the work of Griaule, Lévi-

Strauss, and other French scholars and helped establish personal contacts.

Tardits, who was a student of Africa, prepared a summary and analysis of the Griaule studies of the Dogon. Mendelson, who was especially interested in world view, prepared a comprehensive bibliography of published studies for the comparison of cultures seminar.

The German philosophic analysis of world view was also discussed in the seminar, with contributions from Arnold Bergstrasser and Otto von Simson. A student in the Committee on Social Thought, Victor Gourevitch, prepared a dissertation on Wilhelm Dilthey's ideas on the subject. Karl Mannheim's essay "On the Interpretation of Weltanschauung," originally published in Vienna in 1923, attracted Redfield's attention when it was republished in English translation in the volume *Essays on the Sociology of Knowledge,* edited by Paul Kecskemeti (Mannheim 1952). In general, Redfield found Mannheim's approach to world view convincing but thought that its holistic inclusion of "ethos," "character," and "culture" tended to blur the distinctions among them and to slight the "system of existential conceptions" which Redfield emphasized in his presentations to the comparison of cultures seminar. In 1952–1953 the general subject of the seminar was the world view and ethos of folk cultures. In addition to Redfield's contributions, presentations were also made by Arnold Bergstrasser on world view and the philosophy of history, by Richard Brandt on Hopi ethics, by F. G. Friedmann on the conceptions of Calabrian peasants, and by myself on cultural characterizations in terms of ethos, basic and modal personality, and total culture pattern.

The shaping of a people's world view by the language they speak was another approach to world view that attracted Redfield, especially as formulated by Benjamin Lee Whorf. Towards the end of 1952, we invited the anthropological linguist, Harry Hoijer, to organize an interdisciplinary conference to evaluate the Sapir-Whorf hypothesis. The conference met in Chicago in 1953 and its proceedings were edited by Hoijer in the volume *Language in Culture* and published both as an AAA *Memoir,* and in book form by the University of Chicago Press. Although the consensus of opinion at the conference was rather critical of the Sapir-Whorf theory, the discussions stimulated much new interest and research in the relation of language to other aspects of culture, including ethnolinguistic studies of world view.

Redfield maintained his interest in world view to the very end. In one of his last papers, "Art and Icon," prepared as a lecture for the inauguration of the Museum of Primitive Art in New York City, he returned to Ogotemmeli's cosmological interpretation of a Dogon wooden carving of a couple as one of the texts for his lecture. He was also greatly pleased and stimulated by Kroeber's comments on world view at the comparative civilizations seminar held in the winter and spring of 1958 at the Behavioral Sciences Center in Stanford. After listening to presentations by Redfield (1962) on civilizations, by Arthur Wright (1960) on the Chinese literati self-image of Chinese civilization, by Charles Wagley (1968) on ideal patterns in Latin American culture, and by Ethel Albert (1960) on Urundi world view, Kroeber (1963) brought in a very concise synthesis on "Holism and World View" in which he explicitly related "world view," "self-image," and "ideal pattern" to the process of civilization. By the time Kroeber brought in his formal statement to the seminar, Redfield had already returned to Chicago. As soon as he received a copy of it, he sent me the following comments on it. These comments are notable for their explicit clarity in distinguishing Redfield's conceptions from Kroeber's of "ideal pattern," "self-image," and "world view."[3]

Redfield on Kroeber's "Holism and World View"

It is a pleasure to read in Kroeber's document that you have just sent me several promising suggested developments in new directions of ideas that have interested you and me. The comparison of civilizations by way of the primitive-to-civilized series of holistic entities, the interest in the development, in the course of this series, of specialists who are "definitive formulators," and what he calls "the partial separation of self-image and world view," especially in Europe, are all ideas consonant with themes that we have used and that lead to aspects of answer to the question, "What is generically (not specifically as among cultures) civilizational?"

Among his ideas that appear to me from this document new or freshly accented are the thought (he presented before in the seminar) that it is the self-image that ethnologist and humanist-historian are likely first to encounter, the suggestion that the clarity of the self-image has something to do with the "vigor" of a culture; possible correspondence of self-image and super-ego of persons; the identification of certain written works in Western civilization expressing self-image; the very interesting suggestions as to relations of isolation or culture-contrast to formation of self-image; and—especially to my liking—the recognition (in reference to the Roman plebeians) that a self-image formulated by a literate elite may be so accepted by other classes as to become theirs to defend.

I very much hope Kroeber will develop some of these ideas. Indeed if he would expand this document into a chapter for "our book," I think we—and the scholarly public—would be very fortunate.

He here consolidates the conceptions "world view," "self-image" and "ideal patterns." For his purposes, in summarizing aspects of what was said in the seminar, and for moving into questions in which he is interested, I think he does well in merging them. To me too the concepts are very much alike, "differing only in stress."

Toward the end of his paper he separates "world view" and "self-image." From the context there I understand him to mean by the merged concept (and by "self-image" in cases where the two are by him to be distinguished) "the total" (holistic) view of their way of life which a people holds. In an isolated society, he is saying, this is *all* that is within their view. In at least one case, however, a people views not only its way of life, but views also other ways over those that are not theirs; then its world view includes its self-image and its view of what is outside of its way of life.

Not to disagree, but to clarify minor differences in conception, I note here how I have inclined to use these terms so as to bring out "the differences in stress" among them.

I have meant by "world view" the total "inside view" of everything characteristic of a people. This conception, extremely cogitational and not at all operational, then stands for the way the Watusi, the Hopi, the Chinese, characteristically view everything of which any notice is taken in any kind of order that they have found in it. World views differ in many kinds of respects, and one of these respects was brought to our attention by Arthur Wright: the "self-image" he gave us for the Chinese was one in which "we Chinese" occupied the prominent center. One felt that this prominence was not unconnected with the Chinese awareness of other—and inferior—peoples. One does not feel this "we-people-centered" emphasis in what M. Mead tells us of the world view of the Arapesh. So this difference in stress I would take to be expressed by saying that self-image is the component or aspect of world view which presents a people to itself, and perhaps to others. In self-image the universe, the rest of it, is the setting for the self-presentation. Some world views will be found to be more inevitably so to be reported than will others.

As to "ideal pattern," I at once agree that a self-image is always idealized. However, I should say that we may speak, as did Wagley, of the "ideal pattern" of a single "culture trait," contrasting it with what is "really" expected as to that trait in practice (and, I add, possibly in contrast to another recognized ideal pattern for the *same* trait—see Raymond Smith's discussion of ideals of marriage in Negro British Guiana). But in speaking of "self-image," I think Kroeber is right in saying that this is "an organized and coherent picture or story." Self-image does not refer to a single trait, it is one of the holistic conceptions.

As regards the difference in stress between world view and ideal pattern, I should say simply that as I have used the former term, I have used it so inclusively as to stand for not only the idealized conceptions of a people about themselves and their universe but also the conceptions they have as to how things are likely to work out in "lower" levels of their lives. As Kroeber says, we *begin* by having them talk about ideal patterns. As I make "world view" equal the subjective (insider's) view of their ideal culture, I should like to present this last difference of stress among the terms (Redfield to Singer March 30, 1958).

4. CIVILIZATIONS FROM THE BOTTOM UP

Social and cultural anthropology was not neglected in the project. Although convinced that *it* could not do the job of comparing civilizations without the help of many other kinds of disciplines, Redfield nevertheless believed that anthropology had a special contribution to make to the interdisciplinary effort. That contribution derived from the experience anthropologists accumulated through intensive, observational studies of small communities, and from a comparative and holistic analysis of their generic structures and tendencies to change. Redfield was one of the first anthropologists to recognize that these methods would need extension and revision if they were to be adequate for the study of the great, complex, and historic civilizations. And he pioneered in the development of such extensions and revisions from 1951 to 1958 when he was thinking about civilizations. Nevertheless it was the "little community," and the peasant village community in particular, that provided him with the best point of entry into a civilization. The anthropologist would make his contribution by studying civilizations "from the bottom up," as he often said. There were at least three reasons, I believe, for his preference. He felt, in the first place, that the methods and results which anthropologists developed in their work with the "simpler" societies and cultures in the second period were substantial achievements which should be taken as a foundation for an extended social anthropology of civilizations. In the second place, his own earlier studies in the peasant villages of Tepoztlán and Chan Kom (1930; 1934; 1950), although involving some important departures from the "primitive isolate" model, gave him a personal familiarity with a type of community in which he believed most of mankind lived. Moreover he felt that the results of his Yucatán studies indicated that the constructed folk-urban typology was a fruitful research tool that could be applied to the study of civilizations.

A third reason for the anthropologist to use the small community study as an approach to the study of a civilization, Redfield believed, was that other kinds of scholars, social scientists, and humanists had already preceded the anthropologist in the study of the "great community" and the "great traditions," while the study of the little community, and its cultural tradition within the orbit of a civilization or a nation, had been neglected except for a few anthropological studies.

As an anthropological advocate of an interdisciplinary approach to the comparative study of civilizations, Redfield found himself in the position of an experienced skier about to try his skill on the slopes of an unknown terrain. He preferred to rely on his favorite old skis but was also prepared to learn some new twists and turns if the topography called for them, and was even prepared to add some new modes of transportation if that should become necessary.

In view of Redfield's personal preference for studying a civilization "from the bottom up" through intensive field work in contemporary small communities, his support of the Islamicists and the "Chinese thinkers" may appear out of character. He was delighted, however, to find professional humanists and specialists on historic civilizations who were willing to consider the problems an anthropologist raised. He did not expect or request agreement on his approach to the comparative study of civilizations and was appreciative of what he learned from the Islamicists and the specialists on China. Yet he did feel that these humanistic studies of great traditions and great ideas did not give a picture of a civilization *in vivo*—"in the context of family, neighbors, work, ceremonies, and other circumstances that make up the round of life of a people. It is this close view of a civilization that is provided by the anthropological study of small communities. This is the view of Indian civilization that is taken in the present volume."

The preceding quotation is from our joint foreword to *Village India,* edited by McKim Marriott and published in 1955 both as a memoir of the American Anthropological Association and in the project monograph series by the University of Chicago Press. The *Village India* volume was based on one of the comparison of cultures seminars that Redfield and I organized, with substantial help from Marriott, and conducted during the spring of 1954 at Chicago. Since I have described elsewhere the sequence of events that led to Redfield's and my interest in India, I need not retell that story here (see Singer 1972). I should like, however, to describe briefly how a "little community" approach was, in the case of India, successfully integrated with the humanists' studies of Indian great traditions and provided Redfield with one of the first concrete and developed cases of a compound and historic structure of interaction between a great tradition and little traditions, and between little communities and the structure of a great society.

In 1952–1953, the second year of the comparison of cultures seminar, Redfield pulled together the results of our initial explorations into a systematic account of the "forms of thought" available to anthropologists or other scholars for describing the "little community," the subject of his Uppsala lectures and the book based on them. When we invited the social anthropologists who had recently done village studies in India, we circulated a manuscript copy of *The Little Community* and asked them to consider two questions for discussion at the 1954 seminar: (1) Were the "forms of thought" used in the study of other little communities also useful for the study of Indian villages? and (2) In what ways would anthropology need to change its methods to take account of the relations of a village to the wider society and culture in which it was embedded? The answer to the first question was generally positive, and just about each of the "thought forms" in *The Little Community* was well illustrated by at least one contributor to *Village India*. But it was the answers to the second question that proved to be more novel and interesting. Hardly anyone tried to analyze the Indian village as a "primitive isolate," not even the anthropologist who reported on tribal groups, David Mandelbaum. Everyone, on the other hand, suggested a somewhat different set of "extensions" that connected their village to surrounding villages and towns and to the cities. Networks of kinship and marriage, of caste, trade, pilgrimage, and political administration were among the most important kinds of "extensions" discussed. Oscar Lewis characterized the north Indian intervillage networks as a "rural cosmopolitanism" in contrast with the inward looking Mexican villages.

McKim Marriott studied the relations between some of the little traditions of his village and Indian great traditions, and also included in his account the changing history of social relations of the village with the regional and the national societies.

These explorations of extravillage social and cultural networks in *Village India* went considerably beyond the chapter in *The Little Community* in which Redfield began to analyze the little community within communities. In that chapter he introduced John Barnes's concepts of "activity fields" and "social networks" about which he had learned in Sweden, and Betty Starr's attempt to analyze administrative hierarchies in Mexico. It was the *Village India* seminar and volume, however, that introduced Redfield to the intricately interconnected social and cultural networks from which he was to extrapolate the concepts of "societal structure" and "cultural structure" in his book on *Peasant Society and Culture* (1956a) and in his last lectures on civilization.

Indian village studies were by no means the only concrete examples for Redfield's model of a civilization's societal and cultural structure. As he pointed out in *Peasant Society and Culture*, "Today it is usual for an anthropologist to study a community connected with or forming part of a civilization of national state" (1956a:10). And he refers specifically to many such community studies in different parts of the world which were moving away from the anthropological model of the "primitive isolate" and were struggling with the problems of conceptualizing the relations of the small community to a larger society and culture. In Mexico and Latin America he mentions the work of Beals, Foster, Gillin, Wolf, Wagley, Harris, and Steward; in the United States and Canada he refers to Warner's Yankee City and other community studies and to Miner's study of a French-Canadian parish; in Africa to Evans-Pritchard's Sudanese studies; and in China and Japan to Fei Hsiao-Tung's studies and to those of Fried and Beardsley, which Redfield commented on in a symposium on "Community Studies in Japan and China" (1954).

Community studies in Europe also made important contributions to Redfield's thinking. Barnes's study of a Norwegian parish and Hannsen's related Swedish study have already been mentioned. In addition a number of studies in southern Europe; in Spain by Pitt-Rivers, in the Balkans by Sanders, in Italy by Pitkin, Tentori, and Friedmann came to have a special significance in Redfield's attempt to generalize about "The Peasant View of the Good Life." As he explains in the last chapter of *Peasant Society and Culture*, his preliminary formulation of this generalization was presented in a lecture at Chicago in 1954 and was based on an article by E. K. L. Francis, "The Personality Type of the Peasant according to Hesiod's Work and Days: A Culture Case Study" (1945), his own observations in Chan Kom, and a study of an English village in Surrey by George Bourne, published in 1912 under the title *Change in the Village*.

F. G. Friedmann, who taught philosophy at the University of Arkansas and at Northwestern University and who had worked in southern Italy, circulated Redfield's 1954 lecture for comment among his associates in the southern Italian program. Their criticisms, which Redfield summarizes in *Peasant Society and Culture*, compelled him to amend his preliminary formulations on the peasant "personality type" to take account of the Mediterranean variations and to explain these variations in terms of the probable influence of regional history, ethnic temperament, modal personality, and most importantly, "the kind and duration of the relationships those peasants have had with their gentry" (1956a:73). Redfield's discussion of the criticisms by Friedmann's "band of irregulars" is a model of open-minded consideration of exceptions to a formulated generalization and of careful reformulation that takes serious account of negative instances.[4]

Redfield twice planned to enter the orbit of a civilization through a peasant village, in China in 1948–1949 in cooperation with Fei Hsiao-Tung, and in India in 1955 with the guidance of Nirmal Kumar Bose. Both plans were frustrated, the first by approaching upheavals in Chinese political developments and the second by his falling ill of lymphatic leukemia. The two trips were not without fruit, however. From China the Redfields brought out Fei's manuscript on the Chinese gentry which he entrusted to them with the request that they publish it in the West. Mrs. Redfield revised and edited the manuscript and it was published in 1953 with an introduction by Redfield (Hsiao-Tung 1953).

In India the Redfields first went a conference of anthropologists and social scientists in Madras where they had an opportunity to hear and meet personally with many Indian colleagues, and where Redfield presented a paper on "Primitive and Peasant: Simple and Compound Society" (1956b). After the Madras Conference the Redfields went to Calcutta, where, with the help of Nirmal Kumar Bose and Surajt Sinha, they had started to purchase field equipment for travel in Orissa when illness overtook him and they returned home.

The aborting of Redfield's plans for peasant field studies in China and India did not dampen his interests in peasant communities. On the contrary, through reading, an active and far-flung correspondence, and through participation in seminars, conferences, and lectures, he not only kept in touch with this frontier of anthropological research but also through his lectures and writings considerably influenced its advance. The period from 1950 to 1958 was in fact an extraordinarily creative one, seeing the publication of four books and many important papers. Even after he had learned of the leukemia in the autumn of 1955, and was in and out of the hospital, he kept up his interests and productivity.

One prominent feature of his thinking and writing in this period is that it was directed to an exploration of new methods for a comparative study of civilizations. Another equally prominent feature is that the exploration was guided by the same constructed ideal type of the "folk society," with an added historical dimension, which had guided his studies of the four Yucatán communities. Redfield did not continue to use the "folk society" conception because he believed that civilizations, or even peasant communities, would turn out to be like a folk society. He repeatedly noted that they were very far from being that. But he found that analyzing the degrees and kinds of departure of a civilization or of a peasant community from the constructed folk type was itself an illuminating and fruitful research procedure.

In *The Primitive World and Its Transformations,* delivered as a series of lectures at Cornell University and published in 1953 by Cornell University Press, he employed this procedure to guide his thinking about human history as the story of a single career, "the human career," in which "the emphasized event" is the passage from precivilized to civilized life. What Gordon Childe called the "urban revolution" (Redfield was using the concept as modified by the findings of Braidwood and other archaeologists) is taken as the turning point in the human career; the constructed type of the "folk society" is used as "a provider of suggestions" for characterizing the precivilized societies described by archaeologists as well as the postcivilized societies described by ethnologists and ethnographers. One fruitful consequence of the procedure is that it led to an explicit recognition and analysis of "peasantry" as a human type that emerges concurrently with the rise of cities and that is dependent socially and culturally on cities.

The Little Community, Viewpoints for the Study of a Human Whole, delivered as the Gottesman lectures at Uppsala University in the autumn of 1953 and published in 1955, has been taken by many readers as an exception to the general trend of Redfield's later thought. It has been considered a throwback to his alleged earlier preoccupation with the small folk community. Such an interpretation of the book seems to me mistaken and misses the aim, method, and subject of the book. In one sense, as Redfield makes clear on the first two pages, the book is not primarily about little communities in general or about any particular communities. It is about the "forms of thought" which anthropologists and other scholars can use for characterizing and comparing the different kinds of wholes in which "humanity presents itself to common sense": a person, a people, a nation, a civilization, or a small community. Redfield chose the little community to focus the discussion because

> it is a kind of human whole with which students of man have a great deal of experience, and because it is easier to develop a chain of thought in relation especially to villages and bands than to try to do so also in relation to personalities and civilizations and literatures (1955a:2).

He recognized that some of the "forms of thought" considered in the *Little Community* "are relevant to other human wholes," but he also felt that "the generalization of the problems to other kinds of human wholes is a further and much more difficult problem" (1955a:2).

In the comparison of cultures seminars, the discussion of such "forms of thought" as "total culture pattern," "typical personality," "world view," "value system," and "ethos" had in fact frequently considered their usefulness for characterizing the larger wholes: nations and civilizations. When he came to lecture and write about these thought forms, however, Redfield felt that he could best appraise their value for the bigger job by first trying them out on the "little community." He was still approaching civilizations "from the bottom up" and did not in fact attempt a direct conceptualization of civilizational structures until *Peasant Society and Culture,* his very last lectures, and the *Collier Encyclopedia* article "Civilization" in 1958 (reprinted in *Human Nature and the Study of Society* 1962). And even these exceptions prove the rule for they were direct outgrowths of *The Little Community* volume and the *Village India* seminar and book.

In March, 1955, when Redfield delivered his Swarthmore lectures on *Peasant Society and Culture,* he described them as "a very preliminary exploration of one kind of dependent community, that of the peasants, as a describable type" and as "something of a postscript to *The Little Community.*" In these explorations, however, he went well beyond a review of contemporary studies of small peasant communities. He was in fact charting the frontiers of "An Anthropological Approach to Civilization," as the subtitle of *Peasant Society and Culture* suggested. The timely appearance of social anthropologists who had recently done village studies in India led him to see the frontier passing through "Village India" and into the historic structure of Indian civilization.

5. CIVILIZATIONS AS HISTORIC STRUCTURES

When we turn to Redfield's last writings on civilization, those of 1958, we find striking continuities in them with the structuralist conceptions of the Yucatán studies. In calling attention to these continuities, I do not intend to minimize the difficult problems which Redfield and other anthropologists faced in extending a social anthropology of the rabbits of cultures to the elephants of civilizations. The increase in size, scale, and social complexity; the use of archaeological and historical records; the role of highly developed literary and artistic "texts" and their specialized interpreters—present methodological problems for a social anthropology of civilizations that are not yet completely solved. Even so committed an anthropological student of civilizations as Alfred Kroeber expressed doubts about Redfield's hopes that social anthropology would be able to solve these problems and could develop something more than a "microphysiology" or a comparative history of civilizations (Kroeber 1963:ix–xi). Nevertheless the outcomes of Redfield's exploratory efforts, especially of his collaboration with specialized students of Chinese, Islamic, and Indian civilizations, have justified his hopes. And the recent work of Geertz on Indonesia and Morrocco, Spiro on Burma, Tambiah on Thailand, and Goody and Leach on problems of method, testify to the fruitfulness of a social anthropology of civilizations for a second generation of anthropologists who are neither Redfield's students nor disciples.

The structural approach remained central in Redfield's last thinking about civilizations. He used the generic term "form" to refer both to the organizational features of culture (including Benedict's "culture patterns" and "configurations" and Kroeber's "styles") and to those of society (Radcliffe-Brown's "social structure" and "social system"). He then defined "the form of a civilization" as that which remains the same when everything else changes, "a conceived arrangement of parts that persist when the more particular contents of the parts are altered" (1962:373). The form of a civilization remains the same while its institutions, usages, beliefs, and other contents change. Because the form of a civilization may persist over hundreds or even thousands of years and its persistence may be verified by historical and archaeological evidence, this concept is a diachronic structural concept going beyond the synchronic concept of structure. Redfield called it a "historic structure."

Conceived as a persisting arrangement of kinds of communities and kinds of people in characteristic social relations with one another, a civilization is said to have a "societal structure." Conceived as a persisting form of ideas and cultural products together with the characteristic arrangements for transmitting them from generation to generation and from one group of people to another within the great community of the civilization, a civilization can be said to have a "cultural structure."

Redfield's conception of civilizations as persisting historic structures with characteristic cultural and societal structures obviously echoes the trinity of "community, culture, and society" in *The Folk Culture of Yucatán*. In extending these earlier concepts to the comparative study of civilizations, however, he had to write them large and to project them onto a space-time screen of great proportions. He also took account in these extensions of the greater complexities of structure, cultural as well as societal. The cultural structure of a civilization, which he also called "the structure of tradition," for example, was envisaged as compound and double, embracing components that are universal, reflective, and indoctrinating ("a great tradition") and components that are local, unreflective, and accepting ("a little tradition") (1962:394, 395).

Redfield did not regard his concepts of the historic structure, the cultural structure, and the societal structure of a civilization as operational or as based on direct observation of particular civilizations. He proposed them as somewhat speculative "concepts of cogitation," not even as ideal type concepts, to help guide his and other's thinking about civilizations. Those of us associated with him in the comparative civilizations project found them very useful for this purpose and quickly linked them operationally to field observations and empirical descriptions in particular civilizations.

When I first went to India in 1954 I was surprised and greatly encouraged to find how receptive some Indian scholars were to the Redfield project and especially to his conception of civilizations as historic structures of little and great traditions and of little and great communities. From the research and writing so stimulated, a portrait began to emerge of Indian civilization as a structure maintained through a complex and intricate network of caste and kinship, trade and pilgrimage, government administration and political organization, as well as through cultural and religious media and agents. When Redfield began to receive the results of this research and had a brief opportunity to visit India himself in the autumn of 1955, he readily incorporated many of them into his thinking, adjusted his conceptual scheme to take account of them, and in turn raised new questions for research. Two examples of this positive feedback were his formulation of the more operational concept of "the social organization of tradition" as distinct from "the structure of tradition," and his acceptance of the Cohn and Marriott analysis of Indian civilization as a structure of centers and networks. He recognized the simplifications involved: "The real structure of tradition, in any civilization or part thereof, is an immensely intricate system of relationships between the levels or components of tradition, which we enormously oversimplify by referring to as 'high' or 'low' or as 'great' and 'little' (1962:394).[5]

Redfield formulated his conception of a civilization as a compound historic structure of little and great cultural traditions and of little and great communities with three living civilizations mainly in mind—Chinese, Islamic, and Indian. In 1944 and again in 1947 he had already emphasized the desirability for an area studies program and for a general education program of an enterprise that "would combine the study of books and texts with the field study of the people living in the area today." In such a combination he also recognized that the anthropologist's "culture" and the humanist's "culture" would be linked in a single integrated study of a civilization:

> A literate people expresses its traditional way of life in what is written; and every people expresses it in institutions and customs and everyday behavior. Ultimately the conception of culture as enlightenment through mental and moral training, go back to the same reality; a people with a way of life that is or can be the subject of reflective study.

He also noted in these early and prescient statements that very little research had as yet been done by anthropologists or others along these lines. Among social or cultural anthropologists, Alfred

Kroeber was probably the only scholar who was seriously concerned with a comparative study of civilizations. His massive volume on *Configurations of Culture Growth* was published in 1944 and his series of important papers on civilizations was beginning to appear. Kroeber, however, had not yet turned to the study of civilizations as organized wholes but was concentrating on the different aspects of "high culture" and the fine arts. The relations of the high culture to institutions, customs, and everyday behavior was yet to be explored.

When Redfield arrived at the concept of a civilization as a historic structure in the later 1950s, he acknowledged the influence of two of Kroeber's important ideas—that civilizations follow profiles of formation, florescence, and decline expressed in stylistic configurations; and that civilizations tend to establish in the regions of their dominance a stabilized set of interrelations with tribal, peasant, and urban groups, a set of interrelations which Kroeber (1945) called an *oikumené*. These two ideas represent two of the basic meanings in Redfield's concept of the "historic structure" of a civilization: The first meaning refers to the sequential processes of a civilization coming into being or emerging, of continuing in being, and of becoming something else through transformations. The second meaning of an "historic structure" refers to the more or less simultaneous coexistence of relatively different levels of cultural development as in the coexistence of tribal, peasant, and urban strata within an *oekumené*. In this second sense, the historic structure of a civilization is analogous to the relative temporal order of the strata in an archaeological site. As Redfield started to develop the concept of civilizational structure, he began to shift the emphasis from the first to the second meaning of "historic structure." To paraphrase Whitehead's description of the trend of modern science, Redfield was turning from the concept of a civilization as a procession of cultural forms to the concept of a civilization as a structure of cultural processes. Before, however, he could take this decisive step, he first needed some concrete examples of complex civilizational structures and processes to guide his thinking. These examples came in from the specialists on Chinese, Islamic, and Indian civilizations whose cooperation was enlisted by the Ford project. I shall not attempt to sort out here the detailed contributions which the different groups of scholarly specialists made to Redfield's thinking about civilizations or the stimulus he gave to their researches. Some of these mutual interactions are recorded in the forewords and introductions to the separate project monographs.[6]

The first full length profile of the emergence, growth, and decline of a great cultural tradition within a particular civilization was sketched by Gustave von Grunebaum and his Islamicist colleagues. A professor in Chicago's Oriental Institute and in the department of Oriental languages and civilizations at that time, von Grunebaum associated himself with our project from the beginning and participated regularly in the comparison of cultures seminar. He took the responsibility for identifying the work of specialists on Islamic civilization that promised to lead to an improved understanding and comparing of civilizations. He also assumed the leadership in organizing conferences of Islamicists which discussed with special reference to Islamic civilization some of the basic questions that were being raised in the comparison of cultures seminar.[7]

Professor von Grunebaum's own research, also supported by the project, concentrated on a systematic description and analysis of what he called "the development of culture consciousness in the Islamic World, the way in which and the extent to which the Muslim of the prewesternization period came to see himself as a member of a cultural unit rather than merely as the member of a religious national, or racial group" (von Grunebaum to Singer 6/11/54). In this research von Grunebaum was assisted by one of his students, Marshall Hodgson, who shared many of his interests as well as those of the project in the comparative history of civilizations. Hodgson was especially interested in the problems of interregional comparison in relation to world history, and developed Kroeber's conception of the *oikumené* for this purpose.[8]

From the research and discussions of von Grunebaum and the Islamicists, we began to learn something about how a great cultural tradition is formed; how it is expressed in literature, science, government, urban architecture, and world view; and how it adapts to westernization and to the local and regional cultures in the areas which have become Islamized. From another group of specialists on Chinese civilization we learned about the role of a key set of ideas in a great tradition, in this case Confucianism, and of "the influence of those ideas on patterns of behavior, on the formation of institutions, and on the many men who, by their cumulative efforts, built the great and distinctive civilization of China" (Wright, ed. 1964: introduction). This group was the Committee on Chinese Thought of the Far Eastern Association, or as it was later known, the Association of Asian Studies. Over the period it was associated with our project, from 1951 until 1957, the committee was chaired first by Arthur Wright, then at Stanford, and later by John K. Fairbank of Harvard. "Here was a body of specialists, self-organized and vigorous, whose work led along just the paths conducive to the ends of our more general and inclusive project" (Fairbank, ed 1957: foreword). The Committee on Chinese Thought held two major conferences with our project's support and published two volumes of proceedings. It continued to hold several conferences after this and completed its work in 1962. Fairbank and Wright also maintained a continuing association with Redfield, and Wright participated with Grunebaum and Kroeber in the special comparative civilizations seminar that was held at the Behavioral Sciences Center during the winter of 1958.[9]

Redfield's death in 1958 deprived us of the book on the comparative study of civilizations which he had projected. In a personal letter written about a month before, he referred to this as "a small book on civilizations" which would consist of "perhaps ten essay-like chapters, something like—but in the end probably not much like—the following:

    I.   A Civilization as an Object (a formed thing of the mind)
    II.   Culture and Civilizations: Class and Subclass
   III. Criteria (class and continuum)
   IV. Structures in History (Societal or Cultural)
    V.   Community, Region, Class, Estate
   VI. The Cultivation of Tradition and Self-Image: Knowledge
  VII. The Cultivation of Esthetic Discrimination

6. WAS REDFIELD A STRUCTURALIST?

A former Chicago colleague recently reported that in a 1968 Paris discussion, Lévi-Strauss characterized Redfield as a structuralist. The report did not specify which of Redfield's works were structuralist and in which respects. Lévi-Strauss's interpretation seems to be quite plausible and I shall try to make a case for it, especially concerning Redfield's development of a social anthropology of civilizations.

I have already suggested how Redfield arrived in the late 1950s at the conception of civilizations as persisting "historic structures" by extending Kroeber's conception of an *oikumené* and combining with it the conception of society community within the orbit of a particular civilization such as that of India, China, or Islam. Redfield's structuralism, however, was already explicit in his Yucatán studies and antedated his later work on civilizations. Because this aspect of his folk-urban continuum theory is often neglected or misinterpreted, I should like to summarize it briefly and show how it formed the foundation for his later thinking on civilizations.

In *The Folk Culture of Yucatán* Redfield explicitly distinguishes the terms "society," "culture," and "community." "In so far as any defined human aggregate is characterized by social relations, it is a society; in so far as it is characterized by conventional understandings, it exhibits a culture; and, in so far as it may also be said to occupy a territory, it is a community" (1941:15–16).

Redfield's definition of "society" follows Radcliffe-Brown's concept of social structure. The definition of culture, however, as an organized body of "conventionalized understandings manifest in act and artifact that characterize societies" (1941:110, 132–133) goes considerably beyond Radcliffe-Brown's and other then prevailing definitions of culture. In the 1930s, Radcliffe-Brown, then developing his theory of social structure at Chicago, tried to replace the concept of culture by the notions of "custom" and "social usage" as the standardized behaviors in which the structure of social relations was expressed. Redfield's definition of culture as an organized body of conventional understandings, on the other hand, was both structural and semiotic. It was structural in conceiving culture as an organized structure rather than as an aggregation of discrete customs and beliefs, and it was semiotic in conceiving the organization as a structure of meanings attached to acts and objects. "The meanings are conventional and therefore cultural, insofar as they have become typical for members of that society by reason of intercommunication among the members" (1941:132).

In this sense, a culture is for Redfield an abstraction—the type towards which the meanings of an act or object for different members tend to conform. Although Redfield does not attempt to segregate in this conception of culture the semantic and logical sub-systems, he frequently analyzes culture as an "interrelated web of meanings" in terms of structure, system, and networks. But it is a *semiotic* structure and system, a system of acts and artifacts serving as symbols which have acquired standard meanings for the members of a society as a result of mutual communication. In this respect Redfield's conception of culture is fairly close to the "symbolic interactionism" which derives from Peirce, Dewey, G. H. Mead, and Morris.

Redfield's semiotic and structural conceptions of culture were formulated in both objective and subjective terms. Objectively, the structure of a culture depended on whether the anthropologist in describing one domain of the culture needed to refer in his description to other parts. Subjectively, the structure of the culture expressed the structure of its characteristic outlook or world view, "The insider's total vision and conception of everything."[10] Even in its subjective expression as world view, culture remains for Redfield a structured system of conventionalized meanings attached to acts and artifacts. This is most clearly seen in his essay on "Art and Icon" which suggests that an artifact, a Dogon carving of twins, can be perceived and analyzed both as a work of art, an object with "immanent" meaning, and as an ethnographic symbolic expression of a cosmology and world view.

It was not, however, Redfield's general semiotic definition of culture that was his distinctive contribution to a theory of culture and culture change. It was rather the way in which he used the semiotic concept of culture to guide empirical research on four Yucatán communities that led him to formulate his famous folk-urban continuum theory. This is primarily, but not exclusively, a theory about how particular structures of conventionalized meanings, which Redfield calls "folk" cultures, are transformed by contact and communication with urban kinds of cultures. Redfield was emphatic that the folk-urban theory was not simply a theory about the diffusion and borrowing of discrete culture traits, although he recognizes the involvement of that process. He also used the fashionable term "acculturation" but always added that this referred to more than the exchange of traits between two cultures in contact.

> Contact and communication initiate changes which go on partly under the guidance example provided by the source of the communications and partly of the adaptive necessities of the social situation as it comes to be (1941:361).

In the voluminous critical discussion of the folk-urban theory, little attention has been given to Redfield's semiotic and structural conceptions of culture or to the evidence he adduces for the dependence of cultural organization, disorganization, and reorganization on internal and external processes of communication and their agents.[11] The often facile subordination of these aspects of his Yucatán studies to the better known processes of individualization, secularization, and social disorganization, has tended to submerge one of Redfield's major research problems in the Yucatán studies—"Whether cultures differ as to degree to which the quality of organization is present and as to the nature of the connections among the elements which make the whole an organization rather than aggregation" (1941:133). To be sure, by the 1920s and 1930s anthropologists were beginning to study individual cultures and societies as wholes. Malinowski's "functionalism," Radcliffe-

Brown's studies of social structures and social systems, and Ruth Benedict's "configurations," were among the most influential expressions of this interest. Redfield's folk-urban theory, however, differed from these studies in that it was based on an explicitly defined conception of culture as a semiotic structure, and on a typology of such structures that permitted observation and comparison of degrees of variation in the structures among the Yucatán communities studied.[12]

Redfield analyzed four dimensions of variation in cultural organization: unity—plurality, consistency—inconsistency, connotative interdependence—independence, and universals—alternatives. These are dimensions of variation in the organization of conventionalized understandings or meanings attached to the acts and objects by the members of a given society. Their culture is well organized if the conventionalized meanings of acts and objects can be described in relation to one another as a single whole, if the meanings are consistent with one another in terms of the actions they recommend, if they are shared by all members of the society and are obligatory, and if one set of meanings connotes others. Since it would be difficult to find a culture whose conventional meanings were all so univocal, consistent, interdependent, and universal for all members of the society, Redfield defines a "folk culture" as the *ideal* type towards which a well-organized culture tends. At the opposite pole of variation, that of "cultural disorganization," he posits an ideal-type, "urban culture," with many subcultures, inconsistent meanings, many alternative lines of action, and many "separates," that is, domains of conventional meaning which do not connotatively evoke one another.

In comparing the four Yucatán communities, Redfield was *not* trying to discover which of them represented a folk culture and which represented an urban culture. He was rather trying to discover the *relative* orders of variation in degrees of cultural organization (unity, consistency, interdependency, etc.) among the four communities, and the correlation of these orders of variation with the degrees of contact or isolation from an urban center.

Redfield did not for the most part attempt to *quantify* degrees of cultural organization and disorganization in the four Yucatán communities. He was content to make comparisons of degree based on his own and his coworkers' observations. A typical statement expressing such comparisons is the following:

> The greater degree to which a culture is present in Quintano Roo, as compared with Chan Kom, is to be found in the absence of incompatibles, in the lesser degree to which clusters of ideas exist separately without interconnection with others, and, more generally, in the greater number of associations and interconnections which many acts and ideas have for the natives (1941:139).

In comparing Chan Kom with the railroad town Dzitas, on the other hand, he finds support for the proposition that "there is less organization of culture in Dzitas than in Chan Kom. . . . The meanings attached to acts and objects are less highly standardized by convention, the meanings are relatively few and are less completely connected with one another, and inconsistencies and uncertainties are present among them in the experience of any and all members of the community" (1941:153).

Redfield is quite aware of the nonquantitative and sometimes inexact language of these comparisons. He does not therefore discount them, because he was also aware that the problem of describing and comparing the quality of organization and inner consistency of different cultures did not yet lend itself, at least in the early 1940s, to exact and objective methods. He expressed the hope that such methods would be devised but he also noted that the terms used for referring to the quality of organization of a system of ideas and practices—such terms as "structure," "web," network," "deep," and "shallow"—"do not denote qualities which may be precisely limited and compared; they merely suggest them" (1941:112). Yet, he thought that the use of such terms does serve to organize and record the impressions which the students of the four communities formed of the clearly felt differences between the holistic organization of the culture of the more isolated communities and the aggregational sum of the customs, beliefs, and institutions of the less isolated communities in the town and city (1941:112–113).

In other words, Redfield seems to have recognized even in the Yucatán studies that the description and comparison of cultures as structures of conventional meanings requires the use of a relational logic, that the usual statistical and quantitative methods did not suffice. He identifies the problem more generally in the preface to *The Folk Culture of Yucatán* as one of showing how the language of some social science concepts needs to be differentiated in terms of "more" and "less," "to the extent that" and "in so far as," in order to be useful for the description and analysis of the kind of cultural differences observed among the Yucatán communities. These differences "are not like those among the paint tablets in a paint box; they are like the colors of a spectrum. The concepts—culture, disorganization, etc., etc.—are similarly represented in the materials not by absolute instances and their opposites but by shades of difference that are in some cases very small" (1941:xiv).

Much of the criticism of Redfield's folk-urban typology would have been obviated if the critics had realized that the theory postulated a folk-urban continuum with idealized poles and did not set up a dichotomous classification of communities into folk and urban instances. Some of these critics could also have been spared their criticism of Redfield's Yucatán studies as "impressionistic," "subjective," and "nonquantitative" if they had recognized that these studies were pioneer attempts to develop a relational analysis of the structural properties of cultures as semiotic systems. These attempts paralleled and complemented Radcliffe-Brown's contemporary efforts to develop a relational analysis of the structural properties of societies conceived as systems of social relations. Like Radcliffe-Brown, Redfield explicitly distinguished the concepts of culture and society and of the territorial base of each. He also paralleled Radcliffe-Brown's emphasis on the logical difference between an organized system and an aggregated class, and on the use of synchronic comparison to arrive at generalizations about society and culture. I am not suggesting that Redfield directly followed Radcliffe-Brown in these parallels. Common sources in the writings of Maine and Durkheim must account for some of them, although Radcliffe-Brown's presence in the Chicago department from 1931 to 1937 stirred up American anthropologists and accelerated intellectual invention and variation among them, as Redfield said in the 1937 introduction to the "hail and farewell" volume edited by Fred Eggan (1937, 1955).

Redfield also introduced several significant variations from Radcliffe-Brown's method and concepts. Redfield developed the concept of culture as an abstracted ideal type of organized conventional understandings. In contrast, Radcliffe-Brown in the 1930s regarded American anthropologists' use of the culture concept as vague and unnecessary and preferred to eliminate it in favor of a concept of "social usages" as the discrete customary behaviors in which the structure of social relations was expressed. At the end of his career, Radcliffe-Brown restored the "culture" concept (see his introduction to *Structure and Function in Primitive Society)* but his earlier subordination of culture to social structure remained a trade mark of British social anthropology.

As early as 1937, in his *Natural Science of Society* (1957:92–109), Radcliffe-Brown started to develop a conception of culture as a structure and system of usages, rules, symbols, and values. His insistence, however, that there could be no science of culture, that culture could be studied only as an aspect of social systems led to a neglect of Radcliffe-Brown's anticipations of Lévi-Strauss's structuralism and of other later theories of culture.[13]

While Redfield did not accept such a subordination of culture to social structure, he did attempt in the Yucatán studies to apply some of the social anthropological concepts—especially of kinship as a coordinated social system of kinship terms, behavior, and social organization; and of social statuses and social roles as parts of an organized system of social relations. He did not, however, attempt to describe and compare types of social structure, as Eggan and other students of Radcliffe-Brown were doing at the time (a few kinship diagrams are included in Redfield 1941:196–205). Redfield was more interested in extending Radcliffe-Brown's synchronic method of comparison in order to arrive at generalizations about the *changes* in both cultural and social organization that were stimulated by contacts of a primitive or peasant community with urban, Western civilization. His use of a synchronic, structuralist approach had as its goal the discovery and formulation of generalizations about diachronic processes of cultural change. For Redfield, these processes included not only diffusion and acculturation of discrete culture traits, but also sets of interrelated changes in the structures of conventional meanings that constituted a culture.

That these early insights of Redfield's into the processes of culture change were continuous with his later views of culture change in civilizations, and in fact already adumbrated a semiotic theory of culture change, will become clear, I think, from the review in the next section of the role of compartmentalization in cultural innovation and cultural continuity.

7. COMPARTMENTALIZATION OF INNOVATION AND TRADITION IN CULTURE CHANGE

In spite of the qualifications which Redfield introduced in his ideas about the structure and organization of civilizations as a result of ongoing field research in India and elsewhere, his general conceptual scheme remained intact, as did its continuity with his earlier folk-urban theory. One astonishing example of this underlying continuity and influence of his thinking appeared in my Madras studies. A major research objective of those studies was to find out what happens to the great tradition of Sanskritic Hinduism in a modern metropolitan urban center. This question was suggested by our joint paper on "The Cultural Role of Cities." Written before either of us had visited India, this paper attempted to extend Redfield's diachronic version of the folk-urban theory as he formulated it in *The Primitive World and Its Transformations* to a study of the cultural roles of cities in different civilizations. The paper included the first published effort to apply the great tradition-little tradition analysis to India.

In the course of the Madras studies I came across representatives of Sanskritic Hinduism, including some devout Brahmins, who were also leading innovators in the fields of industry, trade, mass media, science, and technology. Since, contrary to Max Weber's theories, they did not seem to experience deep conflicts between their modern and their traditional activities, I collected information about nineteen industrial leaders and their families to see how these people reconciled the claims of tradition and modernity as they moved to the city from villages and small towns, acquired higher education, and entered industry and the professions. These Madras innovators were able to reduce conflicts and work out successful adjustments in two or three generations by following a series of "adaptive strategies." One of the most important of these strategies was to separate, cognitively and to some extent physically, the work sphere in which they followed a modern culture, from the domestic sphere in which they conformed to their religious and more traditional life styles. I called this adaptive strategy "compartmentalization" and attempted to extrapolate from the operation of this and other associated strategies in contemporary Madras, a picture of how the great tradition of Sanskritic Hinduism was being modernized in an urban center without being completely secularized (see Singer 1972, especially ch. 8, 9, for the details).

Some of my colleagues in Indian studies were not especially surprised by these results, since, as they said, Indian society and culture were proverbially compartmentalized by caste, religion, language, and other divisions. My fellow scholars recognized nevertheless that these preliminary Madras findings called for a revision of the classical theory of Westernization and modernization of "traditional" societies (see, for example Singer, ed. 1973; Singer, Cohn and Srinivas 1966; Srinivas 1962, 1966).

Redfield did not live to see these revisions, but they would not, I am sure, have surprised him either, for, as I discovered in a rather curious way, his own early theory of culture change included a process of compartmentalization. In 1970 I drafted a paper on "Culture Change: Some Convergences in Innovation and Tradition" for a volume on *Theories of Social Change* edited by Daniel Bell to be published by Russell-Sage. The paper traces the parallels and convergences in three types of culture change theories, that of culture history represented chiefly by Kroeber, of acculturation represented by Spicer, and of modernization represented by Redfield. One of the parallels I found while working on this paper was in the notion of "compartmentalization" in Redfield's Yucatán studies, Linton's *Study of Man*, Spicer's and Dozier's Southwest acculturation studies, and in my Madras studies. Not only is the same term, "compartmentalization," often used in these parallels, but it is also used to refer to a similar process of cultural change: namely, a phase in the contact between different cultures in which elements from another culture have entered and coexist with traditional elements of a host culture without close interdependence or incompatibility among the elements. The phase is considered transitional to other phases of cultural change in which the novel elements are eliminated or are reinterpreted and incorporated into the traditional culture. Compartmentalization, then, is an adaptive process, reducing conflicts between new and old traits by keeping them separate and gaining time for internal adjustments, reinterpretation, and selective incorporation into the host culture.

I will describe these parallels, but before I do let me warn the reader that their existence neither proves that the concept of compartmentalization was invented independently by different anthropologists nor that American anthropologists plagiarize one another. Before my first visit to Madras in 1954 I was of course familiar with Redfield's Tepoztlán and Yucatán studies and Linton's *Study of Man*. At that time, however, I did not have any idea that compartmentalization would turn out to be an important process, nor was I especially aware of its previous analysis. Observations and experience in India and later reflections and readings on India led me to see the importance of compartmentalization as a strategy of modernization.

In other words, I do not think of compartmentalization either as an idea that was in the anthropological climate of opinion or as a universal Kantian category of human understanding. It seems to me rather a concept that has turned out to be useful for the description and analysis of more or less similar kinds of cultural change observed in different parts of the world by different scholars—by Redfield in Yucatán, by Linton among the Tanala, by Dozier among the Rio Grande Pueblos, by Spicer among the Yaqui, and by myself in Madras, among others.

In *The Folk Culture of Yucatán* Redfield describes three important examples of compartmentalization: the coexistence of the Spanish Catholic Cult of the Saints with the Mayan pagan Cult of the Beehive, the introduction of Protestantism by some Protestant missionaries, and the influence of the idea of progress. He had opportunities to follow the course of the last two cases in the village of Chan Kom and was thus able to observe the different phases of the process. The coexistence of the saints and beehive cults he could observe only as a "seam" or "scar" on the living culture. Its earlier phases were reconstructed from a comparison of the different degrees of integration in the four communities and from documentary history. Since the integration of Spanish and Mayan cults was greatest in the community most remote and isolated from the city, Redfield reasoned that the cultural disorganization induced by the Spanish conquest was to some extent repaired with lapse of time and withdrawal from intensive contact. The preconquest Mayan culture was not restored through this process, but was "regenerated" and "remade" into a "folk culture" which incorporated both cults with a visible "seam" separating them.

Redfield's analysis of the process of compartmentalization, and his concept of a "folk culture" emphasize the degree and quality of cultural organization and its structural properties, not the historical origins or content of the component culture traits. Compartmentalization is for him a process which produces a low degree of connotative interdependence between the old traits and the new traits; these are "separates" rather than "incompatibles" in the structure of conventional meanings:

> It is not that these discrete groups of ideas [of the Saint and Beehive cults] are inconsistent with one another. It is merely that they are not closely connected with one another. . . . The native does not feel any conflict between the cult of the bee-gods and the cult whereby he assures the well-being and the good will of the souls of the dead. There is no problem of making a choice; both are to be maintained. One is engaged in one sphere of activity and thought, or in the other, but not in both at the same time. It is merely that the cult of the bee-gods does not provide reasons for the cult of the dead, or vice versa (Redfield 1941:136).

In the reorganization of a culture which goes on under isolation, the "separates" can persist long after most or all "incompatibles" have been eliminated, although both eventually are eliminated by the "strain to consistency" and greater interdependence of parts (1941:141, 146).

These examples of Redfield's analysis of "compartmentalization" in the Yucatán studies clearly indicate that he conceived of it as an adaptive process of cultural change which was closely tied to his conception of culture as an organized structure of conventionalized meanings. The "adaptive necessities of the situation as it comes to be" which guide the internal processes of cultural change stimulated by contact and communication with other cultures are nothing else than the disorganization in the structure of conventional meanings resulting from cultural innovation and the subsequent reorganization of that structure that comes with the selection and incorporation of the innovations (1941:134, 361).

Redfield has explicitly noted, in *The Folk Culture of Yucatán*, some similarities between his own analysis of cultural organization and disorganization and Ralph Linton's analysis of the disorganization of primitive and peasant cultures upon contact with modern civilization. Linton describes the process as involving a reduction of the core of "Universals" and an increase in "alternatives" and "specialities." By interpreting Linton's "core of Universals" as "the extent to which the entire society can be described in terms of a single organized body of conventional understandings," and restricting "alternatives" to "elements known to every adult or to all members of a socially recognized group but among which the individual may exercise choice," Redfield can see that his Yucatán studies represent, *"in parvo,* a study of certain aspects of the process of civilization itself" (1941:349).

Redfield did not, however, accept several implications of Linton's kind of analysis, such as, that an increase in number of subcultures is by itself an indication of rapid social change or of cultural disorganization, or that an increase in number of alternatives indicates a low degree of interdependence and consistency of the culture. He did, however, accept Linton's proposition that it is "the conversion of both the universal elements of culture and those which are special to subcultures into Alternatives which is a feature of modern civilization" and he believed that the Yucatán comparisons support that proposition (1941:350).

Another feature of Linton's analysis, not explicitly mentioned by Redfield, which closely parallels my analysis of compartmentalization in Madras, is the suggestion that "alternatives" represent a kind of trial and error zone in which traits are "always on their way into or out from the solid core of Universals and Specialities" (Linton 1936:280–281).

"When a new element is offered to any society, full acceptance is always preceded by a period of trial. During this period both the new trait and the old trait or traits with which it is competing become Alternatives within the total culture complex. They are presented to individuals as different means to the same end. In all cultures the Alternatives serve as a proving ground for innovations" (Linton 1936:280–281).

I found a second set of parallels to the compartmentalization analysis in the work of Dozier and Spicer. In his chapter on the Rio Grande Pueblos in the volume on *Perspectives in American Indian Culture Change* edited by Spicer, Dozier explains the persistence of the native Pueblo culture as a result of the compartmentalization of the Spanish and indigenous traditions. Dozier used the term "compartmentalization" to refer to "the presence in Pueblo culture of two mutually distinct and separate socioceremonial systems" (in Spicer 1961:175). Dozier regarded compartmentalization as an obvious adaptation to Spanish pressure. Although the Pueblos were at first receptive to the contacts, they resisted and rebelled "when it became a matter of the complete eradication of their traditional customs and replacement by Spanish-Catholic patterns." Through compartmentalization, "the Pueblos accommodated to Spanish pressures by separating the ceremonial practices which offended the Spaniards and concealing them behind a facade of the imposed Spanish-Catholic patterns" (Spicer 1961:179).

Dozier credits an earlier article by Spicer, "Spanish-Indian Acculturation in the Southwest" (1954b) as his own source for the use of the term "compartmentalization" to designate a particualr type of acculturative process. In that article Spicer uses the term to characterize the general pattern of Eastern Pueblo adjustment to Spanish contact. "Compartmentalization" summarizes for Spicer the "tendency of all the Eastern Pueblos to accept from the Spanish certain traits and trait complexes which remained peripheral to their major cultural interests and to resist traits which would have altered the main orientations of their culture, and we are referring to the ultimate result of Spanish contact as a native culture added to and modified in limited ways but not changed in fundamental structure" (Spicer 1954b: 665).

After describing how different items in the Eastern Pueblo cultural inventory were affected by Spanish contact, Spicer concludes that the dominant process of Pueblo adjustment was a sort of compartmentalization: The important introductions in subsistence, social organization, and ceremonial were accepted and adapted to Pueblo uses without much modification. Wheat was not integrated into the ceremonial system, the governor pattern was not integrated into the village organization, the Saint's cult and the church building were not integrated into the ceremonial system. They were all employed to satisfy Pueblo interests, but they remained adjuncts rather than intricately linked elements in the whole. It is clear that they could have been abandoned, given a new set of conditions, without any important disruption of Pueblo culture.

> This compartmentalization took place with practically no displacements and with a minimum of formal linkages between the new elements and the old. The conditions which gave rise to this type of adjustment will be discussed . . . (Spicer 1954b: 669–670).

In comparing the Pueblo compartmentalizing pattern of adjustment to Spanish contact with the differing patterns among the Yaqui and Athabascans, Spicer attributes importance to the different conditions of contact. Among the Eastern Pueblos these conditions included direct opposition and supression by missionaries of "the established and widely integrated ceremonials such as the Kachina dances," which "must have given rise to opposition to the innovators as well as to innovations" (1954b: 677).

Spicer's 1954 article was published with supporting comments by Dozier. In these comments Dozier affirms the significance of compartmentalization in Pueblo culture and gives some corroborating examples. He emphasizes that the Pueblos follow both traditions without any apparent conflict:

> That Spanish elements are found in the cultural contents of Pueblo culture cannot be denied, but how such elements are regarded and treated is important. Pueblo Indians affirm that they are good Catholics and also feel that they are conscientious and zealous practitioners of their own native Pueblo religion. This paradoxical situation apparently presents no conflict to the individual Pueblo Indian. He serves each religious tradition separately and, to his manner of thinking, fully and adequately. For example, Pueblo Indians attend mass and other church services in their pueblo. Many families also conduct Catholic prayers in their homes. They prize pictures of Jesus and Catholic saints and many of them are owners of Catholic santos. However, the reverence paid to Catholic saints and the observance of Catholic ritual is separate and distinct from that accorded their own native practices. As further evidence of compartmentalization, it may be pointed out that Catholic prayers are said only in Spanish and holy water is restricted to use at mass or in relation to celebrations honoring Catholic saints (Spicer 1954b: 680–681).

It would be extraordinary if the above parallels in the use of the term "compartmentalization" and in the analysis of the process were independent inventions. Since we know of actual contacts we do not need to argue that hypothesis. As between Redfield and Linton, for example, we know that Sol Tax, a student of Linton's at Madison in the 1920s, was also working with Redfield in Guatemala and facilitating the communication of ideas between them. Redfield, Linton, and Herskovits also served on the SSRC committee which drew up the famous "Memorandum for the Study of Acculturation" in 1935.

When I discussed these parallels with Spicer at the 1973 AAA meetings in New Orleans, he told me that his 1954 analysis of compartmentalization was hammered out in some intensive give-and-take sessions with Dozier. Spicer also mentioned on this occasion that he and his wife had been students of Redfield and Radcliffe-Brown at Chicago in the 1930s, and that he had been stimulated by a paper Redfield had sent him in the 1940s in mimeographed form with a blue cover whose title he did not at the moment recall.

When I returned from New Orleans I found in my office file a copy of the Redfield paper which Spicer mentioned. It was called "Cooperation and Conflict as Modes of Social Integration—In Cultural Change" and was delivered as a lecture on the University of Chicago campus November 30, 1945. As it happens, I had organized the series of public lectures on the "Cooperation and Conflict" theme in different fields at the suggestion of Mrs. Ethel Dummer of Chicago. Mrs. Dummer had been deeply impressed by the symposium volume on *Levels of Integration in Biological and Social Systems* (Jaques Cattell Press: 1942) which Redfield had edited and introduced, and asked me to organize a sequel symposium, with special reference to the problem of cooperation and conflict as modes of integration. The second symposium was not published as such, although some of the individual lectures were. The lectures were recorded by a stenotypist, typed and distributed in a limited number.

The first half of Redfield's 1945 lecture restates in very clear and concise language his conception of culture as a system of conventional meanings, of the dependence of cultural integration on isolation, and of cultural disintegration on contact and communication. Three applications of these views are also presented in the lecture: Linton's description of the introduction of wet rice agriculture among the Tanala, the introduction of Protestantism in Chan Kom, and the relation between the cult of the saints and the cult of the beehive. This part of the lecture summarizes material from *The Folk Culture of Yucatán.*

The second part of the lecture, however, introduces some new material which includes an explicit reduction of the concept of cultural integration to three less general component concepts, as well as a brief account of how cultural integration as a process is related to culture as a structure of standard meanings. Two examples of this structure-process relation are described: the adoption by Guatemalan villages of the Catholic ritual surrounding St. Anthony of Padua, and how the Yaqui in an Arizona village studied by Spicer developed several different myths to interpret their Pascola dances.

Redfield's 1945 reduction of the concept of cultural integration to simpler components includes the earlier concepts of consistency and connotative interdependence, now called "interconnectedness." In a culture with few interconnections, we recognize the "compartmentalization" of institutions and customs. "What you do on Sunday is separate from what you do when you go to your office" (Redfield 1945:7).

A third component of cultural integration Redfield calls "compendence," by which he means the relations of superordination and subordination among the elements of a culture whereby some elements are more pervasive and influential than others. "Compendence" is not explicitly discussed in *The Folk Culture of Yucatán* nor is its relation to the unity of a culture further clarified. It is introduced in the 1945 lecture as an additional structural explanation of the process whereby new elements introduced into a culture became standard, and old elements—institutions, customs, folkways—cease to be standard. Redfield did not think that "compendence" was the only deciding factor in the struggle for survival and adjustment among alternatives in the minds of individual members of a society. He recognized other influential factors—personality, leadership, authority, conservatives vs. radicals. But the fact that Yaqui culture was an organized system with some parts dominant over others, rather than an aggregational sum, seemed to him a major influence in the process of cultural integration: "Men must have around them a world which makes sense" (Redfield 1945:13).

Spicer also employs "compendence" to designate a hierarchical relation among cultural elements in his study of *Potam, a Yaqui Village in Sonora* (1954a). He acknowledges Redfield's 1945 paper as the source of the term, and similarly employs it as one structural explanation for the persistence and revival of Yaqui culture in Sonora as well as Arizona. His analysis emphasizes the ceremonial labor system, and he argues that social unity and direction of change depend on this dominant element (Spicer 1954a:203–208).

As in Redfield's analysis, Spicer does not restrict his structural analysis of cultural integration and disintegration to an analysis in terms of "compendence." He also includes consistency and linkage among the elements as important factors. "Linkage" he defines as "the occurrence of identical or similar cultural forms in different contexts" ("formal linkage"), or as the juxtaposition of different behavior patterns in time and space ("functional linkage"). Flag-waving in different ceremonies by different groups is an example of formal linkage among the groups, and soldiers and students marching together on national Flag Day in Potam are functionally linked.

Spicer's concept of linkage, as he elaborates it, seems to be a comination of Redfield's concept of connotative interdependence with some of Radcliffe-Brown's emphasis on social units and social relations. Absence of linkage is the same as "separateness" or "compartmentalization" of activities (Spicer 1954a:194–196). In Yaqui culture for example, farming is separate from the rest of the culture. One of Spicer's general conclusions from the Potam study is that "the lack of integration between economics and ceremony in Yaqui culture has probably been as adaptive feature," enabling it to survive in a variety of circumstances (1954a:208).

Spicer believes this conclusion applies to his earlier study of a Yaqui village outside Tucson, Arizona (1940) as well as to the Sonora village. He contrasts the two studies, however, in terms of their respective focus on cultural conflict and integration. The Pascua study was "focussed on the nature of conflicts and inconsistencies in the culture of Pascua resulting from 'the splicing' of Yaqui and Anglo-American cultures, as immigrant Yaquis participated in the American wage system but maintained their own social organization and ceremonial life. The focus in the study of Potam is rather on the basis of integration in Yaqui culture, on those features of its structure which may be related to the persistence of the culture under a variety of conditions" (1954a:2).

This sounds like a contrast between a study of compartmentalization and a study of compendence. Indeed, in his Foreword to Spicer's Pascua 1940 study Redfield writes:

> A striking fact about the people of Pascua is then, that their working lives form a separate compartment of their existence. They work outside the system of values which characterize

Pascua as a distinct culture group, but they pray, cure, and associate with one another within that system (Spicer 1940:viii).

Redfield also applauds Spicer for studying the conflict arising in a situation of social change "not simply in the changing forms of customs but as a collection of conflicts of varying intensity in the daily activities of specific persons'" (Spicer 1940:x).

Spicer himself notes that for some persons the intensity of such conflicts was very low and he analyzes the situation of the Yaqui in Pascua in terms of Radcliffe-Brown's notion of "functional inconsistency." He finds that insofar as the inconsistency occurs within the framework of Yaqui culture, the changes in response to a new economic environment can go on without important disorganization. But insofar as Pascuans interact socially with Tucsonans, the conflicts may lead to disorganization and even disappearance of Yaqui culture:

> Pascuans whose lives reveal the job pattern-ceremonial pattern conflict are members of both Pascua society and Tucson society, but the job may have either Tucson or Pascua meanings for them. To the extent that it has Tucson meanings for an individual, he withdraws from Pascua society (Spicer 1940:308).

Spicer's Pascua study was suggested to him in 1936 by John Provinse who had become interested in "the fact that the village maintained an elaborate set of ceremonies annually at Easter and in other ways remained distinct from the surrounding Mexican population, despite apparent assimilation into American economic life. It seemed to him that some explanation was required for this maintenance of cultural integrity" (Spicer 1940:xiv).

Spicer formulated his plan of research "with the assistance and ultimate approval" of Redfield and began fieldwork in July of 1936.[14]

The preceding discussion of parallels in the use of the term "compartmentalization" and in the analysis of the process goes back at least to 1936 when Redfield approved Spicer's proposal for a field study in Pascua, Arizona. By that time Redfield had already done fieldwork in Tepoztlán and Yucatán and published the monograph on Chan Kom, as well as a preliminary paper on "Culture Changes in Yucatán" which described the method and some of the results of the Yucatán studies. His interest therefore in "compartmentalization" developed in the context of his attempt to establish some generalizations about the processes whereby folk cultures and societies are transformed into urban cultures and societies. The more exposed a community is to the center of urban influence the more compartmentalized its culture tends to be. This does not necessarily imply an increase in social disorganization, since increasing urbanization may lead to a greater division of labor and increasing social organization.

In this respect Redfield's conception of compartmentalization as both a structural property of culture and a process of cultural change differs from the culture historical and the acculturation theories of culture change. Without denying that the folk-to-urban transformation involved both diffusion and acculturation, he emphasized that the transformation involved something more, a set of internally related changes of which compartmentalization of the modern urban and the traditional folk traits are an initial phase and their reintegration is a later phase.

In this respect, as well, Redfield's interest in compartmentalization goes back to his Tepoztlán study. The last chapter, as well as briefer references throughout *Tepoztlán* make it quite clear that compartmentalization of modern urban traits and the indigenous traditional traits is a major feature of the analysis. The compartmentalization expresses itself both in spatial terms in the location of each of a set of traits, and of corresponding kinds of professionals with respect to the central plaza, as well as in the different mentalities of the people who have been exposed to the urban influence. The urbanized professionals, tradespeople, and artisans ("los correctos") lived and worked near the center of the plaza, while the traditional type of professionals, midwives, herb doctors, fireworks makers ("los tontos") lived and worked at the periphery. The plaza was therefore the frontier of change between two overlapping culture areas—folk and urban—and "los correctos" represent the psychological expression of the cultural overlap. When "los correctos" went to Mexico City during the Revolution of 1910–1923 they became the "intelligentsia" of a miniature nationalist movement trying to preserve the language and heritage of Tepoztlán. Those who returned to the village after the revolution became like Robert Park's "marginal men," with one foot in each world (Redfield 1930:213).

Although Redfield refers to these processes as "diffusion" in *Tepoztlán*, he conceives the process more broadly then was usual at that time. In his usage "diffusion" includes, besides the communication of culture traits between contemporary groups, changes in "mentality" or "patterns of thinking," as well as the changes in the ways people feel about themselves and others. The sensitiveness, pride, and zeal for reform of "los correctos," for example, were not traits borrowed from the city, but developed in their personalities from the conflicts they experienced.

Redfield's analysis of compartmentalization as a phase in the adaptive response of tribal and peasant cultures to modern, urban, Western cultures not only led him to broaden the concept of diffusion to include acculturation and the processes of selection and incorporation of novel foreign traits in these responses; it also led him in his later work, as he turned to the study of civilizations and their encounters, to a conception of the formation, persistence, and transformation of particular civilizations. This enlarged conception of cultural change obviously drew upon the studies of specialists on particular civilizations—of the ancient Near East, of the ancient Maya, of China, India, and Islam—but—it was already present in embryonic form in his 1930 and 1940 lectures on the folk society.[15]

His typology of transformations of folk societies is restated at the end of Chapter 2 of *The Primitive World and Its Transformations*. The perspective is now all of world history as a single "human career" and includes the non-Western civilizations, living and extinct. Yet the typology of transformed folk societies is practically identical with the types diagrammed in the early lectures: peasants, enclaved folk, minorities, imperialized folk, transplanted folk, world-nomad folk, remade folk, quasifolk, and so on. One reason Redfield was able to maintain so much of the earlier typology was that it was based on the degrees of political and cultural independence and structural organization that a folk society retained after contact, not on any specific features of its cultural content or on the specific kind of civilization encountered. A second reason was that he continued to think of the processes of cultural change involved as recurrent processes of internal disorganization and reorganization and not simply as a diffusion of Western traits:

> The moral order grows by death and rebirth. Or, to change the figure, within the life of the moral order of mankind there is a perpetual anabolism and catabolism (Redfield 1953:48).

When I extrapolated from my Madras observations a cultural-historical conception of how Indian civilization modernizes and innovates, Redfield's metaphor of a cultural metabolism suggested itself almost unconsciously. In any case, the sequence of processes I then formulated still seems to be a plausible generalization: enclavement of foreign imports, ritual neutralization of the foreign enclaves; with compartmentalization and vicarious ritualization foreign imports become a typological option for the indigenous culture, enter the indigenous sphere, are traditionalized (see Singer 1972: ch. 9).

Other anthropologists who have applied the concepts of enclavement and compartmentalization to an analysis of innovation in traditional cultures and civilizations are Geertz to Indonesia, Spicer to the American Indians of the Southwest, H. G. Barnett to the United States Trust Territory of the Pacific Islands, and R. S. Khare to the occupational modernization of some Brahmans in North India. Shils' study of Indian intellectuals also makes implicit use of these ideas.[16]

8. CONCLUSION: THE FUTURE OF CIVILIZATION

Compartmentalization, it turns out, has proved adaptive in all the cases mentioned—among the Maya in Yucatán, the Tanala in

Madagascar, the Rio Grande Pueblos, the Yaqui in Arizona and Sonora. According to the respective analyses of these cases by Redfield, Linton, Dozier, and Spicer, it has provided a defense in depth
against the coercive and sometimes overwhelming contacts of colo-
nizing powers, their soldiers, missionairies, administrators, traders,
and other representatives. By creating a kind of decompression
chamber in the zone of contact, compartmentalization has enabled
the indigenous non-Western cultures to exercise some discretion in
the selection and incorporation of Western traits without aban-
doning their own cultural organization and basic cultural values.

These are of course but a small number of instances in which the
process did prove adaptive within a short-run time perspective.
How far can we generalize from these cases to others, to the long-
run, and to the future? And does compartmentalization also enable
historic civilizations and their great traditions to survive their encounters?

When Redfield went to Tepoztlán in the 1920s and to Yucatán
and Guatemala in the 1930s, he hoped to study some of the recurrent processes of civilization as they occurred, especially the processes whereby the tribal person becomes a peasant, and the peasant
becomes a townsman and urbanite. These synchronic studies, he believed, did suggest some general hypotheses which could be tested
in other areas and times. One of these general hypotheses was that
well-organized tribal and peasant "folk" cultures tend first to disor-
ganize as they come into contact with Western, urban centers of influence and then to reorganize at a new level of integration when
they withdraw from the contacts during a period of protective isolation. A decrease in the degree of consistency, interconnectedness,
unity, and homogeneity of the indigenous culture occurs in the initial phase of the cultural disorganization or disjunction. Compartmentalization between the new and the old traits, and between innovators ("los correctos") and conservatives ("los tontos") constitutes an intermediate phase which is followed by selection, reinterpretation, and incorporation of some of the new traits into the indigenous culture. The original "folk culture" thus tends to be reorganized and remade by urban contacts.

Redfield extended this folk-urban hypothesis in *The Primitive World and Its Transformations* to the history of the human career. In that long-run time perspective, he found it necessary to add a process of "primary civilization," by which the ancient early civilizations were formed from precivilized folk societies and cultures, and a process of "secondary civilization," by which primary civilizations are transformed when they come into contact with one another and with other cultures. The leading cultural innovators in primary civilization Redfield called *literati*, while the innovators in secondary civilization he called *intelligentsia*, a usage he adapted from Gordon-Childe and Toynbee.

In "The Cultural Role of Cities" the theory is further extended to the middle-run perspective of individual civilizations and their systems of urban centers. This extension led to a distinction between two kinds of civilizational change—"orthogenetic," in which literati concentrating in urban centers develop and codify a great cultural tradition from local and regional folk cultures, and "heterogenetic," in which these great traditions are transformed by intelligentsia who are in contact with different cultures and great traditions.

When I studied the fate of the great tradition of Sanskritic Hinduism in what was supposed to be the heterogenetic center of Madras, I found that some individuals and some families played both the roles of literati and of intelligentsia, and that through compartmentalization they were modernizing and Sanskritizing at the same time.[17] Compartmentalization thus operated in Madras through a kind of "internal isolation" to link "heterogenetic" and "orthogenetic" cultural changes to one another.

This linkage does not necessarily assure an undisturbed future for Sanskritic Hinduism in Madras or in India. There are other great traditions, other literati and intelligentsia who have been de-Sanskritizing and challenging the Brahmanical and Sanskritic traditions. Whether a further compartmentalization will lead to a new level of reintegration and the absorption of dissenting sects and movements as in the past, is difficult to predict, particularly since demographic and economic conditions and the prospect of nuclear proliferation must be taken into account.

In his article on "Civilization," written in 1958 for the *Collier En-cyclopedia* (1960), Redfield looked back to the ancient historic civilizations and forward to the prospects of a world civilization. In retrospect he sees the native American civilizations, including the Mayan and Peruvian, as short-lived:

> The Spaniards substantially destroyed their 'great traditions'—their more reflective and creative elites, and they survive today in the more Indian countries of Latin America for the most part in so far as the peasantry or common people of Pre-Columbian times knew and then communicated to their present-day descendants some lesser part of the aboriginal cultur—civilization (1962:413).

Redfield also sees, in agreement with Kroeber, "a far-reaching change in the nature of civilization" that comes about in recent times as a result of "Westernization" and "modernization":

> . . . The historic civilizations were derived from local cultures expanded and matured in relative isolation through very long periods of time. Each became a total way of life, attached to a region, equal to and distinct from the others. Each was, first of all, a tradition, a reach back into history, a set of institutions and convictions resting on the authority of long-shared experience. But what is now sometimes called "world civilization" is another kind of thing. It breaks down the old local traditions; it arises not so much from tradition as from new things—science, technology, the participation of masses in education, standardized entertainment, public life, and organized consumption. The world becomes one interdependent region increasingly characterized by a world-wide way of life that tends to obliterate what is local and traditional. The two conditions of civilization, the arrangement into ancient great civilizations and the newer widespread modernity, co-exist, one upon the other. In so far as the new comes to predominate, some speak of the coming era as that of "post-civilization." (1962:414).

Whether the coexistence of tradition and modernity in the era of "post-civilization" will protect mankind against the increasing threat of ultimate nuclear destruction is a question that Redfield faced in his somber "Talk with a Stranger" (published by the Center for the Study of Democratic Institutions, 1958). He writes in these last words on the question that he could not imagine himself denying the peril:

> I had to admit that the growth of the human spirit might, by destruction, come to an end. It could end by nuclear violence; it could end in abasement to a nihilism of values, a tyranny of doctrine, police power, or material things. What a fragile thing is human spirit!

Taking heart from some words of Camus, Redfield closes with an heroic affirmation:

> We are thrust upward amid dangers and darknesses of our making. We have no promise from the universe that we shall survive. We live for the growing of the human spirit, and in spite of all, we strive toward that growth, up to the last moment of possibility (1963:282).

In the late 1920s and early 1930s when Redfield did his field studies in Tepoztlán and the Yucatán communities, anthropologists were inclined to emphasize the diffusion of discrete traits from one culture to another as the major if not the exclusive form of "conversation" between cultures. Under the influence of this emphasis, modernization of non-Western cultures came to be interpreted as a diffusion of discrete Western traits—railroads, the telegraph, factories, and parliamentary democracy—a process of "Westernization." Redfield's Yucatán studies showed the inadequacy and ethnocentric character of such an interpretation. They demonstrated the importance and feasibility of looking at the process of modernization from the point of view of the traditional societies, their own values and world views, their changing moods and biographies. The traditional societies could no longer be regarded as passive obstacles on the road to progress which must be removed or converted into carbon copies of the "progressive" societies of the West. Partly as a result of Redfield's Yucatán studies, anthropologists and other scholars recognize increasingly that when a non-Western society modernizes, it does more than borrow and imitate some Western techniques and ideas. In addition to the one-way diffusion of Western traits, there has been mutual acculturation, and some structural changes in both the non-Western and the Western societies. The influence of Orientalism on the West in the fields of arts and crafts, literature, religion and philosophy, cuisine, and clothes, for example, is far from ended.

For many non-Western traditional societies, the encounter with the West was traumatic, taking place, as it frequently did, under the coercion of imperial expansion and colonial conquest. In his later thought Redfield came to see that the struggles for independence and the desire to recover some continuity with their ancient indigenous civilizations was for the traditional non-Western societies an inseparable part of the process of modernization. It was this profound perception which led him in the late 1940s to an interest in the rise of the early historic civilizations in the Old and New Worlds, as well as to an interest in the subsequent fates of the surviving historic civilizations in the modern world. He noted that the intellectual elites and great traditions of the Mayan civilization in Yucatán had not survived the Spanish conquest, but in some of the Oriental civilizations—Islamic, Indian, Chinese—he believed that enough of their great traditions had survived to justify direct observational studies of their modernization. But it was not simply a detached scholarly interest in the comparative history of civilizations that motivated Robert Redfield to set up the Ford project, or to travel to China and India. He felt very urgently that with the technical feasibility of nuclear warfare, the fate of all the civilizations and of all mankind depended on our ability to understand and tolerate the diversity of cultures and civilizations, and to turn the "conversation of cultures" into a civilization of the dialogue.

NOTES

[1]For a brief account of the institutional and intellectual resistance to the introduction of area programs in American Universities see my article, "The Social Sciences in Non-Western Studies" (1964).

[2]An early favorable notice of the project was published by D. G. Mandelbaum (1956).

[3]Papers were also presented to the seminar by N. K. Bose on Bengali civilization (1967) and by G. E. von Grunebaum on the analysis of Islamic civilizations (1962).

Kenneth Burke and Talcott Parsons were also active participants in the Behavioral Sciences Center seminar. As a result of the discussions there, Kroeber and Parsons (1958) clarified their previous differences on the relation of "culture" to "social system" and Burke (1968) and Parsons (1968) discovered common ground in symbolic interactionism.

[4]Friedmann's account of his work in south Italian community development was published by Cornell University Press in 1960 under the title *The Hoe and the Book*. His article "La Miseria," an interpretation of Italian peasant outlook, was discussed in the seminar.

[5]Redfield's article on "The Social Organization of Tradition" (1955b) was first published in *The Far Eastern Quarterly* together with my field report on cultural performances in Madras, "The Cultural Pattern of Indian Civilization" (Singer 1955). This report was based on a presentation made shortly after my return from India in the spring of 1955 to a seminar on social and cultural change jointly conducted by Redfield and Raymond Firth. I also brought back from this first trip to India draft papers by V. Raghavan, "Variety and Integration in the Pattern of Indian Culture," and by M. N. Srinivas, "A Note on Sankritization and Westernization." These papers had been written for a conference on Indian studies held in Poona in November 1954, and were published in *The Far Eastern Quarterly* 15, no. 4 (August 1956).

Some empirical studies, inspired by Redfield, of the social organization of tradition in Indian civilization, especially as expressed in cultural performances, networks, and centers, are found in two volumes I edited (1958-59; 1968) and in books by L. P. Vidyarthi (1961); S. C. Sinha, ed. (1970:87-150); and B. S. Cohn (1971).

Applications of the network concept to India are discussed by Redfield in *Peasant Society and Culture* (1956a:50-66); by Cohn and Marriott (1958); by Marriott (1959); by E. Jay (1964); by M. N. Srinivas and A. Beteille (1964); and in my paper "The Social Organization of Indian Civilization" (1964a).

[6]One of Redfield's earliest and most illuminating formulations of his "historic structure" conception of civilizations was presented in autumn, 1956, as a lecture, "Thinking about a Civilization," in the course on Indian civilization. This lecture, which was published in the course syllabus, *Introduction to the Civilization of India* (Chicago: University of Chicago Press, Syllabus Division, September 1957), was later elaborated in the three lectures on civilization which Redfield gave to the comparative civilizations seminar at the Behavioral Sciences Center in the spring of 1958 and were published in the collection of his papers (1962) edited by his wife. The phrase "historic structure" may have been in part suggested by Americo Castro's *The Structure of Spanish History,* which had been mentioned in the comparison of cultures seminar. For some differences between the Kroeber and Redfield concepts of civilization see Singer (1964a).

[7]Three conferences and the publication of their proceedings were supported by project funds: *Studies in Islamic Cultural History* (von Grunebaum, ed. 1953); *Unity and Variety in Muslim Civilization* (von Grunebaum, ed. 1955); and *Classicisme et declin culturel dans l'histoire de l'Islam* (Brunschvig and von Grunebaum, eds. 1957).

[8]Von Grunebaum's studies of the development of Muslim cultural consciousness were pubished chiefly in two volumes of essays: *Islam: Essays in the Nature and Growth of a Cultural Tradition* (1955)and *Modern Islam: The Search for Cultural Indentity* (1962).

Because of an untimely death, Hodgson left much of his work unpublished. His Ph.D. dissertation on *The Order of Assassins* (1955) and *The Venture of Islam: Conscience and History in a World Civilization* (1974) are now available.

[9]The first conference volume published by "The Chinese Thinkers" was *Studies in Chinese Thought* (Wright, ed. 1953). The Fairbank-edited volume followed in 1957. The tables of contents of these and of the committee's subsequent three volumes are given at the end of *Confucianism and Chinese Civilization* (Wright, ed. 1964), which reprints twelve of the original essays together with a new introduction by Arthur Wright.

[10]For Redfield's developing refinements in the conception of world view see p. 132 above.

[11]Eric Wolf's *Anthropology* (1974) is a notable exception.

[12]See, for example Redfield 1941:386 n. 15 for Redfield's contrast with Benedict's "configurations."

[13]For further discussion see Singer 1968 and 1973.

[14]After reading my description of how he and Dozier developed their analysis of compartmentalization, Spicer sent me the following additional recollections:

> All that you write is substantially as it happened in connection with Ed Dozier's and my use of the concept. As I read, however, and began to recall Ed's and my discussions, I was continually surprised at how much we remained strangely unaware of. I had become acquainted with the concept of compartmentalization as Redfield used it in the course he gave in the mid-1930s at Chicago—The Folk Society. Also I taught during the late 1940s and early 1950s a course in Primitive and Modern Society at the University of Arizona, in which I regularly used the concept of the folk-urban continuum and the ideas associated with that. I had reviewed *The Folk Culture of Yucatán* for the *Annals* of the American Academy in 1941 and was thus quite familiar with the concepts of compartmentalization, incompatibles, and separates as developed in that book.
>
> However, when Dozier and I began to make detailed comparisons of acculturation processes among the Pueblos and the Yaquis, we seemed hardly to be aware of Redfield's usage. We had our discussions in the early 1950s. We were using a different framework from the folk-urban continuum and thinking in terms of short term processes—acculturation of particular societies. If we had been asked whether the result of compartmentalization, as we used it, was a higher degree of urbanization (in R. R.'s sense) than before Spanish contact, I suspect that we would have said, "No, the compartmentalization process constituted a successful defense, permitting Pueblo society to remain folk in character." We were of course actually

compartmentalizing our thought and not attempting to see the results of contact in a framework of folk-urban changes. I am amazed, however, that I never referred to Redfield in this connection, since I was familiar enough with his idea" (Spicer to Singer, December 13, 1974).

Spicer's experience is very similar to mine in Madras and perhaps points to a more general psychological process underlying the development and use of concepts.

[15]See, for example, his genetic diagram for the major kinds of transformations of folk peoples as a result of contacts with Western urban civilization, reprinted from a synopsis of the course on "The Folk Society" in *Human Nature and the Study of Society* (1962:253).

[16]See Geertz 1963:61; 1965:51–52,202–208, Spicer 1962:1–2, 344–345, 569, 58lff.; Barnett 1971; Khare 1971; 1973; Shils 1961; Singer ed. 1973.

[17]Redfield noted that in the case of Don Eus of Chan Kom the roles of literati and intelligentsia were combined in the same individual, but explained it as "an early stage in the differentiation of literate types" (1953b:44,170,n.35).

LITERATURTE CITED

Albert Ethel
    1960   Cahiers d'Etudes Africaines 1(2). *Also in* The Ethnography of Communication. Gumpertz and Hymes, eds. American Anthropologist 66, no. 6, pt. 2 (1964).

Barnett, H. G.
    1971   Compatibility and Compartmentalization in Cultural Change. *In* Essays on Modernization of Underdeveloped Societies. A. R. Desai, ed. Bombay.

Bose, N. K.
    1967   Culture and Society in India. Asia Publishing House.

Brunschvig, R., and G. E. von Grunebaum, eds.
    1957   Classicisme et declin culturel dans l'histoire de l'Islam. Paris: Besson–Chantemerle.

Burke, Kenneth.
    1968 "Dramatism." International Encyclopedia of the Social Sciences 7.

Cohn, B. S.
    1971 India: The Social Anthropology of a Civilization. New York: Prentice-Hall.

Cohn, B. S., and McKim Mariott
    1958 Networks and Centres in the Integration of Indian Civilization. Journal of Social Research 1.

Dozier, Edward P.
    1961 Rio Grande Pueblos. *In* Perspectives in American Indian Culture Change. Edward H. Spicer, ed.

Dumont, Louis
    1970 Homo. Hierarchicus: The Caste System and Its Implications. Chicago: University of Chicago Press.

Eggan, Fred, ed.
    1937, 1955 Social Anthropology of North American Tribes. Chicago: University of Chicago Press.

Fairbank, John K., ed.
    1957 Chinese Thought and Institutions. Chicago: University of Chicago Press.

Francis, E. K. L.
    1945 The Personality Type of the Peasant According to Hesiod's Works and Days: A Culture Case Study. Rurual Sociology 10(3).

Friedmann, F. G.
    1960 The Hoe and the Book. Ithaca, N.Y.: Cornell University Press.

Geertz, Clifford
    1960 The Religion of Java. Glencoe, Ill.: The Free Press.
    1963a Agricultural Involution: The Processes of Ecological Change in Indonesia. Berkeley and Los Angeles: University of California Press.
    1963b Peddlers and Princes: Social Development and Economic Change in Two Indonesian Towns. Chicago: University of Chicago Press.
    1965 The Social History of an Indonesian Town. Cambridge, Mass.: The M.I.T. Press.

1968 Islam Observed: Religious Development in Morocco and Indonesia. New Haven: Yale University Press.
1973 The Interpretation of Cultures. New York: Basic Books.

Goody, Jack, ed.
1968 Literacy in Traditional Societies. Cambridge: Cambridge University Press.

Griaule, Marcel
1965 Dieu d'Eau. Translated, with project support, as Conversations
with Ogotemmeli: An Introduction to Dogon Religious Ideas.
Published for the International African Institute by the Oxford
University Press.

Guiteras-Holmes, Calixta
1961 Perils of the Soul: The World View of a Tzotzil Indian. Glencoe,
Ill.: Free Press.

Hodgson, Marshall
1955 The Order of Assassins. New York: Mouton.
1975 The Venture of Islam: Conscience and History in a World Civilization. 3 vols. Chicago: University of Chicago Press.

Hoijer, Harry, ed.
1954 Language in Culture. Memoirs AAA, No. 79. Chicago: University of Chicago Press.

Hsiao-Tung, Fei
1953 China's Gentry: Essays in Rural-Urban Relations. Edited and
revised by Margaret P. Redfield. Chicago: University of
Chicago Press.

Jay, E.
1964 The Concepts of "Field" and "Network" in Anthropological
Research. Man in India 64:137–139.

Khare, R. S.
1971 Home and Office: Some Trends of Modernization among the
Kanya-Kubja Brahmans. Comparative Studies in Society and
History 13(2).
1973 One Hundred Years of Occupational Modernization among the
Kanya-Kubja Brahmans. *In* Entrepreneurship and Moder-
nization of Occupational Cultures in South Asia. Milton B.
Singer, ed. Durham, N.C.: Duke University Press, 1973.

Kroeber, Alfred L.
1944 Configurations of Culture Growth. Berkeley and Los Angeles: University of California Press.
1945 The Ancient Oikoumenê as a Historic Culture Aggregate. *In* The Nature of Culture. Chicago: The University of Chicago Press, 1952.
1963 An Anthropologist Looks at History: Selected Essays: Theodora Kroeber, ed. Berkeley and Los Angeles: University of California Press.

Kroeber, Alfred L., ed.
1953 Anthropology Today. Chicago: University of Chicago Press.

Kroeber, Alfred L., and Talcott Parsons
1958 The Concept of Culture and of Social System. American Sociological Review 23:582–583.

Leach, Edmund Ried.
1968 Dialectic in Practical Religion. Cambridge: Cambridge University Press.

Leslie, Charles
1960 Now We Are Civilized: A Study of the World-View of the Zapotec Indians of Mitla, Oaxaca. Detroit, Mich.: Wayne State University Press.

Linton, Ralph
1936 The Study of Man. New York: D. Appleton-Century Co.

Mandelbaum, D. G.
1956 The Study of Complex Civilizations. *In* Current Anthropology. Chicago: University of Chicago Press.

Mannheim, Karl
1952 On the Interpretation of Weltanschauung. *In* Essays on the Sociology of Knowledge. Paul Kecskemeti, ed. London: Oxford University Press.

Marriott, McKim
1959 Changing Channels of Cultural Transmission in Indian Civilization. *In* Intermediate Societies, Social Mobility and Communication, V. Ray, ed. Seattle: American Ethnological Society.

Marriott, McKim, ed.
1955 Village India. American Anthropolical Association Memoir and University of Chicago Press.

Mendelson, E. Michel
  1957 Religion and World-View in a Guatemalan Village. Microfilm Collection of Manuscripts on Middle American Cultural Anthropoloy, no. 52. Chicago: University of Chicago Library.
  1958 The King, the Traitor, and the Cross: An Interpretation of a Highland Maya Religious Conflict. Diogenes 21.

Orans, Martin
  1965 The Santal. A Tribe in Search of a Great Tradition. Detroit: Wayne State University Press.

Parsons, Talcott
  1968 "Symbolic Interaction." International Encyclopedia of the Social Sciences 7.

Radcliffe-Brown, Alfred R.
  1952 Structure and Function in Primitive Society. London: Cohen and West Ltd.
  1957 A Natural Science of Society. Glencoe, Ill.: Free Press.

Ragavan, V.
  1956 Variety and Integration in the Pattern of Indian Culture. The Far Eastern Quarterly 15(4).

Redfield, Robert
  n.d.   Art and Icon. *In* Aspects of Primitive Art. *Also in* Human Nature and the Study of Society. Margaret P. Redfield, ed. Chicago: University of Chicago Press, 1962.
  1930   Tepoztlán, a Mexican Village: A Study of Folk Life. Chicago: University of Chicago Press.
  1941   The Folk Culture of Yucatán. Chicago: University of Chicago Press.
  1945   Cooperation and Conflict as Modes of Social Integration—In Cultural Change. Lecture. University of Chicago.
  1947   The Study of Culture in General Education. Social Education 11:259–264. *Reprinted in* The Social Uses of Social Science. Margaret P. Redfield, ed. Chicago: University of Chicago Press, 1963.
  1950   A Village That Chose Progress: Chan Kom Revisited. Chicago: University of Chicago Press.
  1953a Relations of Anthropology to the Social Sciences and the Humanities. *In* Anthropology Today. Arthur L. Kroeber, ed. Chicago: University of Chicago Press.

1953b The Primitive World and Its Transformations. Ithaca, N.Y.: Cornell University Press.
1954 Community Studies in Japan and China. Far Eastern Quarterly 14(1). *Reprinted in* Redfield (1962:302ff.).
1955a The Little Community: Viewpoints for the Study of a Human Whole. Chicago: University of Chicago Press.
1955b The Social Organization of Tradition. The Far Eastern Quarterly 15(1):13–21.
1956a Peasant Society and Culture: An Anthropological Approach to Civilization. Chicago: University of Chicago Press.
1956b Primitive and Peasant: Simple and Compound Society. *Published in part in* Society in India. A. Aiyappan and L. K. Bala Ratnam, eds. Madras
1960 Civilization. *In* Collier Encyclopedia. *Reprinted in* Human Nature and the Study of Society. Margaret P. Redfield, ed. Chicago: University of Chicago Press.
1962 Human Nature and the Study of Society. Margaret P. Redfield, ed. (Papers, vol. 1) Chicago: University of Chicago Press.
1963 The Social Uses of Social Science. Margaret P. Redfield, ed. (Papers, vol. 2) Chicago: University of Chicago Press.

Redfield, Robert and Alfonso Villa Rojas.
1934 Chan Kom, A Maya Village. Carnegie Institution of Washington.

Shils, E. A.
1961 *The* Indian Intellectual between Tradition and Modernity. New York: Mouton.

Singer, Milton B.
1951 The Social Sciences. *In* the Theory and Practice of General Education. F. C. Ward, ed. Chicago: The University of Chicago Press.
1953 Shame Cultures and Guilt Cultures. *In* Shame and Guilt: A Psychoanalytic and a Cultural Study. Gerhart Piers and Milton B. Singer, Springfield, Ill., Charles Thomas. New York: Norton, 1971.
1955 The Cultural Pattern of Indian Civilization. The Far Eastern Quarterly 15(1).
1960 The Expansion of Society and Its Cultural Implications. *In* City Invincible. C. H. Kraeling and R. M. Adams, eds. Chicago: University of Chicago Press.

1961 A Survey of Culture and Personality Theory and Research. *In* Studying Personality Cross-Culturally. B. Kaplan, ed. New York: Harper & Row.

1964a The Social Organization of Indian Civilization. Diogenes. *Reprinted in* When a Great Tradition Modernizes: An Anthropological Approach to Indian Civilization. New York: Praeger, 1972.

1964b The Social Sciences in Non-Western Studies. Annals 356:30–44.

1967a On Understanding Other Cultures and One's Own. The Journal of General Education.

1967b Social Anthropology and the Comparative Study of Civilizations. Foreign Area Materials Center.

1968 Culture. International Encyclopedia of the Social Sciences.

1972 When a Great Tradition Modernizes: An Anthropological Approach to Indian Civilization. New York: Praeger.

1973 A Neglected Source of Structuralism: Radcliffe-Brown, Russell and Whitehead. Paper presented in absentia to the A. S. A. Conference, July 1973, in Oxford, England.

Singer, Milton B., ed.

1958-59 Traditional India: Structure and Change. American Philosophical Society.

1968 Krishna: Myths, Rites and Attitudes. Chicago: University of Chicago Press.

1973 Entrepreneurship and Modernization of Occupational Cultures in South Asia. Durham, N.C.: Duke University Press.

Singer, Milton B., and Bernard S. Cohn, eds.

1968 Structure and Change in Indian Society. Chicago: Aldine Publishing Co.

Singer, M.B., B.S. Cohn, M.N. Srinivas

1966 The Modernization of Religious Beliefs. *In* Modernization: The Dynamics of Growth. Myron Weiner, ed. New York: Basic Books.

Singer, Milton B., and Robert Redfield

1954 The Cultural Role of Cities. Economic Development and Cultural Change. *Reprinted in* Man in India (1956). *Also Reprinted in* Redfield, Human Nature and the Study of Society. Margaret P. Redfield, ed. Chicago: University of Chicago Press, 1962.

Sinha, S. C., ed.
1970 Research Programmes on Cultural Anthropology and Allied Disciplines. Anthropological survey of India.

Spicer, Edward H.
1940 Pascua: A Yaqui Village in Arizona. Chicago: University of Chicago Press.
1954a Potam, a Yaqui Village. American Anthropological Association Memoir.
1954b Spanish-Indian Acculturation in the Southwest. American Anthropologist 56:663–684.
1962 Cycles of Conquest: The Impact of Spain, Mexico and the United States on Indians of the Southwest, 1533–1960. Tucson: University of Arizona Press.

Spicer, Edward H., ed.
1961 Perspectives in American Indian Culture Change. Chicago: University of Chicago Press.

Spiro, Melford E.
1970 Buddhism and Society: A Great Tradition and Its Burmese Vicissitudes. New York: Harper and Row.

Srinivas, M. N.
1962 Caste in Modern Indian and Other Essays. Bombay: Asia Publishing House.
1966 Social Change in Modern India. Berkeley: University of California Press.

Srinivas, M. N., and A. Beteille
1964 Networks in Indian Social Structure. Man in India 64:165–168.

Tambiah, S. J.
1970 Buddism and the Spirit Cults in North-East Thailand. Cambridge: Cambridge University Press.

Vidyarthi, L. P.
1961 The Sacred Gayawal. Asia Publishing House.

von Grunebaum, G. E.
1955 Islam: Essays in the Nature and Growth of a Cultural Tradition. American Anthropological Association Memoir. London: Routledge and Kegan Paul, 1955, 1961.

1962 Modern Islam: The Search for Cultural Indentity. Berkeley and Los Angeles: University of California Press.

von Grunebaum, G. E., ed.
　　1953　Studies in Islamic Cultural History. American Anthropological
　　　　　Association Memoir.
　　1955　Unity and Variety in Muslim Civilization. American Anthro-
　　　　　pological Association Memoir. Chicago: University of Chicago
　　　　　Press.

Wagley, Charles
　　1968　Latin American Tradition: Essays on the Unity and the Diver-
　　　　　sity of Latin American Culture. New York: Columbia Uni-
　　　　　versity Press.

Wolf, Eric
　　1974　Anthropology. New York: Norton.

Wright, Arthur F.
　　1960　The Study of Chinese Civilization. Journal of the History of
　　　　　Ideas 21(2).

Wright, Arthur, F., ed.
　　1953　Studies in Chinese Thought. American Anthropological Asso-
　　　　　ciation Memoir. Chicago: University of Chicago Press.
　　1964　Confucianism and Chinese Civilization. New York: Atheneum.

†